T0330166

DEMOGRAPHIC DEVELOPMENTS AND POPULATION POLICIES IN BA'THIST SYRIA

The research leading to the publication of this book has been made possible by the support of the Jewish-Arab Center, at the University of Haifa, Israel, where the author, Onn Winckler, is a scholar.

Demographic Developments and Population Policies in Ba'thist Syria

Onn Winckler

Foreword by
Professor Moshe Ma'oz
THE HARRY S. TRUMAN RESEARCH INSTITUTE
FOR THE ADVANCEMENT OF PEACE

sussex
ACADEMIC
PRESS

BRIGHTON • *PORTLAND*

2 4 6 8 10 9 7 5 3 1
First published 1998 in Great Britain by
SUSSEX ACADEMIC PRESS
Box 2950
Brighton BN2 5SP

and in the United States of America by
SUSSEX ACADEMIC PRESS
5804 N.E. Hassalo St.
Portland, Oregon 97213-3644

British Library Cataloguing in Publication Data
A CIP catalogue record for this book is available from the British Library.

Library of Congress Cataloging-in-Publication Data
Winckler, Onn.
Demographic developments and population policies in Ba'thist Syria / Onn Winckler : foreword by Moshe Ma'oz
p.   cm.
Includes bibliographical references and index.
ISBN 1–902210–16–6 (alk. paper)
1. Demography—Syria.   2. Syria—Population policy.   3. Syria—Economic conditions.
4. Syria—Social conditions.   I. Title.
HB3633.7.A3W558   1999
304.6'095691—dc21   99–10160
CIP

Printed by Biddles Ltd, Guildford and King's Lynn
This book is printed on acid-free paper

Contents

Contents

Figures and Illustrations

Tables

Tables

Foreword

For several generations demographic growth in the Middle East has become one of the most crucial issues of this region. It has influenced not only socio-economic development, but also political changes both within and among the Middle Eastern countries, as well as their relations with the international community. Significantly, the demographic evolution has impacted Arab-Israeli relations too, not only with regard to Egypt, but also in the case of Jordan, as Onn Winckler has already manifested in his previous book in this series (*Population Growth and Migration in Jordan, 1950–1994*). Syria is another important case study of demographic growth – indeed one of the highest in the region – and of its effects on the country's domestic change and regional position. This book traces three major demographic developments and their socioeconomic consequences in Syria during the second half of this century, notably since the Ba'th Revolution of March 1963, i.e., rapid population growth, the rural-to-urban migration movement, and the temporary migration of Syrian labor to other Middle Eastern countries. Each of these developments is described and analyzed within the framework of the overall socioeconomic evolution of Syria. The book convincingly demonstrates that, during the last two decades, the demographic factor has constituted one of the major levers of both structural economic changes and political shifts in internal and foreign affairs in Syria under Ba'th regime. The decisive linkage between socio-economic development and political change is indeed highlighted in this book.

A wide range of official Syrian statistical data as well as other sources are used, including population censuses, demographic surveys, five-year development plans, and Syrian press reports that reflect the authorities' policies on various relevant issues. Other sources are official publications of UN agencies, the World Bank and the IMF, and reports by various commercial companies dealing with demographic and economic issues. Drawing upon these source materials and reflecting original approaches and deep insights, this book provides a unique contribution to better understanding contemporary Syrian society and politics.

Moshe Ma'oz, *The Hebrew University of Jerusalem*

Preface and Acknowledgments

During the last three generations the Syrian population has increased rapidly – in fact – by one of the highest rates all over the Middle East and North Africa region. While in 1922, at the beginning of the French Mandate, the total population of the area now under Syrian sovereignty numbered 1.3 million, it increased to 15.1 million by mid-1997. With a population growth of approximately 3 percent annually, the total Syrian population was estimated to be 15.3 million by the end of 1997, at the time of the writing of this book. These figures show that within a period of less than one century, the Syrian population has increased almost twelve-fold. The main purpose of this book is to describe and analyze the demographic and socioeconomic developments, as well as policies, emerging in Syria within the framework of the demographic developments taking place throughout the Middle East and North Africa region since the Ba'thi Revolution in early March 1963.

The Introduction includes a short description of the demographic developments of the world from the beginning of the twentieth century until the mid-1990s. After an overview of the main demographic trends in the Middle East during the nineteenth and twentieth centuries, Syrian population growth from the beginning of the nineteenth century through the Mandatory period and until 1997 is described, and demographic forecasts of the Syrian population to the first quarter of the twenty-first century are made.

Chapter 1 presents the sources used in this research, mainly the population censuses and demographic surveys which were conducted in Syria during the period under discussion. The accuracy and reliability of the data collected in these censuses and surveys is discussed.

Chapter 2 details the natural increase rates of the Syrian population from the late 1950s onward, including crude birth and total fertility rates; crude death rates, infant and child mortality rates, and life expectancy at birth; distribution of the population by age; rate and age at first marriage, and the stability of the marriage system; trends of contraceptive use; and the economic consequences of the high rates of natural increase.

Chapter 3 concentrates on the spatial distribution of the Syrian population, including the trend of rural-to-urban migration which took place in Syria from the late 1950s onward as part of the overall Middle East urbanization process; the reasons for the unique pattern of the Syrian urbanization process, as compared with those taking place in the other Arab countries; and the economic consequences of the rapid Syrian urbanization process.

Chapter 4 deals with the migration of Syrians to other Middle Eastern countries for purposes of employment, namely, to the Middle Eastern oil-exporting countries (the GCC countries and Libya), as well as to the neighboring countries of Lebanon and Jordan. The chapter discusses migration trends; the scope of Syrian migration to the Middle Eastern labor-receiving countries; their distribution in the host countries according to the number of workers and accompanying family members; the reasons for these migration trends; and the economic consequences of such labor migration.

Chapter 5 describes and analyzes the attitudes of the Syrian authorities towards the three main demographic trends taking place in Syria during the period under discussion, namely: the high rates of natural increase of the population; the spatial distribution of the population, particularly the trend of rural-to-urban migration movement; and the migration of Syrian workers to other Middle Eastern countries. Syrian demographic policy in each of the three components is evaluated in the latter part of the chapter.

The Conclusion traces the effects of the demographic-economic factor on the political changes in Syria from the early 1970s onward, both in internal and external arenas.

This book has evolved out of my research on the demographic developments and socioeconomic policies in the Middle East and North Africa region during the twentieth century; it focuses in particular on these developments in Syria under the Ba'th regime. The book is largely based on my Ph.D. thesis: "Demographic Developments and Population Policy in Syria, 1960–1990," which was written in the Department of Middle Eastern History at the University of Haifa under the supervision of Professor Gad G. Gilbar. In addition, a few parts from chapters 2, 4 and 5 have already been published in English in two articles: "Syria: Population Growth and Family Planning, 1960–1990," *Orient* (Deutsches Orient Institut, Hamburg), Vol. 36, No. 4 (1995), pp. 663–72; and "Syrian Migration to the Arab Oil-Producing Countries," *Middle Eastern Studies* (Frank Cass, London), Vol. 33, No. 1 (1997), pp. 107–18. Excerpts from these two articles are reproduced here.

This research was conducted with the support of the Jewish-Arab Center and the Research Authority of the University of Haifa, as well as with the help of Ms. Ruth and Mr. Carl Barron, for which I am very thankful.

I am deeply indebted to Professor Gad G. Gilbar, the Rector of the University of Haifa, who was not only the Supervisor for my Ph.D. thesis, but also encouraged me to publish this book, as well as to Professor Moshe Ma'oz, the former Director of the Harry S. Truman Research Institute for the Advancement of Peace at the Hebrew University in Jerusalem, for his willingness to write the Foreword and for his useful comments on various topics in the book.

Also my heartfelt gratitude goes to Dr. Ibrahim Geries, the head of the Jewish-Arab Center at the University of Haifa, Mr. Eliezer Rafaeli, Chairman of the Board of Directors of the Center, and to Ms. Zvia Haimovitz, the administrative manager of the Center, for their help in publishing the book. I am also sincerely thankful to my colleagues, Dr. Michael Eppel and Dr. Uri M. Kupferschmidt, for their useful comments on various chapters of the book. I also extend my gratitude to Dr. Mordechai Kedar from Bar-Ilan University, for providing me with the two illustrations which appear in chapter 5. In addition, I would like to thank Ms. Sharon Woodrow for editing the manuscript, Mr. Joshua Rubin for arranging the tables and figures, and Mr. Ori Slonim for his useful help in collecting the material for the research. Finally, I am grateful to the librarians at the Middle East Documentation Unit at Durham University, the Cairo Demographic Center, the Newspaper Archives of the Moshe Dayan Center for Middle Eastern and African Studies at Tel Aviv University, and the University of Haifa Library.

Abbreviations

CAPMAS	Central Agency for Public Mobilisation and Statistics (Cairo)
CBS	Central Bureau of Statistics (Damascus)
CDC	Cairo Demographic Centre (Cairo)
EIU	Economist Intelligence Unit
ESCAP	UN Economic and Social Commission for Asia and the Pacific
ESCWA/ ECWA	UN Economic (and Social) Commission for Western Asia
FUDS	Follow Up Demographic Survey (FUDS – 1976–79)
GCC	Gulf Cooperation Council
GDP	Gross Domestic Product
GFCF	Gross Fixed Capital Formation
GNP	Gross National Product
IBRD	International Bank for Reconstruction and Development
IJMES	*International Journal of Middle East Studies*
ILO	International Labour Office (Geneva)
IMF	International Monetary Fund
JPFHS	Jordan Population and Family Health Survey (1990)
LS	Syrian Pound
MECS	Middle East Contemporary Survey
MEED	*Middle East Economic Digest*
OPEC	The Organization of Petroleum Exporting Countries
SC	Sample Population Census (1976)
SFS	Syria Fertility Survey (1978)
SMCHS	The Syrian Maternal and Child Health Survey (1993)
SPC	State Planning Commission
UAE	United Arab Emirates
UAR	United Arab Republic
UN	United Nations
UNESCO	United Nations Educational Scientific and Cultural Organization
UNFPA	United Nations Fund for Population Activities
UNICEF	United Nations Children's Fund
YAR	Yemen Arab Republic

To
HADAR

Introduction: The Middle Eastern Demographic Transition

The most important demographic development in the world during the twentieth century has been rapid population growth. In 1900, the world's population was estimated at 1.65–1.71 billion.[1] By 1994, it was estimated that the world's population numbered 5.6 billion,[2] representing an increase of 230 percent during less than one century.

The history of the world's population is divided into three main stages of the "Demographic Transition." The first stage, with high crude birth and death rates, ruled most of human history. It seems that until the middle of the nineteenth century, the average total fertility rate was about six. Nevertheless, because mortality levels were also very high, the natural increase rates of the world's population were very low, and sometimes even negative during periods of starvation or epidemic diseases.

The second stage of the "Demographic Transition" began to occur toward the end of the eighteenth century with the beginning of modernization, accompanied by improved public health methods, including preventive medicine, better nutritional habits, and higher per capita income. These developments were all outcomes of the "Industrial Revolution" and thus occurred only in western European countries. However, they led to a marked reduction in mortality rates, gradually raising the average life expectancy from under 40 years to more than 60 years. Nevertheless, the decline in death rates was not followed immediately by a parallel decrease in the fertility rates. As a result, the growing gap between high fertility rates and falling death rates led to a sharp increase in population growth in western European countries, as compared with previous centuries.

The third stage of the "Demographic Transition" was marked by the beginning of a decline in fertility rates caused by the forces of modernization. Eventually, falling fertility rates converged with low death rates, leaving little or even no population growth in many industrialized countries.[3] However, most of the world's countries, including those of the Middle East and North Africa region, have not yet reached the third stage of the "Demographic Transition" and remain in the second stage, which is characterized by high natural increase rates. These developing countries have been the main contributor to the rapid growth of the world's population during the twentieth century, especially in the latter half. By 1994, only 1.164 billion, or 20.7 percent of the world's population, lived in regions classified as industrialized, leaving 79.3 percent in the developing countries.[4]

Similar to other developing areas in the world, the population of the Middle East and North Africa has also increased very rapidly during the twentieth century, especially from the late 1950s onward. By 1830, the total population of the Middle East and North Africa region was estimated at 34 million, increasing to 68 million in 1914, and 79 million in 1930.[5] By 1994, this figure was estimated to be almost 360 million,[6] representing an increase of more than 400 percent during a period of only 80 years, from World War I until 1994. According to demographic forecasts, by the year 2025 the Middle East population is expected to more than double its current size.[7] This dramatic increase in the population of the Middle East and North Africa during the twentieth century was not a consequence of migration, as was the case in North America, for example, but rather the rapid growth of the natural increase rates. These rates are considered to be among the highest in the entire world during the last three decades.

The crude birth rates of the Middle East and North Africa populations, which were very high at the beginning of the Modern Age (about 45 per 1,000 inhabitants), remained at that level until the late 1970s and the early 1980s. During the years 1980–85, the average crude birth rate was 39.7 per 1,000 in Egypt, 44.4 in Iraq, 43.2 in Saudi Arabia, and 44.2 in Jordan.[8] Similarly, the total fertility rates have also remained very high, reaching more than six in many countries in the region during the 1970s and most of the 1980s. Only from the mid-1980s onward, has there been evidence of a reduction in the crude birth and fertility rates among the Middle East and North Africa populations.

The crude death rates, which were very high in the eighteenth century (about 42–44 per 1,000 inhabitants), started to decrease during the nineteenth century, especially from the 1850s onward, dropping to approximately 32–34 by the end of the nineteenth century. Throughout the twentieth century, the crude death rates continued to decline, but in contrast to the previous century the decrease was very rapid, particularly from the late 1950s and early 1960s onward. While in 1960, the average crude death rate of the Middle East and North Africa populations was approximately 20 per 1,000 inhabitants, it dropped by the mid-1990s to about six and even less in the Persian Gulf oil-exporting countries. Thus, within only one generation, the crude death rates in the Middle East and North Africa region were sharply reduced after a slow decline in the second half of the nineteenth century and the first half of the twentieth century.

There are many reasons for such a marked reduction in the crude death rates in the Middle East and North Africa region over the last two centuries. Initially, the decrease was a result of the elimination of starvation and devastating epidemics. At the end of the nineteenth century and throughout the twentieth century, the further reduction in the crude death rates can be attributed primarily to the massive improvements in health services, both in quantity and quality. During the second half of the twentieth century, the rise in the standard of living and the substantial increase in per capita income have also contributed to this sharp reduction in the crude death rates.[9]

The outcome of this increasing gap between the crude birth and death rates has been rapid growth in the natural increase rates throughout the Middle East and North Africa populations. While at the beginning of the twentieth century the average natural increase rate in this region was estimated at one percent, by the beginning of the 1980s this rate grew to more than 3 percent, and in some countries reached almost 4 percent during the late 1980s and the early 1990s. Thus, the "Demographic Revolution" in the Middle East and North Africa region was, more than anything else, a revolution in the crude death rates.

This rapid population growth during the second half of the twentieth century has had various negative impacts on the economic and social life of the over-populated Middle Eastern countries, mainly Egypt, Turkey, and Iran, and, to a lesser extend, Jordan and Syria. The term "overpopulated" does not necessarily relate to the size of the population, but mainly represents the ratio between the population on the one hand, and the available economic resources, on the other. For example, although the total population of Saudi Arabia is almost four times that of Jordan, which is considered to be an overpopulated country, the former, due to its huge oil resources, is not considered as such and does not share the problems engendered by high natural increase rates.

The first and the most important consequence of the high natural increase rates of the Middle East and North Africa populations during the second half of the twentieth century has been the creation of a wide base of the age pyramid. During the late 1970s and the early 1980s, more than 40 percent of the Middle East and North Africa populations were below the age of 15, making them large consumers of public and other services, such as health-care and education. Yet, their economic contribution is marginal, if any, particularly in the urban areas. The direct result of this process has been very low crude economically active rates, due to the low percentages of the working age population (15–64) within the total population, as well as the tendency of the vast majority of the Middle Eastern women not to work outside the home.

Another major negative result of the rapid population growth has been the increase in open and disguised unemployment, as the expansion of the labor force has outpaced that of the available jobs in the productive sector. Consequently, the work force in the overpopulated Middle Eastern and North

African countries is cheap, in turn creating a negative incentive for the integration of new and modern technology in the fields of agriculture, industry, and public services. In order to diminish the high rates of unemployment, the governments of the overpopulated countries have attempted to augment the number of available work opportunities by absorbing large numbers of employees into the governmental bureaucracy as well as in other public sector establishments. Although this step succeeded in bringing about some reduction of the open unemployment rates in the short run, it increases the level of disguised unemployment and inefficiency within the public sector in the long run.

Another devastating consequence of the rapid population growth in most of the Middle Eastern countries has been the increasing pressure on natural resources. Since most of the Middle East is comprised of desert, this has meant a steady decline in the ratio between population, on the one hand, and water and agricultural lands, on the other. While this problem is clearly evident in Egypt and Jordan, it also exists in Iraq, Syria, and the Gulf countries. As a result, in many Middle Eastern countries, the steep increase of water for domestic use has caused a steady reduction in the amount available for agricultural purposes, transforming these countries from agricultural exporters to large-scale food importers. This, in fact, constitutes the most important reason for the food gap in all of the Middle Eastern and North African countries during the last generation, which has forced them to spend billions of dollars annually on the import of basic foodstuffs.[10]

The rapid population growth and the scarcity of agricultural lands in the rural areas are the main factors accounting for the acceleration of the urbanization process throughout the Middle East region during the last two generations. The rate of urbanization in the Middle East is rising faster than in any other region in the world, and it seems that this trend will continue in the coming decade as well. The proportion of the urban population within the total population in the Middle East rose from 27.7 percent in 1950 to 46.8 percent in 1980, and will continue to grow to almost 60 percent by the year 2000.[11]

As a result of the rapid urbanization process, the larger cities in the Middle East, mainly the capitals, have been forced to absorb large numbers of rural migrants, above and beyond the swelling ranks of the urban population itself. Thus, the urbanized areas have experienced rapid expansion, primarily due to uncontrolled sprawl. This expansion has far outpaced the capacity of the authorities involved to adequately provide basic public services for these uncontrolled new urban neighborhoods. One of the most critical problems facing the larger cities in the overpopulated countries of the Middle East from the 1950s onward is a chronic housing shortage, which has led to a dramatic rise in housing prices and an increase in the construction of informal dwelling units. Moreover, since most of the major cities in the Middle East are located near the main water sources, their expansion has been at the expense of the culti-vated lands located around them. This phenomenon is very prominent in Cairo, where a large quantity of agricultural land has been virtually "swallowed" by the new urban areas.

The negative results of the rapid population growth in the Middle East have contributed to the creation of the "vicious circle of poverty." The main links in this "vicious circle" are as follows: In a developing economy with high rates of natural increase, the saving capability of the population is limited due to the low level of per capita income; the low level of per capita income is a reflection of a very low productivity level; the very low productivity level is the result of capital shortage; and capital shortage is the result of the limited saving capacity, caused mainly by the high natural increase rates of the population.[12]

Today, there is no longer any doubt that rapid population growth constitutes the most critical socioeconomic problem in many Middle Eastern and North African countries. The main reason for the acute nature of the demographic problem, as compared with other socioeconomic problems, is that while it is possible to change economic policy within a relatively short period of time, say, a few years, as indeed occurred in Egypt during the mid-1970s (*al-infitah al-iqtisadi* – the "open door" policy),[13] or in Syria during the second half of the 1980s and the beginning of the 1900s,[14] it takes at least two generations to change demographic trends and reproductive behavior, mainly as a result of the wide-based age pyramid of the population.

Until these changes take hold, the authorities of the overpopulated countries in the Middle East are forced to absorb and support their bulging populations with inadequate resources. Since this process is irreversible, the governments of these countries must plan the development of their economies, infrastructure system, environmental conditions, housing projects, education and health services to support populations which will, at least, double their current size. It is doubtful whether some Middle Eastern countries will be able to support their growing populations in the first quarter of the twenty-first century without causing a substantial reduction in both per capita income and the standard of living.

As in other Middle Eastern countries, the Syrian population has grown rapidly during the twentieth century, but especially from the late 1950s onward. At the beginning of the nineteenth century, the population of the Syrian region was estimated at 800,000.[15] During the nineteenth century, the rate of popula-tion growth in the Syrian region was very low, and it seems that during the first half of the century, it was even close to zero. It was only in the middle of the century that the Syrian population started to increase, albeit at a slow pace, mainly due to low natural increase rates and large-scale emigration to areas outside the region.[16] According to the population census data conducted by the Ottomans during the years 1872–74, the total population of the Syrian region was 973,120.[17] From these data, it appears that during the first three-quarters of the nineteenth century, the Syrian population increased by only 20 percent. Since the Ottomans did not organize a comprehensive population registration system, the French Mandate authorities conducted a population census in 1922, shortly after they established their control over Syria and Lebanon. According to the census data, the total Syrian population, excluding the Alexandretta *sanjak* (district), numbered 1,298,319 (986,829 in the State of Syria, 261,162 in the Governorate of Ladhaqiya, and 50,328 in the Governorate of Jabel-Druze).[18] By 1936, according to the French Mandatory official figures, the Syrian population numbered 2,096,486, including the *sanjak* of Alexandretta.[19]

In 1947, the first population census taken in independent Syria placed the total population at 3.043 million. This figure increased to 4.565 million, according to the census data of 1960. From the early 1960s onward, due to the high natural increase rates, the population growth rate in Syria has been among the highest in the entire Middle East and North Africa region: 6.305 million in 1970, 9.046 million in 1981, and 13.812 million in 1994, according to the census of that year, which is the latest one conducted to date in Syria. According to data published by the Syrian Central Bureau of Statistics (CBS), by mid-1995 the Syrian population numbered 14.186 million (see Appendix 1), and reached 15.1 million, two years later, in mid-1997.[20]

With population growth of about 3 percent annually, the total Syrian population was estimated to be 15.34 million by the end of 1997, at the time that this book is being written. These data show that during the last 75 years, from the establishment of the French Mandate until 1997, the Syrian population has increased almost twelve-fold. A population forecast prepared by the World Bank indicates that by the year 2000, the Syrian population will reach 16.9 million and then 30.4 million by the year 2020 (see Appendix 3).

Several questions will be addressed in this book regarding the Syrian rapid population growth: What have been the economic and social consequences of the rapid population growth in Syria during the last generation? Were the Syrian authorities aware of the implications of the rapid population growth? And what measures, if any, were taken in order to reduce the high fertility rates?

In addition to rapid population growth, two other major demographic trends have taken place in Syria during the period under discussion. The first was the rapid urbanization process. During the years 1960–94, the percentage of the urban population within the total Syrian population increased from 37 percent to more than 51 percent. The main questions are: What were the reasons for the steady rise in the percentage of the urban population within the total Syrian population? Are these reasons unique to Syrian society alone, or are they similar to those in the other Middle Eastern countries, which were also undergoing a rapid urbanization process during that period? In addition, as will be discussed in chapter 3, while in almost all of the other Middle Eastern countries, the urbanization drive was mainly from the rural areas to the major cities, particularly to the capitals, in the case of Syria, the rural-to-urban migration drive was concentrated primarily in the provincial towns. What were the reasons for this unique phenomenon?

Another important question to be explored in relation to the Syrian urbanization process concerns why the pace of urbanization during the 1940s and 1950s was, to a great extent, slower in Syria than in most other Middle Eastern countries. Moreover, in Syria the urban scene is much more balanced, as compared with most other Middle Eastern countries.[21] What is the reason for this unique urbanization pattern? Is it related to the geographical structure of the country?

The third demographic trend which took place in Syria during the last generation was the temporary migration of Syrians to other Middle Eastern countries for purposes of employment, mainly following the "oil boom" of October 1973. The questions to be addressed are: What were the incentives for the migration of hundreds of thousands of Syrians to other Arab countries for purposes of employment? In which countries were the Syrian migrants concentrated? How did the joining of Syria in the anti-Iraqi coalition during the Gulf crisis affect the scope of the Syrian migration to the Gulf countries? What were the economic consequences of this migration trend, and how did it impact on the Syrian labor market, especially during the second part of the 1970s and first half of the 1980s, when the migration trend reached its peak? Finally, and perhaps most importantly, what was the Syrian government's attitude towards the labor migration phenomenon?

The Conclusions deal with the most interesting issue regarding the demographic developments in Syria from the early 1970s onward: the effects of the demographic factor on the political and economic decision-making in Syria under Hafiz al-Asad. The questions to be addressed include: Was there any connection between the economic recession which took place in Syria during the second half of the 1980s and the rapid population growth? What was the connection, if any, between the economic recession and the economic liberalization drive which took place in Syria from the mid-1980s onward? Was there any connection between the decision of Asad to join the anti-Iraqi coalition during the Gulf crisis and the economic recession of the late 1980s? What was the connection, if any, between the economic deterioration and the changing Syrian attitudes towards the Middle East peace process?

Each of the three demographic trends discussed in the book are tied to both of the others. Therefore, one trend cannot be treated separately from the other two, not only in the case of Syria, but also with regard to other Middle Eastern and North African countries. This is mainly due to the fact that development in one trend necessarily affects the direction of the two other trends. Thus, the book deals with all the three demographic trends, and how they relate to each other.

The starting point for the period under discussion was chosen for its strong impact on Syrian demographic developments, namely, the implementation of the socialist policy in Syria after the Ba'thi revolution of March 1963. The changing socioeconomic policies in Syria under the Ba'th regime, including the provision of large-scale public services, either free of charge or heavily subsidized, as well as governmental subsidies of basic foodstuffs, have had a significant effect on overall demographic development. They have brought about a drastic and rapid reduction of the crude death rates, in parallel to a rapid increase in the life expectancy of the population. The implementation of a socialist economy has also strongly affected the spatial distribution of the population. Overall, throughout the last three and a half decades, one can see a close connection between demographic developments and the implementation of socioeconomic policies in Syria, and it is this connection that constitutes the main focus of this book.

1

Sources for Syrian Demographic Trends and Developments

Population Growth and Natural Increase

Population censuses and registration of births, deaths, marriages, and divorces, as well as changes in place of residence, which are the most important sources of data for demographic analysis and research, have had a very short history in most Middle Eastern and North African countries, including Syria. Only three countries in this region conducted modern population censuses prior to the end of World War II (in 1882 in Egypt, 1886 in Tunisia, and 1927 in Turkey). Due to the absence of population census data, it is impossible to conduct comprehensive demographic research in most Middle Eastern and North African countries for the period preceding the end of the 1950s and the early 1960s.

But, this does not mean that there are no general population estimates for those countries which lack population census data before the middle of the twentieth century. These estimates are based on the partial censuses that were conducted in most Middle Eastern countries, including Syria, during the first half of the twentieth century. Many of these censuses were carried out under the Mandatory rule of Britain or France. However, these censuses have their share of limitations and inaccuracies. For example, nomadic and semi-nomadic populations may be markedly under-reported. Other elements of the population – such as young children, and especially young girls – may also be under-reported. Together with age misreporting, this produces noticeable distortions in the apparent age–sex distributions of the population of many countries in the Middle East, including Syria.[1]

Demographic Research in the Syrian Region under Ottoman Rule

Until the middle of the nineteenth century, the flimsy rule of the Ottoman Empire over the provinces, including the Syrian region, refrained from conducting comprehensive population registration. Moreover, since the Ottoman rule provided almost no social services, there was likewise no need to determine the demographic characteristics of the population, such as crude death rates and the overall health condition of the population. As a result, there is only very limited demographic data on the populations of the Ottoman areas. Stanford Shaw notes that: "No problem has perplexed students of modern Ottoman history more than that of determining the state of the empire's population during its last century."[2] The only sources regarding the scope of the population in many regions of the Ottoman Empire during the beginning of the nineteenth century are the sporadic estimates of European travelers, such as Volney, Seetzen, Burckhardt, and others.[3] However, these estimates are general, and it is obvious that they cannot serve as a primary source for comprehensive demographic research. With regard to the Syrian region in particular, it seems that the main reason for the lack of population registration until the mid-nineteenth century was the flimsy structure of Ottoman rule in this area.

During the nineteenth century, as part of the reforms movement (the *Tanzimat*) which took place in the Ottoman Empire, demographic data were substantially improved. A census was undertaken by Sultan Mahmud II (1808–39) as part of his efforts to create a new army and bureaucracy following the destruction of the *Janissart* Corps in 1826. Since only men served in the army and paid taxes, only they were included in the census. However, due to the Ottoman-Russian war, the census was not fully completed until 1831. In their attempt to determine the exact number of Muslim and non-Muslim men in each *sanjak* (district), *kada* (county), and *nahiya* (locality) of the Empire, the Ottoman authorities registered Muslim males in three categories: those under 16, those aged 16–40, and those over 40. Jews and Christians were also recorded, according to their socioeconomic status, since they were subject to head tax. Females were not recorded in this census.[4]

The knowledge of the size and changes in the composition of the spatial distribution of the population throughout the Empire region became much more important during the latter part of the nineteenth century. This was due mainly to administrative reasons, as roads, railways, and a variety of professional schools were planned in accordance with the spatial distribution of the popu-lation in the various provinces of the Empire.[5] As the Ottoman control over the provinces improved during the last quarter of the nineteenth century, population registration improved as well, including that of the Syrian region.

The Ottoman authorities kept the population registration in the provincial capitals of the Empire, where they were published in the *Salname* (provincial yearbook), as well as in the *Defter Nüfus* (population register) in the capital of the Empire, Istanbul. The *Salname* of the Syrian province appeared almost every year during the period 1868/9–1900/1.[6] Population records for the

Sanjaks (districts) of Sham and Hamma were first published in 1882–83. While the Ottoman authorities collected data on the population of *Wilayet* Syria (province) much earlier, the Syrian *Salnames* published only the number of households, rather than the total population, and included no other demographic data or characteristics of the population. Moreover, the number of inhabitants of the *Sanjaks* of Hawran and Karak were not published until the 1330 (1912) *Nüfus*. In addition, Ottoman sources often listed as the total population of the *Wilayet* Syria what was in fact only the population of *Sanjak* Sham and part of *Sanjak* Hama.[7]

In the introduction of the 1960 Syrian population census, it is stated that several population counts were conducted in the Syrian region by the Ottoman rule in the years 1854, 1884 and 1905. While all the former censuses conducted by the Ottoman authorities were for tax and military purposes and thus included only males, the 1884 census was the first actual enumeration of the whole population, with both males and females. The results of this census constituted the basis of the Ottoman Civil Registration system. The next census in 1905 was very similar to that of 1884, and new civil registration data was established according to the new figures.[8] However, the results of this census, as well as the data drawn from the Ottoman civil registration system, were only partial, particularly in the remote provinces, including the Syrian region. Although Stanford Shaw claims that "There is little evidence of large-scale avoidance of registration and counting by men as well as women in the heavily populated centers of the empire," he added that "the counts in the mountain and desert areas were still no more than estimates." Moreover, there was a substantial undercounting of females in the countryside.[9] Since during the late nineteenth century and the beginning of the twentieth century, the majority of the population in the Syrian region lived either in the mountains or in the countryside, it seems that the figures provided by the Ottoman censuses regarding the Syrian region can be treated, at best, as no more than broad estimates. Moreover, since the present-day Syrian boundaries were never constituted as one administrative unit under the Ottoman rule, even if the Ottoman figures regarding this area were accurate and reliable, they would not be of much use.[10]

In light of the partial and discontinuous population registration system in the Syrian region during the late Ottoman period, it seems that it is impossible to conduct comprehensive demographic research on this region under the Ottoman rule. Thus, the only possibility is to give a general description of the number of inhabitants in the area, and some outline of their spatial distribution in the late Ottoman period. Indeed, this is precisely what McCarthy, Gerber, Shaw, Karpat, and others[11] have done.

Demographic Research in Syria under the French Mandate

1922 Population Census

Since the Ottoman authorities had not conducted a comprehensive population registration system, the French Mandate authorities decided to conduct a population census in Syria and Lebanon in order to provide the proper basis for building an administrative system, as well as to collect taxes from the population. Law No. 8305 of July 20, 1921 specified that a population census of the Levant was to be carried out to ensure equitable distribution of the taxes and national income. The census system set up committees for the enumeration of every 15,000 people, based on the figures of the previous Ottoman censuses. These committees were instructed to register the number of houses in every village. Each committee was required to prepare a report which included the exact time when the enumeration was carried out. The conduct of the census extended for several months, and its results were recorded in three categories: Syrians residing in a city or village, absent Syrians, and foreigners.[12] However, there were many defects in the 1922 census. Robert Widmer commented on the quality of the census:

> The census of 1921–22, which was taken throughout the territories under the French Mandate, can scarcely be considered as even an approximation.[13]

Several factors accounted for the inaccuracies in the 1922 census data. First, many religious sects falsified the number of adherents in order to increase their proportionate representation in the parliament or the administrative system. Second, some of the old fears of military conscription, as well as of any sort of administrative inquiry, also influenced the declarations to the census committees. Third, estimates of the Bedouin population could not be accurate since there were no means by which to enumerate the itinerant tribes.[14] In addition, the Mandate authorities conducted several local censuses in order to achieve better registration of the Syrian population. These censuses covered the following: the city of Hasakah in 1924; the rural area of Ladhaqiya in 1925; the city of Ladhaqiya in 1928; the city of Kamishli in 1929; and the province of Suwayda in 1932.[15]

Civil Registration during the Mandatory Period

Syria has one of the oldest civil registration systems among Middle Eastern countries. Law No. 176/1923 entrusted the Ministry of Interior with the role of recording all vital demographic events. According to the law, every Syrian citizen was to be registered with the Department of Civil Registration (established in 1923) on the events of birth, death, marriage and divorce, as well as change in place of residence. The Department issued to every citizen an identity booklet containing the holder's name, sex, place of residence, place of birth, civil status and religion. Statistics relating to demographic events have been published since 1944. The earlier figures published by the French Mandate on the total Syrian population related to the year 1938, based on adding births to and deducting deaths from the original figures of the 1922 census.[16] Insofar as these demographic statistics were based on the 1922 census, they can only be considered as unreliable and inaccurate.

Demographic Research in Independent Syria

After independence (1946), the quality as well as the quantity of the Syrian demographic and economic data substantially improved. This improvement has found expression in the five population censuses, as well as in the demographic surveys that have been conducted since 1947. In addition, since independence, a variety of international bodies and organizations have conducted and published research on the demographic trends and developments, as well as other socioeconomic issues, in Syria. This includes various establishments and departments of the United Nations (UN), mainly ESCWA (Economic and Social Commission for Western Asia), the Population Division of the UN, and UNFPA (UN Fund for Population Activities). Thus, while it is almost impossible to conduct comprehensive demographic research on Syria prior to its independence (mainly as a result of lack of demographic and other related socioeconomic data), the improvement of the data since the 1950s, and especially following the 1960 census, enables the conduct of such research.

Civil Registration in Independent Syria
Despite improvement in data collection, even after independence the Syrian Civil Registration data continued to suffer from high rates of under-reporting. Moreover, it appears that in the major provinces of the country, the Civil Registration data were much more accurate than in the remote provinces. Thus, for example, while in Damascus city during the period from March 31, 1960 until April 1, 1961, the recorded crude birth rate was 47.18 per 1,000 and the crude death rate was 9.42 per 1,000, the records of both crude birth and crude death rates in Deir al-Zur, al-Raqqa, Darʻa, and other remote provinces, were far from accurate. For example, the crude death rate was reported as 1.98 per 1,000 in the province of Deir al-Zur, and even less in al-Raqqa, as only 1.50 per 1,000.[17] Such low recorded crude death rates are clearly impossible in any given Middle Eastern country, including the capital rich Gulf oil-exporting countries even today.

The ECWA report from 1980 on the demographic situation in Syria, includes a cautionary statement regarding the data published by the Syrian Civil Registration:

The data published [by the Syrian Civil Registration] are considered unreliable and inadequate. For example, the crude birth rate of 28.2 per 1,000 and the crude death rate of 4.1 per 1,000 for 1970, which were calculated on the basis of the Civil Registration figures, are clearly too low.[18]

The UNFPA report from the same year also addressed the rate of under-reporting in the Syrian Civil Registration:

Currently, the recording of vital events by a resident's declaration is observed mainly for marriages and divorces. Other vital events are often unregistered, or registration is delayed beyond the legal period . . . In some areas, delayed reports were estimated to total one-third to one-half of all registrations.[19]

There are many reasons for these high rates of under-registration in the Syrian Civil Registration, the most important of which are as follows: First, it was impossible to register a birth unless both parents were on the population register. In addition, a death was not recorded unless the person was registered when he was born. Moreover, registration in Syria was a costly operation to the public, especially in those cases when the registration office was located at a long distance.[20] During the early 1970s there were about 175 registration centers, serving more than 13,000 population settlements. This excluded a rather large segment of the population, mainly in the small and remote villages and small urban settlements, from registering their vital demographic events.[21]

The Syrian Central Bureau of Statistics (CBS)
The Syrian Central Bureau of Statistics was established in 1968 under Legislative Decree No. 87/1968 as the legal authority for the collection, compilation, consolidation and coordination of all data in relation to national development, including the conduct of population censuses and demographic surveys. The CBS is placed directly under the Office of the Prime Minister. The central office of the CBS is in the capital city of Damascus, and another 13 regional directorates are located in each of the provinces of the country.

The main functions of the CBS are:

1   Establishing a comprehensive and unified statistical system that ensures the collection, as well as the publication, of accurate and up-to-date vital socioeconomic data.
2   Reporting the results of the various socioeconomic development plans.
3   Preparing periodical reports and studies in various socioeconomic fields for the Office of the Prime Minister and the State Planning Commission, as well as for other concerned ministries.[22]

In addition, the CBS publishes the Syrian annual *Statistical Abstract*, which covers a wide range of topics, including a chapter on demographic trends and developments with up-to-date data.

The Population Studies and Research Center

The Population Studies and Research Center, established in 1972, is attached to the CBS and is responsible for carrying out and analyzing demographic surveys and censuses. The Center was responsible for the conduct of the 1978 Syria Fertility Survey, as well as for the preparation of the 1981 and 1994 population censuses.

Population Censuses

Before discussing the major demographic developments which have taken place in Syria since independence, it is necessary to examine the accuracy and reliability of the data collected in the population censuses, which constitute the main data base for the research. During the period under discussion, five censuses have been conducted in Syria, the first in 1947, following independence, and the latest in September 1994.

1947 Population Census

The main purpose for the implementation of the 1947 population census was to establish election lists. It included only the sedentary population, but there was an investigation of sorts of the nomadic population as well. However, the results of the census have been never published, other then those regarding the distribution of the population by sex and religion.[23] Moreover, even after conducting this census, the results were not used as a means for checking the records of the Civil Registration, which continued to be based on the 1922 census data.[24]

1960 Population Census

The 1960 population census was the first demographic investigation to be conducted scientifically in covering the entire Syrian region and its resident population. The need for reliable and up-to-date demographic data was underscored in the late 1950s when the preparation of the First Five-Year Development Plan (1960–65) required reliable data regarding the total population of Syria, the distribution of the population among the various provinces, and the age pyramid of the population. Law 35/1960 was promulgated on February 9, 1960 for the establishment of a technical body to ascertain the requirements, schedules, and procedures for conducting a comprehensive population census. Law 159/1960 was then published on May 24, 1960, providing for a general population census to be conducted in both the regions of the United

Arab Republic (UAR)[25] on the night of September 20–21, 1960.[26] The census was conducted by the Directorate of Statistics and Census under the direction of the Central Statistical Committee. The territorial divisions consisted of the 11 *mohafazas* (provinces) of the country and the two main cities, Damascus and Aleppo. The provinces were subdivided into *mantika* (district) and *nahiya* (sub-district), which comprised several villages.[27]

Despite this being the first comprehensive demographic investigation conducted in Syria, there were apparently some serious defects in the census data. A large number of nomads and semi-nomads, as well as foreign refugees, were missed by the enumeration. In addition, as a result of the lack of accurate and reliable data, the annual natural increase rate, which had been officially adopted by the authorities during the 1950s, was reported as 2.2 percent. The 1960 census data was not used either for the evaluation of this reported natural increase rate, or for the establishment of a new rate, which was essential to the organization of the socioeconomic development plan.[28]

1970 Population Census
Legislative Decree No. 323/1969 on December 17, 1969 established that a population and housing census would be carried out every ten years. By the end of January 1970, the Prime Minister issued a decree setting up an advisory committee, composed of the Deputy Ministers of Planning, Interior, Education, Municipalities, Finance, Labor, and Agriculture, in order to assist the CBS in conducting the census.[29] The census was conducted in September 1970 by the CBS on a *de facto* basis. The questionnaires, as well as the methods used for the organization of the census, were probably similar to those used in the previous census. The main difference between the two censuses was that the data collected in the 1970 census were computer-tabulated. In addition, the territorial divisions in the 1970 census changed, and two new provinces were added: Tartus, which was divided from Ladhaqiya, and Quneitra, which was divided from Damascus.[30]

Regarding the quality of the census data, it was believed that they were more accurate than those of the former census and that more information was provided on various aspects of the demographic characteristics and the spatial distribution of the population among the various provinces, as well as between urban and rural areas. The 1970 census also suffered from under-enumeration, which was estimated at about 2 percent among the urban population and as high as 11 percent in the countryside.[31]

1976 Sample Population Census (1976 SC)
The purpose of the 1976 sample census was to draw a numerical picture of the structural composition of the Syrian population; to trace the socioeconomic factors affecting it; and to obtain indicators comparable to the data collected in

the two previous censuses.[32] A questionnaire similar to that used in the 1970 census was completed by a systematic sample of about 300,000 people living in one-third of the dwelling units in the country. An additional question was asked in the 1976 SC regarding the number of births in the previous 12 months, thereby providing new important data on the fertility trends among Syrian women. In terms of the quality of the data, tests showed an improvement over the 1970 census data in depicting the age pyramid of the population,[33] which is one of the most important tools used to calculate the age-specific fertility rates, as well as the crude death and infant and child mortality rates.

1981 Population Census
The fourth census in Syria was conducted on September 8, 1981. The census had been delayed for one year as a result of organizational problems. About 3,000 people assisted in conducting the census.[34] The questionnaire used in the census consisted of four different parts covering the following issues:

1   Personal questionnaire (sex, age, relationship with head of household, nationality, civil status, occupation, level of education, etc.).
2   Family size and composition.
3   Information on dwelling units.
4   Information about relatives living abroad.[35]

1994 Population Census
The latest population census in Syria was conducted on September 3–9, 1994. As in the previous censuses, a housing census was taken prior to the population census, on August 14–23, that year.[36] The census was again conducted by a staff of approximately 3,000. The Syrian authorities emphasized the importance of the census, since its data would constitute the basis for future socioeconomic development plans.[37]

Demographic Surveys

Since the population censuses undertaken in many Middle Eastern and North African countries have not been conducted at smaller intervals than every ten years, and in most cases at even broader intervals, information on current rates of population growth and other demographic characteristics has to be obtained from other sources. In most developed countries, this information can be obtained from the Civil Registration, making it possible to analyze the relative contribution of fertility and mortality to population changes. However, in most Middle Eastern and North African countries, as in Syria, the data in the Civil Registration are not complete (except in Egypt, Algeria, Tunisia, and Kuwait).

Therefore, in order to follow the demographic changes in the periods between the population censuses, the authorities in these countries have conducted periodical demographic surveys. During the period under discussion in this book, the Syrian authorities conducted four of these demographic surveys, obtaining from each household retrospective measures of vital demographic events. These included crude birth and death rates, infant and child mortality rates, age-specific fertility rates over a given period preceding the interview date (usually 12 months), employment patterns, educational level (mainly of females, since this is the most important factor affecting fertility level), the desired number of children, and knowledge and use of contraceptives.[38]

Infant and Child Mortality Survey in Damascus – 1973
This survey was conducted in early 1973 and was limited to the city of Damascus. The main aims of the survey were to provide data on infant (age 0–1) and child (1–5) mortality rates in the city of Damascus during the years 1968–72, according to the following socioeconomic characteristics: level of mother's education, level of family income, and mother's occupational characteristics. The survey covered 10,151 households with a population of 120,600, among which 9,282 eligible women were selected.[39]

Follow-Up Demographic Survey, 1976–1979 (1976–79 FUDS)
The 1976–79 FUDS was conducted in order to provide up-to-date information regarding fertility rates, mortality rates, internal and external migration, and the rate of population growth of the Syrian population. The preparation of the survey was spread over a period of three years, from October 1976 to October 1979. In order to take into account socioeconomic differentials among the various regions of the country, the participants in the survey were selected according to three strata:

1 Inhabitants of the major cities with more than 100,000 people (Damascus, Aleppo, Homs, Hama, and Ladhaqiya).
2 Inhabitants of the provincial towns with 20,000–100,000 people, such as Dar'a, Idlib, Tartus, al-Suwayda, and al-Hasakah.
3 Inhabitants from the rural areas.

In order to narrow the deviation rate of the survey, the fieldwork was conducted through seven rounds to the household participants, twice a year, in October and April. The survey included one percent of the total Syrian population at that time. Since it was a follow-up survey, the number of participants differed from year to year. In the first year, the number of participants was 48,315. In the second year, their number was 49,098, and in the third year, 48,444.[40]

Syria Fertility Survey – 1978 (1978 SFS)

The 1978 SFS, which was carried out as part of the World Fertility Survey (WFS) program, was designed to obtain data on total fertility rates, age-specific fertility rates, crude death rates, infant and child mortality rates, knowledge and use of contraceptives, and other related factors in order to enhance the understanding of changing dynamics in demographic trends of the Syrian population. The 1978 SFS, together with the data obtained from the 1976–79 FUDS, was designed to provide sufficient background demographic information for political decision-makers to prepare a suitable national population policy in Syria.[41]

The survey, conducted by the CBS, consisted of two components. The first was a large-scale household survey with an extended questionnaire listing basic demographic characteristics of the Syrian population (children ever-born, crude death rates, infant and child mortality rates, and total and age-specific fertility rates). The second component was an individual survey based on a sub-sample of the households covered in the first phase. The survey was carried out by 15 teams from June to August 1978, with 14,670 households containing 97,510 persons. Every third household in each group was selected for the individual questionnaire. Among the 4,915 selected households, 4,646 eligible women (aged 15–49) were identified, and 4,487 were successfully interviewed, representing a response rate of 96.6 percent.[42] The results of the survey were published in 1982.

The Syrian Maternal and Child Health Survey (1993 SMCHS)

The 1993 SMCHS was conducted by the CBS in collaboration with the State Planning Commission (SPC) and the Ministries of Health and Labor and Social Affairs, within the framework of the Pan-Arab Project for Child Development (PAPCHILD) of the League of Arab States. The 1993 SMCHS was carried out during June–July 1993 with a nationally representative sample. Data were collected from 19,971 households, and complete interviews covered 4,814 ever-married women aged 15–54 and 4,356 children under the age of five. The main aims of the survey were to provide health policy-makers, as well as health professionals, with accurate and comprehensive data on mothers and children in order to identify the health problems of the Syrian population and to help in formulating strategies and policies for overcoming these problems.[43]

Spatial Distribution of the Population

As in other demographic issues, also in the field of the spatial distribution of the Syrian population among the various provinces, as well as between urban centers and rural areas, there is a lack of accurate and reliable data for the Otto-man period. This makes the conduct of comprehensive research on the spatial distribution of the population in the Syrian region during the Ottoman period an impossible mission. Regarding the Mandatory era, until the late 1930s, there is also a lack of accurate and reliable data on the spatial distribution of the popu-lation. However, in 1938 the Civil Registration began to publish annual estimates for the total population in each of the provinces, but not for the percentage of the urban and rural populations, either in the various provinces or in the entire country. Moreover, since the Civil Registration data were based on the 1922 census results, their accuracy and reliability were poor.

During the period between receiving independence (1946) and the conduct of the 1960 census, there are estimates in the annual Syrian *Statistical Abstract* regarding the distribution of the Syrian population among the various provinces, but not regarding the percentage of the urban and rural populations in each of the provinces. These estimates were based on the Civil Registration records. However, since the conduct of the 1960 census, there are relatively reliable and accurate data on both the distribution of the Syrian population among the various provinces and the proportion of the urban and rural populations in each of the provinces. These data, which are published annually in the Syrian *Statistical Abstract*, are based on the results of the population censuses and the Civil Registration records during the periods between the conduct of the censuses. Another important source of data on the spatial distribution of the Syrian population (as well as for the other Middle Eastern and North African countries) is provided by the annual estimates of the UN for both the total population of the major cities (over 100,000 in-habitants) and the distribution of the total population among urban and rural areas. These estimates appear on a regular basis in the annual UN *Demographic Yearbook*.

Migration Trends

Until the "oil boom" of October 1973, interest in the field of movement of workers between Arab countries was rare. The dramatic rise in the number of migrants moving from the poorer over-populated countries to the rich Arab oil-exporting countries for purposes of employment after the "oil shock," and the important consequences of this phenomenon, both for the labor-exporting and the labor-receiving countries, caused a rapid increase of interest in this phenomenon. Since the mid-1970s, a large number of organizations have been dealing with this important topic.

The most prominent of these organizations are the World Bank, the ILO, and ESCWA. These international organizations have conducted research dealing with a variety of issues: the number of migrants and their accompanying family members; the distribution of the migrants by countries of origin and host countries; the scale of the workers' remittances, which in some of the labor-exporting countries constituted the largest foreign exchange earner (primarily in Egypt, Jordan, and the YAR); and the consequences of large-scale migration on the socioeconomic developments, both in the labor-exporting and the labor-receiving countries, mainly for those cases in which the migrants and their accompanying family members constituted the majority of the total population, such as in Kuwait, Qatar, and the United Arab Emirates (UAE).

It seems that the major difficulty in the research of Syrian migration abroad, especially to other Arab countries, is that the Syrian authorities did not publish official figures, or even estimates, regarding the number of Syrian workers abroad, not to mention their distribution according to the host countries. In other Middle Eastern labor-exporting countries, the data and the official estimates published by the authorities, in some cases even on a regular basis, constitute the major source for determining the number of migrant workers, the scale of their remittances, and their distribution according to the host countries. In the case of Jordan, for example, the official estimates regarding the number of Jordanian migrant workers in other Middle Eastern countries appear in the official annual *Statistical Yearbook*.[44] The Egyptian authorities also publish data and other information regarding Egyptian migrant workers in other Middle Eastern countries.

One major problem with the available data is that some labor-importing countries tend to underestimate the number of foreign workers, due to the large number of foreign workers, or even perhaps for political reasons. For example, according to Saudi Arabian official data, the number of foreign workers in the Kingdom in 1975 was 400,000. However, a government expert was reported to have said that the number of foreign workers in Saudi Arabia at that time was actually over one million.[45]

Another basic difficulty with the data is that since the mid-1970s, the censuses conducted by the GCC countries have tended to give a broad view, at least in their official publications, on the national and non-national populations without breaking down the foreigner groups by their countries of origin.[46] Moreover, in most of the labor-receiving countries, the population censuses were taken at large intervals of at least ten years, and in some cases at even broader intervals. In Saudi Arabia, which is the largest labor-importing country all over the Middle East, the first population census was taken in 1962–63. However, most of the census results were never published, besides those regarding a few cities, which were later published by the Saudi Department of Statistics.[47] The second census was conducted 12 years later, in 1974. But, there were indications of serious defects in the reliability of the data.[48] The third and the latest census of the Kingdom was conducted 18 years later, in 1992. In all of these censuses, as well as in other Saudi official publications, there is a lack of information regarding the distribution of foreigners by their country of origin. The most extreme case as far as lack of data is found in the Sultanate of Oman, which conducted its first population census ever in 1993. Among the GCC countries, only Bahrain and Kuwait conducted population censuses on a regular basis, mostly in intervals of five years.

Further complicating the issue is the fact that agreements between labor-importing and labor-exporting countries in the Arab world are highly irregular. In fact, migration as part of the formal system constitutes only a small percentage of the migration that actually takes place. For example, although Egypt agreed to supply Qatar with 9,000 workers a year as per a 1974 agreement, this is not necessarily an indicator of the actual number of Egyptians working in Qatar at that time.[49]

An additional important source of data is provided by unofficial studies on foreign workers in the major oil-exporting countries, as conducted by commercial bodies. In addition, the newspapers, both local and foreign, constitute a major source of information and up-to-date data, insofar as they contain reports and articles on various issues relating to the number of foreign workers and their distribution by nationalities; labor and migration regulations and laws; the deportation of illegal foreign workers; and interviews with officials in these fields. In spite of the severe difficulties with these sources, they provide indications of the trends of Syrian migration to other Arab countries for purposes of employment, as well as the Syrian authorities' policies towards this phenomenon.

With regard to the Ottoman and Mandatory periods, it is almost impossible to conduct a comprehensive demographic investigation as the result of lack of sufficient and accurate data. However, the tremendous improvements, in both quantity and quality, of the demographic and other socioeconomic data on Syria since receiving independence, especially following the 1960 census, will enable us to implement comprehensive research on the demographic developments and policies in Ba'thist Syria.

Economic Data

Accurate and reliable economic data have a tremendous impact on the conduct of comprehensive demographic research, since without them it is impossible to calculate important topics such as the per capita income and GDP, or the distribution of the labor force according to the various economic activities. However, a number of sources have pointed to the fact that the Syrian data which appears in official publications regarding various socioeconomic topics are often neither accurate nor complete, and sometimes retroactively changed.[50] With regard to unemployment rates, for example, which is one of the most important indicators used to analyze whether the rate of population growth is higher than economic expansion, Eliyahu Kanovsky notes that: "In Syria, as in many other less developed countries, the unemployment figures are not very meaningful."[51]

Another major problem in this regard is the high rate of smuggling of both cash and consumer goods into the country.[52] One of the main reasons for this is the huge difference between the official and the unofficial exchange rates of the LS (Syrian Pound) to the US dollar. In addition, the income of Syrian workers in the Gulf oil-exporting countries is often transferred on a large scale via unofficial channels.[53] The data regarding the actual income on these migrants obviously do not appear in any official statistics.

Thus, as a result of the substantial amount of smuggling, it is impossible to calculate the real per capita income and GDP, as well as the actual unemployment rates, both of which constitute essential indicators for analyzing demographic pressures and the real standard of living of the population. All of these obstacles clearly make the conduct of comprehensive socio-demographic research on Syrian society more difficult, but in no way will they prevent the successful implementation of such research.

2

Population Growth

Natural Increase of the Population

It seems that until 1840, the annual natural increase rate of the Syrian population was near-zero (this stagnation in the population growth was the outcome
of the crude death rates being almost equally as high as the crude birth rates,
leaving no room for population growth). Since 1840 through the end of the
World War I, the natural increase rate in the Syrian region was estimated to be
one percent.[1] Under the French Mandate, the natural increase rate of the Syrian
population rose rapidly, primarily as a result of the sharp reduction in the crude
death rates. During the years 1938–47, the annual natural increase rate in Syria
was estimated at 2.27 percent. After independence, the natural increase rate
continued to rise and was estimated to be 2.70 percent during the years
1947–60.[2] This was mainly due to a sharp reduction in the crude death rates as
a result of steady improvement in the health-care facilities in parallel to a
constant increase in the standard of living of the population.

Since 1960 and until the mid-1980s, the fertility levels in Syria continued to
be very high, in fact, one of the highest in the entire Middle East and North
Africa region. In 1960, the crude birth rate in Syria was estimated to be 47.9
per 1,000, and the total fertility rate was 7.3. Ten years later, in 1970, the crude
birth rate was estimated to be 47.8 per 1,000, slightly decreasing to 45.8 in 1980.
Similarly, the total fertility rates also continued to be very high: 7.6 in 1970 and
7.3, ten years later, in 1980.

However, from the mid-1980s onward, the crude birth and fertility rates in
Syria started to decrease. In 1985, the crude birth rate in Syria was estimated
by the World Bank to be 45.3, slightly decreasing to about 44 in 1990, according
to the same source. Similarly, the total fertility rates also decreased slightly:
from 7.3 in 1980 to 6.4 in 1990 (see table 2.1). By the beginning of the 1990s,
according to the various estimates, despite the increasing involvement of the
Syrian authorities in family planning activities,[3] the fertility rates in Syria
continued to be one of the highest all over the Middle East and North Africa
region. By 1992, the crude birth rate in Syria was estimated by ESCWA at 43.8

per 1,000, and the total fertility rate was 6.9. In Egypt, for example, at the same year, the crude birth rate was estimated to be 29.2 per 1,000,[4] and the total fertility rate was 4.17 – more than 30 percent less than in Syria.[5] In Jordan in the same year, the crude birth and the total fertility rate were estimated to be 37.85 and 5.87, respectively.[6] According to these figures, it seems that at the beginning of the 1990s, one can find only in a few countries in the Gulf higher crude birth and total fertility rates than in Syria. Moreover, these countries are large exporters of oil and are operating pro-natalist policies, due both to very small national populations and severe shortages of manpower.

According to the 1993 SMCHS, the total fertility rate in 1993 was only 4.2,[7] while this rate for the same year was estimated by the World Bank to be as high as 5.8 (see table 2.1). While the Population Division of the UN estimated the crude birth rate in Syria in 1993 to be 41.1,[8] it later updated the estimate for that particular year, placing it at only 33.2 per 1,000 (see table 2.1). Three years later, in 1996, according to ESCWA figures, the crude birth rate in Syria was 29.3 and the total fertility rate was 4.0. These rates represent a reduction of 33 percent in the crude birth rate and a parallel decline of 42 percent in the total fertility rate, as compared with ESCWA figures from 1992 (see table 2.1).

There are no earlier examples among the Middle Eastern and North African countries from which to conclude that societies can decrease their crude birth and total fertility rates by tens of percent within a period of only two or even five years. There is one example, that of Egypt, which points to a sharp reduction in the fertility levels within a relatively short period of time. During the late 1960s, the crude birth rate dropped from 40.9 in 1966 to 35.1 in 1970,[9] representing a reduction of 17 percent within a period of only four years. However, it appears that this drop was short-lived. It has been suggested that the decline was caused primarily by the traumatic events of the June 1967 War and the War of Attrition which followed (1969–70), bringing about severe security as well as economic hardships that caused a dramatic decrease in the per capita GDP and income.[10] However, with the recovery of the Egyptian economy during the mid-1970s, combined with the "oil boom" and the return of the oil fields in Sinai to Egypt, the crude birth and fertility rates in Egypt again increased, reaching almost 40 per 1,000 by the late 1970s and the early 1980s.[11]

In Syria, according to the above-mentioned figures and estimates, the reduction of the crude birth and fertility rates during the early 1990s was much sharper than in Egypt during the late 1960s. In addition, by the beginning of the 1990s, Syrian society was not experiencing any traumatic events, either on the military front or in socioeconomic life. On the contrary, the economic situation in Syria at that time was showing substantial improvement. Moreover, with regard to the age distribution of the population (see table 2.17), it is not

Table 2.1   Syria: Natural increase rates, 1960–96

Year	Crude birth rate (per 1,000)	Crude death rate (per (1,000)	Natural increase (%)	Total fertility rate
1960	47.9	17.7	3.0	7.3
1965	47.9	16.0	3.2	7.6
1970	47.8	13.5	3.4	7.6
1975	45.9	10.3	3.6	7.5
1976	45.8	9.1	3.7	7.5
1977	45.8	8.5	3.7	7.5
1978	45.7	8.5	3.7	7.5
1979	46.4	8.3	3.8	7.3
1980	45.8	8.3	3.8	7.3
1981	47.5	8.0	4.0	7.2
1982	45.7	7.0	3.9	7.2
1983	46.5	7.2	3.9	7.2
1984	45.4	8.0	3.7	7.0
1985	45.3	8.0	3.7	6.9
1986	45.3	8.3	3.7	6.8
1987	45.2	7.0	3.8	6.8
1988	44.7	7.0	3.8	6.7
1989	45.0	7.0	3.8	6.6
1990	44.0	7.0	3.7	6.4
1992	43.8	6.5	3.7	6.9
1993	33.2	5.8	2.7	5.8
1994	28.0	5.4	2.3	4.7
1996	29.3	4.9	2.4	4.0

Sources:

Crude birth rates

1960–70: Syrian Arab Republic, Office of the Prime Minister, Central Bureau of Statistics, *Statistical Abstract – 1973* (Damascus, 1974), p. 60, table 9/2 [hereafter: Syria, *Statistical Abstract*].

1975: The World Bank, *World Tables, The Third Edition, Vol. 2 – Social Data from the Data Files of the World Bank* (Baltimore and London: The Johns Hopkins University Press, 1984), p. 87 [hereafter: World Bank, *World Tables, the third edition*].

1976: Syria, *Composition and Growth of Population*, p. 24.

1977: Syria, *Rates of Natural Increase*, p. 14, table 3.

1978: ESCWA, *Population Situation in the ESCWA Region, 1990* (Amman: 20 May 1992), p. 185, table 11.4 [hereafter: ESCWA, *Population Situation, 1990*].

1979: UN, *Demographic Yearbook – 1982* (New York, 1983), p. 272 [hereafter: UN, *Demographic Yearbook*].

Table 2.1 Sources *(continued)*

1980: ECWA, *Demographic and Related Socio-Economic Data Sheets for Countries of the Economic Commission for Western Asia*, No. 3 (Beirut, May 1982), p. 164, table 2 [hereafter: ECWA, *Demographic Data Sheets*].

1981: World Bank, *World Tables, the third edition*, p. 87.

1982–83: UN, *Demographic Yearbook – 1983*, p. 291.

1984–87: World Bank, *World Tables, 1989–90 edition*, p. 547.

1988: ESCWA, *Population Situation, 1990*, p. 185, table 11.4.

1989: World Bank, *World Development Report – 1991*, p. 256, table 27.

1990: World Bank, *World Development Report – 1992*, p. 270, table 27.

1992: ESCWA, *Demographic Data Sheets*, No. 7 (1993), p. 134, table 3.

1993: UN, *Demographic Yearbook – 1996*, p. 323.

1994: ESCWA, *Demographic Data Sheets*, No. 8 (1995), p. 118, table 3.

1996: ESCWA, *Demographic Data Sheets*, No. 9 (1997), p. 110, table 3.

Crude death rates

1960–75: World Bank, *World Tables, the third edition*, p. 87.

1976: *Population Policy Compendium, Syrian Arab Republic*, p. 4.

1977: Syria, *Rates of Natural Increase*, p. 14, table 3.

1978: *Population Policy Compendium, Syrian Arab Republic*, p. 4.

1979: ESCWA, *Statistical Abstract of the Region of the Economic and Social Commission for Western Asia, 1978–1987* (Baghdad, December 1989), p. 397 [hereafter: ESCWA, *Statistical Abstract, 1978–1987*].

1980:ECWA, *Demographic Data Sheets*, No. 3 (1982), p. 165, table 3.

1981: World Bank, *World Development Report – 1983*, p. 187, table 20.

1982: World Bank, *World Development Report – 1984*, p. 257, table 20.

1983: UN, *Demographic Yearbook – 1984*, p. 366.

1984: UN, *Demographic Yearbook – 1986*, p. 216.

1985: World Bank, *World Development Report – 1987*, p. 257, table 28.

1986: ESCWA, *Statistical Abstract, 1978–1987*, p. 397.

1987: UNICEF, *The State of the World's Children – 1989* (Oxford and New York: Oxford University Press, 1989), p. 102, table 5 [hereafter: UNICEF, *The State of the World's Children*].

1988: UN, *Demographic Yearbook – 1991*, p. 360.

1989: World Bank, *World Development Report – 1991*, p. 256, table 27.

1990: World Bank, *World Development Report – 1992*, p. 270, table 27.

1992: ESCWA, *Demographic Data Sheets*, No. 7 (1993), p. 135, table 4.

1993: UN, *Demographic Yearbook – 1994*, p. 406.

1994: ESCWA, *Demographic Datat Sheets*, No. 8 (1995), p. 119, table 4.

1996: ESCWA, *Demographic Data Sheets*, No. 9 (1997), p. 111, table 4.

Total fertility rates

1960–75: World Bank, *World Tables, the third edition*, p. 87.

1976: World Bank, *World Tables, 1989–90 edition*, p. 546.

Table 2.1 Sources *(continued)*

1977: UNFPA, *Syrian Arab Republic*, p. 70.

1978: ESCWA, *Population Situation, 1990*, p. 185, table 11.4.

1979: ESCWA, *Statistical Abstract, 1978–1987*, p. 397.

1980–82: World Bank, *World Tables, 1989–90 edition*, p. 547.

1983: UNICEF, *The State of the World's Children – 1986*, p. 145, table 5.

1984–87: World Bank, *World Tables, 1989–90 edition*, p. 547.

1988: World Bank, *World Development Report – 1990*, p. 231, table 27.

1989: UNICEF, *The State of the World's Children – 1991*, p. 111, table 5.

1990: World Bank, *World Tables, 1993 edition*, p. 584.

1992: ESCWA, *Demographic Data Sheets*, No. 7 (1993), p. 134, table 3.

1993: World Bank, *World Tables, 1995 edition*, p. 651.

1994: ESCWA, *Demographic Data Sheets*, No. 8 (1995), p. 118, table 4.

1996: ESCWA, *Demographic Data Sheets*, No. 9 (1997), p. 110, table 3.

Table 2.2 Syria: Age-specific fertility rates, 1960–93 (per 1,000 women)

Year Age	1960	1970	1978	1988	1993
15–19	122.0	153	124	51	61
20–24	329.8	318	302	255	164
25–29	377.8	380	341	354	255
30–34	314.6	339	312	342	189
35–39	197.4	260	246	275	129
40–44	76.6	135	135	162	64
45–49	7.3	45	42	70	11
Total fertility rates	7.13	7.6	7.5	7.5	4.2

Sources:

1960: Syria, *Statistical Abstract – 1973*, p. 60.

1970: Syria, *Composition and Growth of Population*, p. 34, table 3.5.

1978: Syria, *Statistical Abstract – 1995*, p. 56, table 4.2.

1988: ESCWA, *Population Situation, 1990*, p. 185, table 11.4.

1993: Syria, *Statistical Abstract – 1995*, p.56, table 4.2.

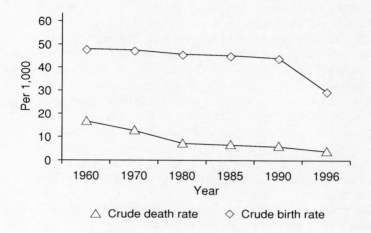

△ Crude death rate   ◇ Crude birth rate

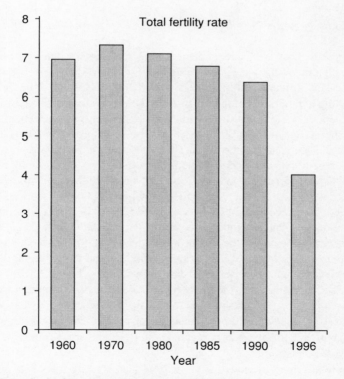

Total fertility rate

Figure 2.1   Syria: Natural increase rates, 1960–96

reasonable that in a normal state of society, without any traumatic events, fertility rates would drop by tens of percent within only a few years.

The only explanation for these contradictory figures is that the estimates regarding fertility rates in Syria during the late 1980s and the early 1990s were exaggerated by a considerable extent. In any case, from the late 1980s onward, there are many indications for a gradual reduction in fertility rates among the Syrian population, as was actually the case in many other Middle Eastern countries (for example, Egypt, Jordan and Tunisia) during that period. The only question remaining refers to the exact rate of decrease.

This reduction was due to four main factors: The *first* is the large improvement in the educational level of the whole population, especially for women. The *second* factor is the sharp rise in the rate of contraceptive use, and the *third* is the increased level of governmental activity in the area of family planning. The *fourth* reason is the growing proportion of the urban population within the total population, since the fertility rates among urban women are substantially lower than those of rural women (see below).

The Fertility Gap between Urban Centers and Rural Areas

One of the most widespread demographic phenomena among developing countries all over the world, including those of the Middle East, is a wide gap in the crude birth and fertility rates between urban centers and the rural areas. According to the results of the 1976–79 FUDS, while the crude birth rate in the urban centers was 38.5 per 1,000, and the total fertility rate was 6.0, in the rural areas these rates were 47.1 per 1,000 and 8.6, respectively (see table 2.4). Similar data collected by the Syrian CBS shows that during the years 1973–78, the average total fertility rate in the urban centers was 6.0, as compared with 8.7 in the rural areas. According to these data, the highest fertility rates were found in the northeast and the southern provinces (8.4), and the lowest, as was expected, in the capital city of Damascus (4.7). This also represents a high correlation between the proportion of the urban population in the region and the fertility level: the higher the proportion of the urban population, the lower the fertility rates (see table 2.3). One can also find the same trend in the 1978 SFS figures (see table 2.5), as well as in data from the early 1990s. According to the 1993 SMCHS data, while the total fertility rate in the urban centers was 3.6, it was as high as 5.1 in the rural areas.[12] The difference in the fertility rates between urban centers and rural areas was also reflected in the average family size: 6.6 in the rural areas, as compared with 6.0 in the urban centers, according to the 1981 census data.[13]

There are many reasons for the wide gap in fertility rates between urban centers and rural areas, one of which is that in the countryside children serve as

Table 2.3 Syria: Age-specific fertility rates per 1,000 women, according to level of education, age, and place of residence, 1973–78

Background characteristics	Total fertility rate	Age group						
		15–19	20–24	25–29	30–34	35–39	40–44	45–49
Level of education								
Illiterate	8.6	175	357	384	366	283	150	51
Literate	4.3	109	310	136	99	142	59	9
Primary and over	3.2	27	99	179	166	98	61	*
Place of residence								
Urban	6.0	109	256	292	261	186	97	24
Rural	8.7	140	343	392	378	315	175	64
Region of residence								
Damascus city	4.7	91	204	251	213	121	54	11
Aleppo city	6.9	153	323	318	268	216	105	22
Northeast	8.4	142	322	364	350	304	199	78
West	6.9	74	282	342	307	265	118	8
Center	7.8	143	295	345	351	269	152	54
South	8.4	128	361	408	351	294	144	56
Total	7.3	124	302	341	312	246	135	42

Source: Syria, *Statistical Abstract – 1984*, p. 62, table 6/2.
* Less than 50 cases.

Table 2.4 Syria: Crude birth and total fertility rates, according to type of residence, 1976–79

Year	(1) Crude birth rate (per 1,000)			(2) Total fertility rate		
	Urban	Rural	Total	Urban	Rural	Total
1976/77	40.5	46.7	43.7	6.4	8.6	7.5
1977/78	37.0	49.1	43.3	5.8	9.1	7.4
1978/79	38.2	45.4	41.9	5.9	8.1	7.0
1976–1979	38.5	47.1	43.0	6.0	8.6	7.3

Sources: 1. *Follow-Up Demographic Survey, 1976–79*, p. 40.
     2. Ibid., p. 52.

Table 2.5 Mean number of children ever born to ever-married women in Syria aged 45–49, by background characteristics, 1978

Background characteristics	Mean number of children	Number of women
Level of education		
No schooling	8.0	451
Some schooling	6.6	69
Place of residence		
Urban	7.9	251
Rural	7.8	269
Region of residence		
Damascus city	7.3	91
Aleppo city	7.6	50
Northeast	7.7	133
West	7.6	57
Center	8.3	127
South	8.4	62
Pattern of work		
Before and after marriage	7.4	89
After marriage only	7.4	34
Before marriage only	7.8	42
Never worked	8.0	359
Total	7.8	520

Source: *Syria Fertility Survey – 1978*, p. 53, table 5.14.

an important labor force, while in urban centers their contribution to the family income is marginal, if any. However, it seems that the most important reason for this gap is the large difference in women's educational level between urban centers and rural areas.

Women's Education and Fertility Levels

The most important factor affecting the fertility rates in Syria, as in other Middle Eastern countries, is women's educational level. In all the demographic surveys and censuses conducted in Syria, as well as in other Middle Eastern countries, there are significant differences in the fertility rates between educated and non-educated woman, insofar as the higher the women's educational level, the lower the fertility rate. According to the 1970 census data, the average number of children ever born to women without any formal education was 5.7, as compared with 3.4 for women with primary school education, 2.6 for those with preparatory (or intermediate) school education, and only 1.9 for women with some form of higher education. Another important result obtained from the census was that the differences between the various provinces had almost no effect on fertility trends.[14] The 1976 CDC (Cairo Demographic Centre) Survey, which was conducted in the capital city of Damascus during June–July 1976, also pointed to a very similar trend.[15]

Similar findings are also revealed in the 1978 SFS. According to the survey data, while the mean number of children ever born to women in the age group of 45–59 without any formal education was 8.4, it dropped to 6.4 for those with an incomplete primary school education. The lowest number of children was among those with a primary school education, only 3.5, representing a gap of more than 100 percent between women without any formal education and those

Table 2.6 Mean number of children ever born to ever-married women in Syria, according to age, place of residence, and level of education, 1978

Background characteristics	Age 15–19	20–24	25–29	30–34	35–39	40–44	45–49
Level of education							
No schooling	0.9	2.3	3.9	5.9	7.4	8.0	8.4
Incomplete primary	0.7	1.9	3.5	4.9	6.1	6.4	6.4
Complete primary	0.2	0.9	1.8	3.1	3.7	(3.9)	(3.5)
Secondary and over	–	(0.7)	(1.0)	2.1	3.0	(4.0)	(3.7)
Place of residence							
Urban	0.9	2.0	3.5	5.1	6.6	7.5	8.0
Rural	0.7	2.2	3.8	5.8	7.3	7.9	8.3
Region of residence							
Damascus city	0.7	1.8	3.1	4.5	6.0	6.8	7.5
Aleppo city	0.8	2.2	3.9	5.3	6.9	7.3	7.7
Northeast	0.8	2.1	3.5	5.4	6.7	7.9	8.2
West	0.9	2.0	3.8	5.5	7.4	8.0	8.1
Center	0.9	2.2	3.9	5.7	7.2	7.9	8.5
South	0.8	2.2	3.9	5.9	7.4	8.1	8.2
Total	0.8	2.1	3.7	5.4	6.9	7.7	8.1

* Figures in parentheses are based on less than 20 cases.

Source: *Syria Fertility Survey – 1978*, p. 54, table 5.15.

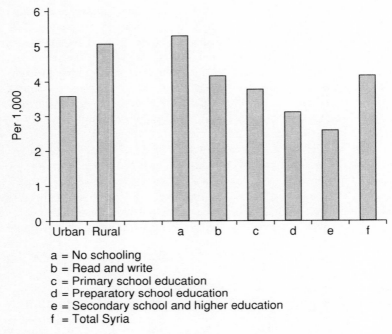

a = No schooling
b = Read and write
c = Primary school education
d = Preparatory school education
e = Secondary school and higher education
f = Total Syria

Figure 2.2 Total fertility rates in Syria, according to place of residence, and mother's educational level, 1993
Source: *Syrian Maternal and Child Health Survey*, 1993, p. 16.

who have at least primary school education (see table 2.6). The same gap continued to exist throughout the 1980s and the early 1990s. As reported in the 1993 SMCHS, the total fertility rate among women without any schooling was 5.3, in comparison with 4.2 among those who could only read and write, 3.8 among those with a primary school education, 3.1 among those with a preparatory education, and only 2.6 for those with secondary and higher education (see figure 2.2).

The most important question in this regard is: What are the reasons for the close connection between fertility rates and women's educational level? It seems that there are six main factors accounting for this association:

1   **Delay of the age at first marriage:** In general, there is a high correlation between the age at first marriage and the woman's level of education. In most cases, educated women tend to delay their marriage at least until they complete their education. In the case of those with higher education, this means delaying the first marriage at least until the age of 23–24, thereby

substantially reducing the reproductive years within the marriage system. Moreover, educated women tend to choose their husbands by themselves and generally oppose arranged marriages. On the contrary, among uneducated women in traditional societies, one finds the opposite trend: marriage at a relatively early age and much dependence upon the family wishes,[16] meaning more reproductive years within the marriage system.

2 **Employment outside the home:** There is a high correlation between women's educational level and labor force participation rates: The higher the woman's educational level, the higher her tendency to work outside the home. Naturally, educated women wish to pursue their education in the context of a career, and thus, their labor force participation rates are substantially higher. Since a large number of children generally acts as a hindrance to a woman's career, the trend among career women is to have fewer children. According to the 1970 census data, the average number of children ever born to women who were economically active in non-agricultural professions was 3.9, in comparison with 5.4 children for those who were engaged in agriculture. The highest number of children was found among economically inactive women, with an average of 5.6.[17]

3 **Participation in decision making:** Education usually increases the communication between husband and wife, making wives more influential in the decision-making process within the family. Accordingly, the wife plays a more significant part in deciding the size of the family, understanding the connection between the number of children and the per capita income in the family.

4 **Wider scope of interests:** In addition to their tendency to work outside the home, educated women are inclined to enjoy social life, as well as to raise the family standard of living. These two factors have a major influence on the number of children desired.

5 **Lower infant mortality rates:** Educated women are more competent in taking care of their children, who are, as a result, less exposed to illness and epidemics. Consequently, the mortality rates among infants of educated mothers are significantly lower than those among infants of illiterate mothers (see below). Educated women are thus more inclined to have a small number of children because they do not fear as much about their loss.

6 **Better knowledge of contraceptives:** Educated women are much more likely to be aware of contraceptive methods and their proper use, as compared with uneducated women. Therefore, if an educated woman prefers a small family, she has the knowledge about how to limit the number of her children.[18]

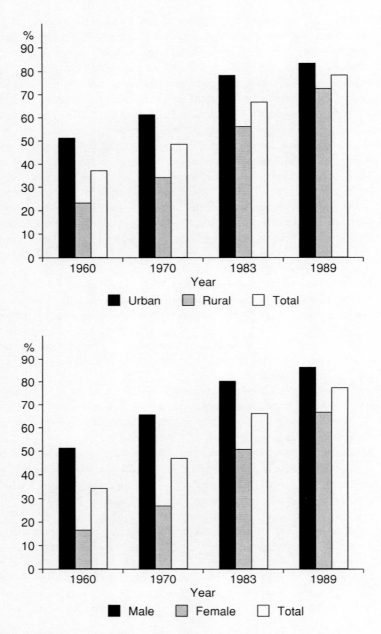

Figure 2.3 Syria: Distribution of the population (10 years and over), according to literacy/illiteracy, 1960–89

Table 2.7 Syria: Distribution of the population (10 years and over), according to sex, place of residence, and level of education, 1960–93 (in percentages)

Year	sex	Total Literate	Literate and over Urban	Literate and over Rural	Illiterate Urban	Illiterate Rural
	M	51.6	68.1	41.3	31.9	58.7
1960	F	16.8	34.6	6.1	65.4	93.9
	T	34.4	51.7	23.8	48.3	76.2
	M	65.6	76.3	56.8	23.7	43.2
1970	F	26.8	46.2	11.7	53.8	88.3
	T	46.6	61.7	34.4	38.3	65.6
	M	76.9	84.0	69.7	16.0	30.3
1978	F	45.8	63.8	28.4	36.2	71.6
	T	61.6	74.1	49.2	25.9	50.8
	M	80.1	85.4	74.7	14.6	25.3
1983	F	50.8	68.1	30.1	31.9	69.9
	T	65.7	77.0	54.5	33.0	45.5
	M	86.4	90.2	85.3	9.8	14.7
1989	F	66.2	74.3	57.6	25.7	42.4
	T	77.2	82.4	71.6	17.6	28.4
	M	88.8	na		na	
1993	F	69.4	na		na	
	T	79.4	na		na	

na = no data available

Notes: M = Male   F = Female   T = Total

Sources:

1960–70: Syria, *Composition and Growth of Population*, p. 11, table 1.9.

1978–93: Syria, *Statistical Abstract – 1995*, p. 64, table 12/2.

Mortality Rates and Life Expectancy

The study of a country's mortality trends requires reliable statistical data on various characteristics of its population, such as life expectancy according to sex, distribution of the population by sex, and most importantly, accurate and up-to-date data on the age pyramid of the population. However, these data do not exist in Syria for any period preceding the 1960 census. In this respect, Syria is no different from any of the other Middle Eastern countries, with the exception of Egypt, Kuwait and Tunisia, where demographic data have nearly complete coverage since the late 1940s. Consequently, it is almost impossible to analyze demographic trends in general, and mortality trends in particular, among most Middle Eastern and North African countries, including Syria, previous to the early 1960s, when most of these countries conducted more or less comprehensive censuses and demographic surveys.[19]

These data reveal that the primary factor accounting for the extraordinarily high natural increase rates in Syria over the last four decades, as in the other Middle Eastern and North African countries, is the sharp reduction of the crude death rates. These rates dropped from 17.7 per 1,000 in 1960 to 15.6 in 1970, 8.3 in 1980, and reached a low of 4.9 in 1996, one of the lowest throughout the Middle East and North Africa region. As a result of the sharp drop in the crude death rates, in parallel to a minor decline in the crude birth rates throughout the 1960s and the 1970s, the natural increase rate of the Syrian population increased

Table 2.8 Infant (0–1) mortality rates in Syria, 1960–96

Year	Infant mortality rate (per 1,000 live births)
1960	132.0
1965	115.5
1969	99.4
1975	77.2
1980	67.0
1985	52.4
1988	48.0
1990	42.6
1992	44.2
1993	35.0
1994	29.6
1996	29.1

Sources:
1960–65: World Bank, *World Tables, the third edition*, p. 87.
1969–75: World Bank, *World Tables, 1989–90 edition*, p. 546.
1980: UN, *Demographic Yearbook – 1983*, p. 374.
1985: World Bank, *World Tables, 1993 edition*, p. 587.
1988: UN, *Demographic Yearbook – 1991*, p. 332.
1990: World Bank, *World Tables, 1993 edition*, p. 587
1992: ESCWA, *Demographic Data Sheets*, No. 7 (1993), p. 135, table 4.
1993: *Syrian Maternal and Child Health Survey*, 1993, p. 21.
1994: ESCWA, *Demographic Data Sheets*, No. 8 (1995), p. 119, table 4.
1996: ESCWA, *Demographic Data Sheets*, No. 9 (1997), p. 111, table 4.

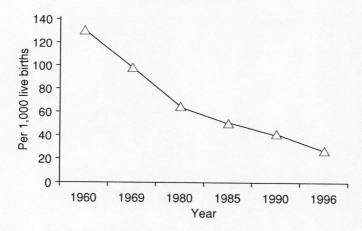

Figure 2.4   Infant (0–1) mortality rates in Syria, 1960–96

extremely rapidly during this period: from 3.0 percent in 1960 to 3.7 percent in 1975, reaching a peak of 4.0 percent in 1981 (see table 2.1). However, due to the decline in the crude birth and fertility rates over the last decade, the natural increase rates also declined to 3.7 in 1987, and only 2.4 in 1996, according to ESCWA estimates (see table 2.1). Thus, in Syria, as in the other Middle Eastern and North African countries, the demographic revolution was, first and foremost, a revolution in crude death rates.

There are two main factors accounting for the sharp reduction of the crude death rates in Syria, as well as in other developing countries, including those of the Middle East and North Africa, during the latter part of the twentieth century. The first is the marked decline in infant (aged 0–1) and child (aged 1–5) mortality rates. During the years 1950–55, the average infant mortality rate per 1,000 live births was 160, slightly decreasing to 145 on average during the years 1955–60.[20] From the early 1960s onward, there has been a substantial drop in the infant mortality rate: In 1960, this rate was estimated to be 132.0 per 1,000 live births, decreasing to 67.0 in 1980, and reaching as low as 29.1 in 1996 (see table 2.8). Likewise, the under-5 mortality rates also fell very sharply: from 270 per 1,000 live births on average during the years 1950–55, to 239 on average during the years 1955–60,[21] 218 in 1960,[22] 88 in 1980,[23] 71 in 1985,[24] and as low as 39 in 1993.[25]

The meaning of these low rates of both infant and child mortality is that while almost 30 percent of the infants born in Syria just a few decades ago did not survive their fifth birthday, this rate decreased sharply to only a few percent by the beginning of the 1990s. This huge reduction in infant and child mortality

Table 2.9   Life expectancy at birth in Syria, 1960–96

Year	Life expectancy at birth (years)
1960	49.7
1965	53.0
1970	54.6
1975	56.8
1980	65.0
1985	64.0
1988	65.4
1990	66.3
1992	66.1
1993	67.5
1994	69.9
1996	70.0

Sources:
1960–1965: World Bank, *World Tables, the third edition*, p. 87.
1970–1975: ECWA, *Demographic Data Sheets*, No. 2 (1978), country page.
1980: World Bank, *World Tables, the third edition*, p. 87.
1985: World Bank, *World Tables, 1989–90 edition*, p. 547.
1988–90: World Bank, *World Tables, 1993 edition*, p. 587.
1992: ESCWA, *Demographic Data Sheets*, No. 7 (1993), p. 135, table 4.
1993: World Bank, *World Tables, 1995 edition*, p. 651.
1994: ESCWA, *Demographic Data Sheets*, No. 8 (1995), p. 119, table 4.
1996: ESCWA, *Demographic Data Sheets*, No. 9 (1997), p. 111, table 4.

rates constituted one of the most important factors accounting for the overall decrease in fertility rates in Syria from the late 1980s onward.

The second factor responsible for the significant drop in crude death rates in Syria over the last four decades was the rise in the average life expectancy of the population. In 1960, average life expectancy at birth in Syria was estimated to be 49.7 years (48.5 years for males and 51.0 years for females).[26] From the early 1960s onward, life expectancy in Syria increased considerably, reaching 54.6 years by 1970 and 65.0 years in 1980 (for both sexes). This trend also continued in the 1980s and the first half of the 1990s: by 1988, average life expectancy at birth in Syria was estimated by the World Bank to be 65.4 years, increasing to 67.5 years in 1993 (see table 2.9), and reaching 69.95 years in 1996 (68.81 years for males and 71.10 years for females), according to ESCWA estimates.[27]

There have been many factors contributing to the sharp drop in the infant and

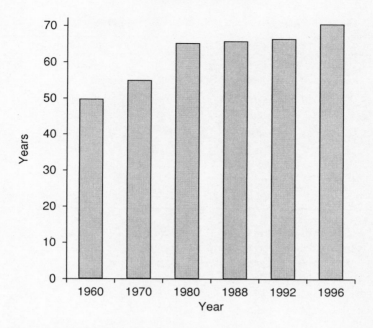

Figure 2.5   Life expectancy at birth in Syria, 1960–96

child mortality rates, and for the rapid increase in life expectancy in Syria over the last four decades. The two most important factors are as follows:

1   **Improvements in medical care:** Among the most significant factors in the improvement of health-care in Syria has been the reduction in the ratio of population per physicians and nurses. The per capita physician ratio fell from 1:4,224 in 1946 to 1:966 in 1993 (see table 2.10). Likewise, the per capita nurse decreased rapidly: from 1:6,666 in 1960 to 1:1,440 in 1980[28] and 1:728 in 1993.[29] Moreover, the ratio of population per hospital-bed also declined sharply, from 1:1,986 in 1949[30] to 1:911 in 1993.[31] It must be emphasized that this massive improvement, in both urban centers and the countryside, has been one of the most prominent aims of the socioeconomic agenda of the Ba'th regime since the revolution of March 1963.[32]

2   **Increase in the standard of living:** One of the most important indicators of the impressive increase in the standard of living in Syria was the rise in the per capita GNP from $290 in 1968[33] to $1,150 in 1991.[34] Furthermore, at the beginning of the 1990s, there was a substantial improvement in the

Table 2.10   Per capita physician ratio in Syria, 1946–93

Year	Number of physicians	Per capita physician
1946	670	4,224
1958	942	4,692
1968	1,437	4,088
1975	2,400	3,065
1980	3,880	2,314
1985	6,163	1,666
1990	11,682	1,037
1991	11,808	1,061
1993	13,863	966

Sources:

1946: Syria, *Statistical Abstract – 1983*, p. 330, table 1/11.

1958: Syria, *Statistical Abstract – 1958*, p. 63, table 9.

1968–80: Syria, *Statistical Abstract – 1983*, p. 330, table 1/11.

1985: Syria, *Statistical Abstract – 1988*, p. 390, table 1/11.

1990: Syria, *Statistical Abstract – 1991*, p. 352, table 1/11.

1991–93: Syria, *Statistical Abstract – 1994*, p. 360, table 1/11.

overall Syrian economy, and the GDP increased by almost 7 percent annually during the period of 1990–94, resulting in an annual increase of more than 4 percent in the per capita GDP. By 1995, the annual per capita income in Syria was just under $1,000, which is still low in comparison with developed countries, but a substantial improvement over previous years.[35]

Differences in Mortality Rates and Life Expectancy between Urban Centers and Rural Areas

As in the field of fertility, so in the fields of mortality rates and life expectancy: There are significant differences between urban centers and rural areas. According to the 1976–79 FUDS, while the total Syrian crude death rate was 8.2 per 1,000 inhabitants, it was only 6.7 in the urban centers, as compared with 9.6 in the rural areas, representing a gap of 43 percent (see table 2.11). Differences in crude death rates were found not only between urban and rural dwellers, but also between the various provinces of the country. During the years 1965–70, the crude death rate and the infant mortality rate in the Damascus province were estimated to be 11.4 and 93.5, respectively, as compared with 18.3 and 122.3 in the Idlib province and 17.4 and 125.8 in the

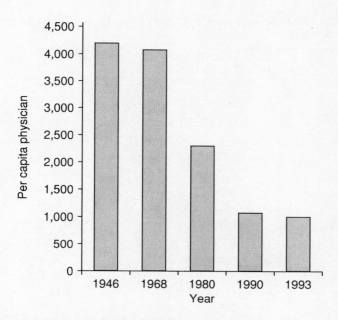

Figure 2.6   Per capita physician ratio in Syria, 1946–93

Table 2.11   Syria: Crude death rates, according to type of residence, 1976–79

Type of Residence		1976/7	1977/8	1978/9	1976–79
Urban	M	7.7	6.1	6.1	6.6
	F	5.7	7.1	7.4	6.7
	T	6.7	6.6	6.8	6.7
Rural	M	9.8	10.3	10.2	10.0
	F	8.8	9.5	9.7	9.3
	T	9.3	9.9	9.8	9.6
Total	M	8.8	8.3	8.0	8.4
	F	7.3	8.4	8.6	8.1
	T	8.1	8.3	8.3	8.2

Note: M = Male   F = Female   T = Total.

Source: *Follow-Up Demographic Survey, 1976–79*, p. 79, table 21.

Table 2.12   Infant mortality rates and crude death rates in Syria, according to regions, 1965–70

Regions	Infant mortality rate (per 1,000 live births)	Crude death rate (per 1,000)
Region I	93.3	11.4
Damascus	93.3	11.4
Region II	109.2	14.9
al-Suwayda	99.4	15.0
Darʿa	100.3	13.8
Homs	99.4	12.5
Hama	99.4	12.5
Tartus	103.4	14.3
Ladhaqiya	107.4	14.5
Idlib	122.3	18.3
Aleppo	106.5	13.9
Region III	114.1	15.6
al-Raqqa	112.0	15.1
Deir al-zur	109.0	15.7
al-Hasakah	125.8	17.4

Source:

Mahmoud Farag, "Mortality Level and Differentials Associated with Socio-Economic Development in Syria," in Cairo Demographic Centre, *Mortality Trends and Differentials in some African and Asian Countries*, Research Monograph Series, No. 8 (Cairo, 1982), p. 344, table 9.7 [hereafter: Farag, "Mortality Level"].

al-Hasakah province (see table 2.12). The conclusion indicated by these data is that the higher the proportion of the urban population in a given province, the lower the crude death and infant mortality rates will be.

According to the 1978 SFS, the indirect estimates for child mortality rates suggest that there were about 15 more survivors to the age of one year for every 1,000 live births among urban women than among rural women. It also appeared from this survey that the particular province of residence was influential in determining infant and child mortality rates. While the percentage of children who have died in Damascus city was 9.16, it increased to 12.47 in Aleppo city, and 14.38 in the south provinces, representing a gap of 57 percent in child mortality rates between Damascus city and the south provinces.[36] Similar findings are also evident in the 1993 SMCHS: While the under-5 mortality rate in the urban centers was 38.8 per 1,000 live births, it increased to 40.6 in the rural areas.[37] However, this small difference indicates the huge

Table 2.13 Life expectancy at birth in Syria, according to place of residence and sex, 1976

Place of residence		Life expectancy at birth (years)	
		Males	Females
Damascus city	Urban	63.9	67.7
Aleppo city	Urban	61.4	65.2
	Urban	61.0	64.8
Northeast region	Rural	56.0	59.6
	Total	–	–
	Urban	62.8	66.6
West region	Rural	58.9	62.8
	Total	–	–
	Urban	64.7	68.6
Center region	Rural	58.5	62.4
	Total	–	–
	Urban	62.8	66.6
South region	Rural	60.1	63.9
	Total	–	–
	Urban	62.8	66.6
Total Syria	Rural	57.8	61.7
	Total	60.1	64.0

Note: Based on the 1976 Sample Census
Source: Syria, *Rates of Natural Increase*, p. 13, table 2.

improvements in health-care in the rural areas during the 1980s and the early 1990s.[38]

Differences in life expectancy have also been found between urban centers and rural areas, as well as between the various provinces of the country. According to the 1976 SC, the life expectancy at birth in the capital city of Damascus was 63.9 years for males and 67.7 for females, as compared with 58.9 years for males and 62.8 years for females in the rural areas of the west region, and 58.5 years for males and 62.4 years for females in the rural areas of the center region (see table 2.13).

Women's Education and Infant and Child Mortality Rates

Another important factor affecting infant mortality rates is the mother's educational level. According to a survey conducted at the beginning of the 1980s by the CBS, it appeared that while the infant mortality rate among infants of illiterate mothers was 64 per 1,000 live births, it decreased to only 29 among infants of educated mothers.[39] One can find a similar tendency in the 1978 SFS[40] and the 1993 SMCHS, in which children of mothers with no schooling were found to have the lowest chances of survival. According to the 1993 SMCHS, while the under-5 mortality rate among children of mothers with no schooling was 43.9 per 1,000 live births, it decreased sharply to 37.9 among children of mothers with a primary school education, and only 31.8 among children of mothers with a preparatory school education and over.[41] One can also find the same trend in Jordan. According to the 1990 JPFHS figures, while the mortality rate among infants of illiterate mothers was 38.7 per 1,000 live births, it dropped significantly to only 23.9 among infants of mothers with more than a secondary school education.[42]

Marriage and Divorce

The rate of marriage and the average age at first marriage play a very important role in determining fertility rates, especially among traditional societies in which there are virtually almost no births outside the marriage system. In Syria, as in other Middle Eastern countries, the median age at first marriage is relatively low.

According to Law No. 59/1953 (article 16), the minimum age for marriage in Syria is 18 years for males and 17 years for females. However, this law was not observed by a large proportion of the population, especially females, among whom a substantial percentage were married earlier than the legal minimum age. According to the results of the 1976 CDC Survey conducted in Damascus city, 2.7 percent of ever-married males and as high as 34.9 percent of ever-married females married below the legal minimum age.[43]

According to the 1960 census data, the mean age at first marriage for females was 19.51 years. This figure increased to 20.67 years in 1970 and 21.53 years, according to the 1976 SC.[44] These data show that from the early 1960s onward, the mean age at first marriage for females in Syria has increased significantly. This trend was also apparent in the 1978 SFS: While 52.5 percent of the women in the age group of 45–49 who were participating in the survey married before the age of 20, this rate dropped to 42.8 percent in the age group of 20–24. In addition, there was also a large decline in very early marriage (under the age of 15), from 17.4 percent among women in the age group of 45–49, to only 7.7 percent among those in the age group of 15–19. The survey data also show that the median age at first marriage (the age by which half of the women of any given cohort have entered into a first marriage) rose from 18.4 years for women in the age group of 30–34, to 20 years for women in the age group of 20–24.[45]

From the 1993 SMCHS data, it appears that the trend of delayed marriage continued, and even strengthened, during the 1980s and the early 1990s. According to the survey data, while 43 percent of ever-married women in the age group of 45–49 were married before the age of 17, this rate dropped to 23 percent among those in the age group of 20–24. Similarly, the median age at first marriage increased from 18 years among women in the age group of 35–39, to 20 years among those in the age group of 25–29.[46] This increase has been one of the most important factors contributing to the reduction in fertility rates from the mid-1980s onward, simply as a result of the decline in the reproduction period.

The main question is: What are the factors shaping the age at first marriage? It seems that there are four such factors:

1 **Woman's educational level:** As in other demographic areas, the woman's educational level constitutes the most important factor in relation to age at first marriage. According to the 1970 census data, the median age at first marriage among women without any formal education was 18.6 years, increasing to 19.6 years among women with a preparatory school

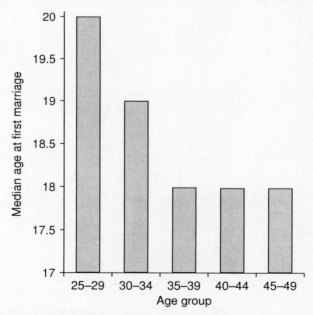

Figure 2.7   Median age at first marriage for women aged 25–49 in Syria, 1993
Source: Syrian Maternal and Child Health Survey, 1993, p. 75.

education, 22.3 years among those who had a secondary school education, and reaching as high as 25.5 years among women with higher education (see table 2.14).

The same trend also appeared in the 1976 CDC Survey in Damascus city: The median age at first marriage among women without any formal education was 17.9 years, as compared with 19.3 years among those with a secondary school education, and 25.6 years among women with higher education.[47] This tendency also appeared in the 1978 SFS, which showed that while the median age at first marriage among women without any formal education was 18.53 years, it increased to 24.73 years among those with a secondary school education and above (see table 2.15). All these surveys and censuses reveal that the higher the woman's educational level, the higher the age at first marriage. It seems that the most prominent reason for this phenomenon is that educated women tend to delay marriage until after completing their education.

2 **Place of residence.** Another important factor, albeit less so than education, is the place of residence. One can find that throughout all the age groups, the median age at first marriage among urban women was higher than among rural women. According to the 1978 SFS, the median age at first marriage for urban women was 21.16 years, as compared with 19.32 years among rural women (see table 2.15). The same tendency also appeared in the 1993 SMCHS.[48] The relatively large gap in the median age at first marriage between urban centers and rural areas constitutes one of the most important factors accounting for the higher fertility rates among rural women.

3 **Province of residence.** Differences in the median age at first marriage also exist between the various provinces of Syria. Since the 1960 census, the

Table 2.14 Median age of women at first marriage in Syria, according to level of education, and place of residence, 1970

Level of Education Governorates	Without formal education	Primary education	Preparatory education	Secondary education	Vocational and technical education	Higher education
Damascus	18.7	18.4	19.4	22.4	23.9	26.2
Aleppo	18.4	18.4	19.9	22.6	24.0	25.8
Hama	18.1	18.1	19.3	22.4	23.6	26.3
Homs	18.2	18.3	19.5	22.2	23.6	25.3
Others	18.8	18.5	19.8	22.5	23.4	25.9
Total	18.6	18.3	19.6	22.3	23.6	25.5

Source: Farag, "Differentials in Age at First Marriage in Syria," p. 499, table 24.3.

data indicate that the highest median age at first marriage has been in the capital city of Damascus. For example, according to the 1978 SFS, the median age at first marriage in Damascus was 22.20 years, as compared with 19.17 years in the south provinces and 19.32 years in the northeast provinces (see table 2.15). It appears from all the censuses and the demographic surveys conducted in Syria since 1960, that there is a strong correlation between the proportion of the urban population within the total province's population and the median age at first marriage, insofar as the higher the proportion of the urban population, the higher the median age at first marriage.

4   **Women's pattern of work.** Another prominent factor shaping the age at first marriage in Syria is the woman's pattern of work. According to data collected in the censuses and demographic surveys conducted in Syria, similar to those which have been conducted in other Middle Eastern countries, the median age at first marriage among working women is higher than among those who do not work outside the home. As reported in the 1970 census, for example, it appeared that the median age at first marriage among economically inactive women was 18.6 years, as compared with 19.4 years among economically active women.

Moreover, occupation also constitutes an important factor in shaping the age at first marriage. According to the same source, the median age at first marriage among women working in agriculture was 18.8 years, as compared with 21.2 years among those working in non-agricultural professions (see table 2.16). The reason for this is that in most cases, women with higher education tend to work outside the home, and the combination of higher education and working outside the home lead to a higher median age at first marriage.

The stability of marriage also constitutes an important factor in shaping the fertility rates, since in Syria, as in the other Middle Eastern countries, there are almost no births outside the marriage system. As in other traditional societies, in Syria the stability of the marriage system is very high. According to the 1978 SFS, 92.9 percent of the ever-married women reported that they were still married to their first husbands. Among the remaining 7.1 percent, 3.7 percent had their first marriages ended by the death of the husband, and 3.1 percent by divorce or separation.[49] In the 1993 SMCHS, marital stability was measured by the proportion of ever-married women whose first marriage ended as a result of divorce or widowhood. According to the survey data, about 95 percent of all the first marriages were still intact at the time that the survey was taken, and among the ever-married women whose first marriage was dissolved, 36 percent remarried.[50]

However, also in the area of marriage stability, there are significant

Table 2.15 Syria: Percentage of ever-married women, according to age, place of residence, and level of education, 1978

Age Background Characteristics	15–19	20–24	25–29	30–34	35–39	40–44	45–49	Median age at first marriage
Level of education								
No schooling	32.2	70.1	88.7	95.2	96.4	97.9	99.0	18.53
Incomplete primary	17.8	60.3	82.5	90.5	92.1	94.8	98.4	20.20
Complete primary	5.5	21.0	55.7	81.7	81.0	78.3	*	24.21
Secondary and higher	*	42.3	31.7	61.4	77.8	*	*	24.73
Place of residence								
Urban	21.8	56.4	79.1	91.1	91.8	95.6	97.1	21.16
Rural	23.8	64.7	86.6	94.3	97.8	98.5	99.2	19.32
Region of residence								
Damascus city	21.3	50.9	72.9	86.2	90.6	94.6	94.6	22.20
Aleppo city	30.9	68.3	87.6	91.4	92.7	96.7	97.5	19.22
Northeast	26.0	64.0	87.0	93.8	97.1	99.1	99.5	19.32
West	10.8	48.5	79.1	93.2	92.8	96.6	98.9	22.11
Center	21.4	60.7	82.8	95.1	94.9	96.3	98.8	19.87
South	25.4	68.0	86.9	94.3	97.2	98.3	98.8	19.17

* Less than 20 cases

Source: *Syria Fertility Survey – 1978*, p. 38, table 4.4.

Table 2.16 Median age of women in Syria at first marriage, according to economic activity, and place of residence, 1970

Governorates	All women	Economically inactive women	Economically active women		
			Total	Agricultural	Non-agricultural
Damascus	18.2	18.2	21.4	18.4	22.0
Aleppo	18.4	18.4	19.2	18.8	20.5
Homs	18.7	18.7	19.2	18.6	21.2
Hama	18.8	18.7	19.2	19.0	21.5
Others	18.8	18.8	19.2	18.9	20.8
Total	18.6	18.6	19.4	18.8	21.2

Source: Farag, "Differentials in Age at Marriage in Syria," p. 500, table 24.4.

differences between urban centers and rural areas. Throughout the period under discussion, the marriage stability rates were higher in the rural areas than in the urban centers. The highest rates of divorce were measured in the capital city of Damascus. By 1990, for example, the percentage of divorce certificates within the total marriage contracts was 22 cent in Damascus city, as compared with 7 percent in the Damascus rural area, 8 percent in the Aleppo province, and only 5 percent in the Tartus and Dar'a provinces.[51]

Economic Consequences of High Rates of Natural Increase

The high rates of natural increase of the Syrian population, a process which has been ongoing for more than four decades, has created a wide base of the age pyramid. In 1960, the percentage of the population below the age of 15 *vis-à-vis* the total Syrian population was 46.3 percent, rising to 49.3 percent ten years later, in 1970, due to the rising natural increase rates during the 1960s. However, since the late 1980s, as a result of the decreasing fertility rates, the percentage of the young population within the total population has also declined, from 48.5 percent, according to the 1981 census, to 44.7 percent in 1995, according to the CBS figures (see table 2.17).

Despite this decline, the percentage of the population below the age of 15 of the total Syrian population is still very high in comparison with developed countries, in some cases even more than double. According to UN sources, the international average of the under-15 population as a percentage of the total

Table 2.17 Distribution of Syria's population, by age, 1960–94

Year	Total	0–14	%	15–64	%	65+	%
1960	4,565,121	2,111,385	46.3	2,233,961	48.9	219,775	4.8
1970	6,304,685	3,106,120	49.3	2,922,559	46.3	276,006	4.4
1981	9,046,144	4,385,266	48.5	4,371,766	48.3	289,112	3.2
1990	12,116,000	5,968,000	49.3	5,616,000	46.3	532,000	4.4
1994	13,812,284	6,174,486	44.7	7,223,033	52.3	414,765	3.0
1995	14,186,000	6,342,000	44.7	7,418,000	52.3	426,000	3.0

Sources:
1960: UN, *Demographic Yearbook – 1970*, pp. 296–7.
1970: UN, *Demographic Yearbook – 1975*, pp. 240–1.
1981: Syria, *Statistical Abstract – 1990*, p. 51, table 1/2.
1990: Ibid., p. 60, table 10/2.
1994: Syria, *Statistical Abstract – 1995*, p. 53, table 1/2.
1995: Ibid., p. 62, table 10/2.

population at the beginning of the 1990s did not exceed 32 percent. The share of the under-15 population was at that time 36 percent in Latin America, 45 percent in Africa, 21 percent in North America, and only 20 percent in Europe, the lowest rate worldwide.[52] In France, for example, the percentage of the under-15 population within the total population in 1990 was only 20.1.[53] The reason for these very low percentages in Europe and North America is their correspondingly low crude birth and total fertility rates.

The direct result of the high percentage of the young population in Syria, as in most other developing countries, including those of the Middle East and North Africa, has been very low crude economically active rates of the population. According to the 1960 census, this rate was 26.3 percent (46.0 percent for males and 5.4 percent for females).[54] Almost three decades later, by 1988, this rate dropped to 23.58 percent (42.14 percent for males and only 4.46 percent for females),[55] mainly due to an accelerating natural increase rate of the Syrian society during the 1960s and the 1970s. One year later, by 1989, this rate increased to 26.2 percent as a result of the rise in the crude economically active rate among women to 8.3 percent.[56]

However, despite this increase, the crude economically active rates among Syrian women remained very low, even in the late 1980s and early 1990s. By comparison, in 1992, this rate was 35.7 percent among Cyprus women, and reached as high as 42.2 percent among Japanese women one year later, in 1993.[57] At that year, the overall crude economically active rate was 53.1 percent in Japan, 49.9 percent in Hong Kong, and 49.4 percent in the United Kingdom.[58] As a result, in the developed countries, the total crude economically active rates of the population are almost double those of the developing countries, including Syria or any other Arab country.

Children and teenagers are large consumers of public services, such as health-care and education, while their productive contribution is marginal, if any, particularly in the urban centers. In a country such as Syria, where public services are largely free of charge or are heavily subsidized, the high percentage of the young population has far-reaching consequences and a substantial negative impact on the rate of economic growth.

As a result of this process, Syria, like many other Middle Eastern countries also suffering from high fertility rates during the 1980s, has been unable to reach a balance between economic growth and population growth. In a country with an annual natural increase rate of more than 3 percent, the annual increase rate of the GDP has to be at least 6 percent in order to achieve significant economic growth. This is because more than half of the increase will be "swallowed" by the natural increase rate. However, such a GDP growth rate was far beyond the capacity of the Syrian economy during the 1980s. This was reflected in two main indexes: The first was the drop in the per capita GDP from LS 8,281 in 1980 to LS 7,386 ten years later, in 1990 (in constant prices of 1985).[59] The second index was the drop in the per capita GFCP (Gross Fixed Capital Formation) from LS 1,954 in 1980 to only LS 888 in 1990 (in constant prices of 1985).[60]

Another negative consequence of the rapid population growth was the continuing decline of the per capita agricultural land under cultivation. While during the years 1960–94 the cropped area in Syria increased by 40 percent (from 3.48 million hectares to 4.85 million hectares), at the same time the population size more than tripled. This resulted in a gradual drop of the per capita cropped area: from 0.76 hectares for the total Syrian population in 1960 to less than half, only 0.35 hectares, in 1994. Similarly, the per capita cropped area of the rural population also decreased sharply, from 1.21 hectares to 0.72 hectares during the same years (see table 2.18). This process, it must be emphasized, occurred despite the massive urbanization process which took place during that period.[61] The direct result of this process was increasing food imports, which amounted to $414 million already in 1978.[62]

Due to the economic structure of the Syrian villages, which are almost solely based on agriculture (despite the government's efforts to further develop industry in the countryside), those who became expendable due to the cultivated land shortages were forced to look for alternative employment in the urban centers, especially in the largest cities, where there were more varied employment opportunities than in the countryside. In addition, the rapid population growth in Syria, as in the other countries in the Middle East region, brought about a reduction in the available water for agricultural purposes. The cut of a

Table 2.18   Per capita cropped area in Syria, 1960–94

Year	Total Population (in thousands)	Rural Population (in thousands)	Total cropped area (thousands of hectares)	Per capita cropped area: Total population	Per capita cropped area: Rural Population
1960	4,565	2,880	3,480	0.76	1.21
1966	5,451	3,412	3,127	0.57	0.92
1970	6,305	3,564	3,291	0.52	0.93
1975	7,355	3,937	3,700	0.50	0.93
1980	8,797	4,608	3,893	0.44	0.84
1985	10,267	5,276	3,970	0.39	0.75
1990	12,116	6,029	5,466	0.45	0.91
1994	13,844	6,732	4,852	0.35	0.72

Notes: The data for the total and rural population taken from table 3.1; the data for the cropped area taken from Appendix 2.

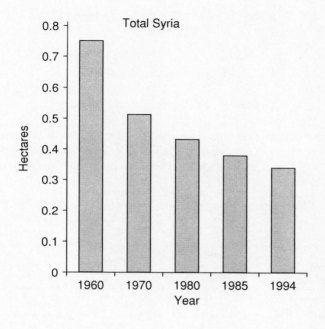

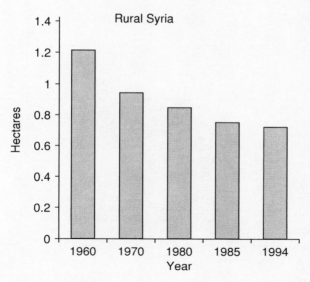

Figure 2.8   Per capita cropped area in Syria, 1960–94

large volume of the Euphrates water by Turkey,[63] combined with the rapid increase in domestic use due to the rapid population growth, has created a severe water shortage in Syria over the last decades.

Contraceptive Use

Knowledge of Birth Control Methods

The use of modern birth control methods on a large scale in the Middle East in general, and in Syria in particular, is relatively a new phenomenon. In the early 1970s, according to a report made by UNESCO, despite the fact that the trade,

Table 2.19 Percentage of ever-married women in Syria who heard of any contraceptive method, according to age, and background characteristics, 1978

Current age Background characteristics	Less than 25	25–34	35–44	45 and over	All
Level of education					
No schooling	59.0	70.9	74.2	64.5	68.3
Incomplete primary	94.9	98.5	97.6	92.9	96.6
Complete primary	95.0	94.4	98.6	95.0	95.4
Secondary and over	100.0	100.0	100.0	100.0	100.0
Place of residence					
Urban	91.4	93.7	93.6	84.1	92.0
Rural	61.1	66.1	65.0	53.9	62.9
Region of residence					
Damascus city	98.0	99.6	98.6	95.6	98.4
Aleppo city	79.6	86.0	86.0	76.0	83.0
Northeast	45.9	54.3	55.3	39.1	50.2
West	94.3	94.0	90.4	80.7	91.5
Center	78.6	81.1	79.1	67.7	78.1
South	85.1	85.7	84.2	75.8	84.2
Pattern of work					
Before and after marriage	60.8	68.3	60.5	60.0	63.4
After marriage only	83.0	83.1	77.3	73.5	79.9
Before marriage only	64.4	77.9	88.1	64.3	74.3
Never worked	81.2	84.0	85.3	70.5	81.9

Source: *Syria Fertility Survey – 1978*, p. 89, table 8.3.

promotion, and use of contraceptives were officially banned in Syria,[64] contraceptives were available and used in the major urban centers, mostly by middle-class families.[65] Nevertheless, it seems that the overall rate of contraceptive use during that period in Syria was relatively very low, and hence the impact on the overall fertility rates in the national level was quite marginal.

The first source which provides us with comprehensive and accurate data on the rate and distribution of contraceptive use in Syria is the 1978 SFS. Since knowledge of contraceptive methods can be regarded as a precondition for use, it is helpful to know the extent to which Syrian women were aware of various methods of contraception. According to the 1978 SFS, 77.7 percent of the respondents reported that they had heard about some method of birth control.

However, as in other demographic fields, there was also a large differential between urban and rural women in terms of awareness about birth control methods. While the rate of awareness among the former was 92.0 percent, it fell to only 62.9 percent among the latter. The highest rate of awareness was measured in the capital city of Damascus (98.4 percent), and the lowest in the northeast region (50.2 percent). The data from this survey reveal that the higher the proportion of the urban population in the region, the higher the rate of awareness of birth control methods (see table 2.19).

Another important factor shaping the rate of awareness of birth control methods is the age of the woman. According to the 1978 SFS, the highest rate of awareness was found among women in the age group of 35–44 (80.3 percent), and the lowest in the age group of 45 and over (only 68.5 percent).[66] Throughout the 1980s and the early 1990s, the rate of awareness about birth control methods increased sharply. According to the 1993 SMCHS, 92.7 percent of the respondents reported that they had heard about at least one modern birth control method, and 93.9 percent reported that they heard about at least one birth control method of any kind, including traditional methods. Among the modern methods, the most familiar was the pill (91.9 percent) and the IUD (89.1 percent – see table 2.21).

Use of Birth Control Methods

According to the 1978 SFS, 33.1 percent of ever-married women reported ever using either "modern" or "traditional" methods of family planning, and 29.5 percent of the respondents were reported to be currently using some method of contraceptive during the time that the survey was taken. This level of use represents 20 percent of all currently married women.[67] During the 1980s, however, the rate of contraceptive use in Syria rose dramatically. According to the 1993 SMCHS, 56.2 percent of the respondents reported ever-using some method of birth control, and 44.3 percent reported ever-using a modern method. The rate of current use of any method was measured at 39.6 percent, and 28.3 percent reported current use of a modern birth control method (see table 2.21). The tremendous increase in the rate of contraceptive use among Syrian women constitutes the main reason, even more important than that of delay in age at first marriage, for the sharp reduction in fertility rates during the last decade.

The most important question is: What are the critical factors shaping the rate of contraceptive use among Syrian women? This question is particularly important to the Syrian authorities, who have, since the late 1980s, been investing a considerable effort in order to reduce the fertility rates. The two most important factors are:

Table 2.20 Percentage of ever-married women in Syria who have ever used any contraceptive method, according to current age, and background characteristics, 1978

Current Age Background characteristics	Less than 25	25–34	35–44	45 and over	All
Level of education					
No schooling	8.4	17.4	27.8	21.1	19.0
Incomplete primary	39.4	69.3	71.8	71.4	58.9
Complete primary	38.6	70.9	84.8	80.0	59.1
Secondary and over	55.6	78.0	97.2	85.7	76.5
Place of residence					
Urban	37.9	60.2	64.9	51.0	54.4
Rural	9.1	12.2	13.7	7.1	11.1
Region of residence					
Damascus city	53.2	79.5	80.6	75.8	72.3
Aleppo city	31.4	55.8	61.7	42.0	48.5
Northeast	6.0	13.4	18.4	7.5	11.8
West	29.5	34.8	35.6	19.3	32.1
Center	17.3	27.3	29.9	16.5	23.8
South	20.7	30.8	34.2	24.2	27.8
Pattern of work					
Before and after marriage	10.8	19.2	21.8	15.3	17.6
After marriage only	25.5	33.7	34.1	29.4	31.8
Before marriage only	12.6	33.7	35.8	21.4	25.9
Never worked	28.0	42.9	48.2	32.0	38.6

Source: *Syria Fertility Survey – 1978*, p. 91, table 8.5.

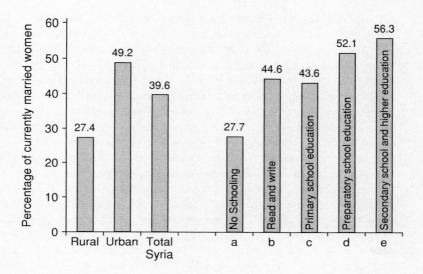

Figure 2.9   Contraceptive use in Syria, according to place of residence, and level of education, 1993

Source: "Syria 1993: Results from the PAPCHILD Survey," p. 299, table 9.1.

Table 2.21   Knowledge and use of contraceptives among currently married women in Syria, 1993 (in percentages)

Method	Knows method	Ever used	Currently using
Pill	91.9	29.5	9.9
IUD	89.1	24.7	15.7
Injection	44.2	0.6	0.0
Diaphragm/cream/jelly	36.8	1.4	0.2
Condom	42.4	1.8	0.3
Female sterilization	59.3	2.2	2.2
Male sterilization	26.3	0.3	0.0
Calendar method	64.0	13.0	6.7
Withdrawal	46.1	4.0	1.0
Breast feeding	72.8	12.6	3.5
Other traditional	0.7	0.3	0.1
Any method	93.9	56.2	39.6
Any modern method	92.7	44.3	28.3

Source: "Syria 1993: Results from the PAPCHILD Survey," p. 250, table 5.1.

1   **Woman's educational level.** As in other demographic areas, the most prominent factor influencing contraceptive use is the woman's educational level. According to the 1978 SFS, the rate of ever-use of any contraceptive method among women without any formal education was 19.0 percent, increasing to 59.1 percent among women with a primary school education, and reaching as high as 76.5 percent among women with a secondary school education and over (see table 2.20). The same trend was also found in the 1993 SMCHS: While the rate of ever-use of any contraceptive method among illiterate women was 27.7 percent, this rate increased to 52.1 percent among women with a preparatory school education, and 56.3 percent among those with a secondary school education and higher (see figure 2.9).

2   **Place of residence.** Another factor heavily affecting the rate of contraceptive use, albeit less so than educational level, is the place of residence. As in other demographic areas, large differences were found between urban centers and rural areas. According to the 1978 SFS, the rate of ever-use of contraceptives in the urban centers was 54.4 percent, as compared with only 11.1 percent in the rural areas (see table 2.20). However, during the 1980s and the beginning of the 1990s, the differences in the rate of contraceptive use between urban centers and the countryside somewhat diminished. According to the 1993 SMCHS, the rate of contraceptive use in urban centers was 49.2 percent, as compared with 27.4 percent in rural areas (see figure 2.9).

3

The Spatial Distribution of the Population

The Rate of the Syrian Rural-to-Urban Migration Movement

One of the most prominent demographic characteristics of developing countries throughout the entire world during the second half of the twentieth century has been the rapid urbanization process. This process, however, is a relatively new phenomenon in world history, started by the Industrial Revolution which took place in western European countries during the latter part of the eighteenth century. Urbanization is one of the basic conditions in the process of modernization and industrialization, as well as an essential element in the process of cultural and social change.[1]

At the beginning of the nineteenth century, the share of the urban population within the total world's population was estimated at approximately 3 percent, increasing to about 15 percent by the beginning of the twentieth century, and expected to reach 50 percent by the end of the century: 40 percent in developing countries and 78 percent in developed countries.[2] While in 1950, the number of inhabitants of the urban centers among the developing countries throughout the entire world was estimated to be 275 million, their number increased to more than 800 million in 1975. According to demographic projections, by the end of the twentieth century, their number will reach 2.12 billion, representing 66 percent of the total world's urban population.[3]

In contrast to the developed countries, the rapid urbanization process in the developing countries began only in the late 1930s and early 1940s. Moreover, whereas in the developed countries the "pull" factors were the dominant incentives for this movement, in the developing countries the "push" factors were the main reasons for the rapid movement from rural areas to urban centers. In addition, while in the developed countries the urbanization process was gradual and continuous over more than 150 years (from the late eighteenth century until the middle of the twentieth century), in the developing countries, including those of the Middle East, it was a very rapid process, occurring during less than two generations. With regard to the rate of the urbanization process in the Middle East, Saad Eddin Ibrahim has stated:

> It took the West 150 years to reach this point. It is taken the Arab World only fifty years.[4]

This pattern of rapid urbanization process has had very significant consequences for various socioeconomic and political aspects of life in these countries. However, it has to be emphasized that despite the acceleration of the urbanization process in the Middle East and North Africa region during the second half of the twentieth century, the main contributor to the increasing population in the largest Middle Eastern and North African cities has been the high rates of natural increase of the urban populations themselves.

In Syria, as in many other Middle Eastern and North African countries, one of the most important aspects of the socioeconomic changes that have been taking place during the second half of the twentieth century is the rapid urbanization process. The aim of this chapter is to examine and analyze the urbanization process in Syria from the late 1950s onward, with a view to studying the causes and the consequences of this process, as well as its relationship to the overall socioeconomic developments which took place in Syria during that period.

Although the urbanization process in Syria is a relatively new phenomenon, Syria has a long history of urban settlements. Already in 1849, the population of Damascus was estimated to be 150,000, and that of Aleppo 77,000 four years earlier, in 1845.[5] During the second half of the nineteenth century and the beginning of the twentieth century, the population size of the major Syrian cities continued to increase. By 1915, the Damascus population was estimated to be 201,470 and that of Aleppo about 200,000.[6]

In contrast to Egypt and Iraq, in which the acceleration of the urbanization process began in the late 1930s and early 1940s, in Syria the massive urbanization process started almost two decades later, in the late 1950s. According to the 1947 census, the urban population constituted 31.5 percent within the total Syrian population, increasing to 33.1 percent in 1952, and reaching 36.9 percent, according to the 1960 census results, representing an increase of only 5.4 percent within 13 years (see table 3.1). This is substantially lower than the rate of urbanization in most of the other Middle Eastern and North African countries during the same period.

The slow rate of urbanization in Syria during the 1940s and early 1950s was mainly due to the rapid expansion of the agricultural sector,[7] in parallel to the low pace of industrial development in the major urban centers during that period. In 1950, according to official Syrian estimates, the percentage of the industrial sector within the total Syrian NDP (Net Domestic Product) was 10 percent, increasing by only 3 percent, to 13 percent, by 1968. Moreover, the majority of Syrian industry at that time consisted of small-scale workshops and handicrafts, with each employing only a few workers. The number of factories using modern technology methods and employing a sizable workforce was very small, and thus their influence on the overall development of the Syrian industrial sector was quite marginal.[8]

Bent Hansen described the development of Syrian industry as follows:

> Some industrial development did take place during the 1950s and 1960s, but Syrian industry is still in its infancy, and by 1964 the structure of industry was much the same as in 1950.[9]

The political instability throughout the 1950s and most of the 1960s, in parallel to the nationalization of many privately-owned factories, which began with the July 1961 Socialist Decrees,[10] and continued after the Ba'thi revolution in March 1963, also contributed to the slow rate of industrial development in Syria during that period. Within the framework of these circumstances, not only were the "push" factors from the rural areas to the urban centers non-existent as a result of the rapid agricultural expansion and increasing demands for agricultural workers, but "pull" factors in the urban centers were weak and unattractive as well. In addition, the enlargement of the Syrian army during the 1950s required increasing manpower. Many of those who joined the army originated from rural areas, thus releasing some pressure on the sources of employment in the countryside.[11]

From the late 1950s and early 1960s onward, there was a massive acceleration of the urbanization process in Syria, and during the years 1960–70 the percentage of the urban population within the total Syrian population increased from 36.9 percent to 43.5 percent (see table 3.1). The 1970 census data indicated that with the exception of the Bedouin, there were almost a million inhabitants who were living in areas other than their place of birth, representing approximately 16 percent of the total Syrian population at that time. While these figures also included those who migrated from one rural area to another, the vast majority of the movement was from the rural areas to the urban centers. It also appeared from the census data that two-thirds of the population movement (640,000 out of 969,000) occurred during the 1960s. These figures indicate a large scale of rural-to-urban migration movement in Syria during the 1960s.[12]

One of the most important reasons for the acceleration of the Syrian urbanization process during the 1960s, especially during the first half of the decade, was the substantial slowdown in agricultural development. In 1961, the level of agricultural production was similar to that of 1953. As a result of the rapid population growth during that period, the per capita production sharply dropped.[13] By 1970, the total cropped area[14] in Syria was 3.29 million hectares,

Table 3.1 Syria: Distribution of the population, according to urban/rural areas, 1947–94 (in thousands)

Year	Urban population	%	Rural population	%	Total
1947	1,026	31.5	2,231	68.5	3,257
1952	1,136	33.1	2,298	66.9	3,434
1960	1,685	36.9	2,880	63.1	4,565
1967	2,362	41.6	3,318	58.4	5,680
1968	2,475	42.2	3,392	57.8	5,867
1969	2,599	42.9	3,461	57.1	6,060
1970	2,741	43.5	3,564	56.5	6,305
1971	2,849	44.1	3,615	55.9	6,464
1972	2,982	44.7	3,694	55.3	6,676
1973	3,121	45.3	3,773	54.7	6,894
1974	3,266	45.9	3,855	54.1	7,121
1975	3,418	46.5	3,937	53.5	7,355
1976	3,543	46.6	4,053	53.4	7,596
1977	3,769	48.0	4,076	52.0	7,845
1978	3,950	48.8	4,152	51.2	8,102
1979	4,141	47.9	4,506	52.1	8,647
1980	4,189	47.6	4,608	52.4	8,797
1981	4,264	47.1	4,786	52.9	9,050
1982	4,370	47.0	4,925	53.0	9,295
1983	4,587	47.7	5,024	52.3	9,611
1984	4,783	48.1	5,151	51.9	9,934
1985	4,991	48.6	5,276	51.4	10,267
1986	5,208	49.1	5,404	50.9	10,612
1987	5,428	49.5	5,541	50.5	10,969
1988	5,672	50.0	5,666	50.0	11,338
1989	5,855	50.0	5,864	50.0	11,719
1990	6,087	50.2	6,029	49.8	12,116
1992	6,594	50.9	6,364	49.1	12,958
1994	7,112	51.4	6,732	48.6	13,844

Sources:

1947: "L'Explosion Demographique en Syrie," *Syrie & Monde Arabe*, Vol. 22, No. 253 (Fevrier 1975), p. 6.

1952: Étienne De-Vaumas, "La Population de la Syrie," *Annales de Geographie*, Vol. 64, No. 341 (Jan–Fev 1955), p. 79 [hereafter: De-Vaumas, "La Population de la Syrie"].

1960: Syria, *Statistical Abstract – 1987*, p. 53, table 1/2.

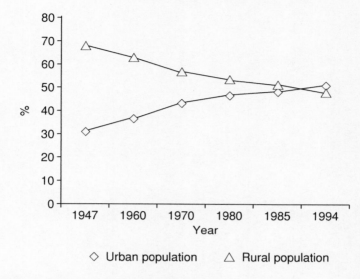

Figure 3.1 Syria: Distribution of the population, according to urban/rural areas, 1947–94

as compared with 4.65 million in 1958, representing a decrease of almost 30 percent (see Appendix 2).

The main reason for the slowdown in the Syrian agricultural sector in the late 1950s and throughout the 1960s was not economic, but rather political. It was caused by a combination of several factors, namely: The establishment of the United Arab Republic (UAR) in February 1958; the initiation of the Agrarian Reform Law in September of that year; the political instability in Syria during the period between the breakdown of the UAR in September 1961 and the Ba'thi revolution a year and a half later, in early March 1963; and the frequent changes of the Agrarian Reform Law during that year and a half period.[15] As a result, the scale of investment in agriculture sharply decreased, and in some cases farmers even refrained from cultivating their own lands.[16]

Sources for table 3.1 *(continued)*
1967–74: UN, *Demographic Yearbook – 1975*, p. 175.
1975–82: UN, *Demographic Yearbook – 1984*, p. 177.
1983–89: UN, *Demographic Yearbook – 1989*, p. 155.
1990: Syria, *Statistical Abstract – 1990*, p. 60, table 10/2.
1992: Syria, *Statistical Abstract – 1992*, p. 61, table 11/2.
1994: *Syria, Statistical Abstract – 1994*, p. 63, table 11/2.

Table 3.2 Syria: Distribution of the population, according to provinces, and urban/rural, 1960–95 (in thousands)

Year		1960		1970		1981		1990		1994		1995	
Province		Population	%	Population	%	Population	%	Population	%	Population	%	Population	%
Damascus city	U	530	100	837	100	1,112	100	1,397	100	1,552	100	1,489	100
	R	–	–	–	–	–	–	–	–	–	–	–	–
	T	530	100	837	100	1,112	100	1,397	100	1,552	100	1,489	100
Damascus rural areas	U	74	15.6	182	29.3	332	36.2	527	42.0	644	44.4	nd	
	R	399	84.4	439	70.7	585	63.8	727	58.0	807	55.6	nd	
	T	473	100	621	100	917	100	1,254	100	1,451	100	1,730	100
Aleppo	U	474	49.5	708	53.8	1,112	59.7	1,607	64.3	1,883	65.9	nd	
	R	483	50.5	609	46.2	757	40.3	894	35.7	973	34.1	nd	
	T	957	100	1,317	100	1,879	100	2,501	100	2,856	100	3,035	100
Homs	U	150	37.4	254	46.5	408	50.1	593	52.8	701	53.9	nd	
	R	251	62.6	292	53.5	407	49.9	531	47.2	600	46.1	nd	
	T	401	100	546	100	815	100	1,124	100	1,301	100	1,247	100
Hama	U	118	36.4	175	34.0	248	33.7	330	33.6	376	33.7	Nd	
	R	206	63.6	340	66.0	489	66.3	651	66.4	740	66.3	Nd	
	T	324	100	515	100	737	100	981	100	1,116	100	1,120	100
Ladhaqiya	U	111	21.1	149	38.2	232	41.8	315	42.9	367	44.0	nd	
	R	416	78.9	241	61.8	323	58.2	420	57.1	467	56.0	nd	
	T	527	100	390	100	555	100	735	100	834	100	766	100
Deir al-Zur	U	58	26.2	89	30.4	125	30.6	164	30.8	186	31.1	nd	
	R	163	73.8	204	69.6	284	69.4	369	69.2	413	68.9	nd	
	T	221	100	293	100	409	100	533	100	599	100	722	100
Idlib	U	51	15.3	85	22.1	122	21.0	163	20.2	187	20.0	nd	
	R	282	84.7	299	77.9	458	79.0	644	79.8	750	80.0	nd	
	T	333	100	384	100	580	100	807	100	937	100	922	100

Region		1960		1970		1981		1990		1994		1995	
		No.	%	No.	%	No.	%	No.	%	No.	%	No.	%
Al-Hasakah	U	58	16.4	96	20.5	194	29.0	331	37.0	416	40.4	nd	nd
	R	295	83.6	372	79.5	476	71.0	563	63.0	614	59.6	nd	nd
	T	353	100	468	100	670	100	894	100	1,030	100	1,050	100
Al-Raqqa	U	15	8.4	39	16.0	135	38.8	304	65.4	361	69.7	nd	nd
	R	163	91.6	205	84.0	213	61.2	161	34.6	157	30.3	nd	nd
	T	178	100	244	100	348	100	465	100	518	100	566	100
Al-Suwayda	U	24	24.0	39	27.9	57	28.6	78	29.5	91	30.3	nd	nd
	R	76	76.0	101	72.1	142	71.4	186	70.5	209	69.7	nd	nd
	T	100	100	140	100	199	100	264	100	300	100	270	100
Dar'a	U	22	13.1	33	14.2	77	21.2	147	28.3	193	31.3	nd	nd
	R	146	86.9	199	85.8	286	78.8	373	71.7	423	68.7	nd	nd
	T	168	100	232	100	363	100	520	100	616	100	623	100
Tartus	U	–	–	55	18.2	89	20.1	131	21.8	155	22.5	nd	nd
	R	–	–	247	81.8	354	79.9	471	78.2	534	77.5	nd	nd
	T	–	–	302	100	443	100	602	100	689	100	596	100
Quneitra	U	–	–	–	–	–	–	–	–	–	–	nd	nd
	R	–	–	16	100	26	100	39	100	45	100	nd	nd
	T	–	–	16	100	26	100	39	100	45	100	50	100
Total	U	1,685	36.9	2,741	43.5	4,253	47.0	6,087	50.2	7,112	51.4	nd	nd
	R	2,880	63.1	3,564	56.5	4,800	53.0	6,029	49.8	6,732	48.6	nd	nd
	T	4,565	100	6,305	100	9,053	100	12,116	100	13,844	100	14,186	100

nd = no data available

Sources:

1960–81: Syria, *Statistical Abstract – 1985*, p. 54–55, table 2/1.

1990: Syria, *Statistical Abstract – 1990*, p. 61, table 11/2.

1994: Syria, *Statistical Abstract – 1994*, p. 63, table 11/2.

1995: Syria, *Statistical Abstract – 1995*, p. 63, table 11/2.

During the 1970s and 1980s, however, the rate of urbanization in Syria slowed down, and the percentage of the urban population within the total population increased by only 6.7 percent during these two decades, from 43.5 percent in 1970 to 50.2 percent in 1990. This tendency also continued during the first half of the 1990s, and according to the 1994 figures the percentage of the urban population within the total Syrian population was 51.4 (see table 3.1).

While several factors accounted for the decrease in the rate of urbanization over the last two and a half decades, the two most important were: First, the migration of tens of thousands of Syrian workers, of whom a large number were from the rural areas, to the Gulf states, as well as to Lebanon and Jordan,[17] caused substantial relief of employment pressures in the countryside. The second reason was the significant improvement in the Syrian agricultural sector during that period, with the total cropped area increased from 3.29 million hectares in 1970 to 5.47 million hectares in 1990 (see Appendix 2). This massive increase in cultivated land, especially from the mid-1980s onward, created a large number of work opportunities in the countryside, contributing to a further reduction in the pressures for rural-to-urban migration movement.

Another major reason for the slowing down of the urbanization process from the late 1970s onward was the government's policies towards the countryside. Since the early 1960s, but particularly after Asad came to power in late 1970, the Syrian authorities devoted more attention and allocated larger sums of money for the development of public services in the countryside and the remote provinces. Furthermore, the completion of the Agrarian Reform in 1969, in addition to the regaining of political stability and the confidence which Asad's regime imparted to the farmers regarding ownership of their lands without fear of land expropriation, all contributed to bringing about a reduction in the rate of urbanization.

A new phenomenon in the urbanization process in Syria has been occurring with increasing frequency from the mid-1980s onward: migration from the cities to villages located near the major urban centers. The *al-Tuwani* village, located in the Damascus rural province, constitutes one example of this prevalent phenomenon. By mid-1985, the village's population numbered 4,000. However, as the result of a shortage in cultivated land in this region, only about 10 percent of the labor force in the village made their living in agriculture, while 90 percent were engaged in non-agricultural professions, many of whom were employed in varied governmental establishments. Until the early 1980s, large numbers of those who were not engaged in agriculture were living permanently in the capital city of Damascus, due to inadequate basic services in the village. As a result of substantial improvements in public services in the village during the late 1970s and early 1980s, in parallel to increasing housing prices in Damascus city, many of them returned to live in the village, while continuing to work in Damascus city.[18]

In contrast to most of the other Middle Eastern and North African countries, in Syria one of the most important factors accounting for the increasing percentage of the urban population within the total population from the 1970s onward was the rapid population growth in small and medium provincial towns. In the rural province of Damascus one can find a relatively large number of examples of this process.[19] As a result, the percentage of the urban population within the total province's population increased from 15.6 percent in 1960 to 36.2 percent in 1981, and reached as high as 44.4 percent, according to the 1994 figures (see table 3.2).

The Pattern of Rural-to-Urban Migration

In Syria, in contrast to other Middle Eastern and North African countries, which were also witness to a large rural-to-urban migration, the major proportion of the migration movements occurred within the borders of the provinces themselves, rather than from the rural areas to the capital or to the second largest city. In Egypt, Jordan and Iraq, for example, as in most of the other developing countries, the vast majority of the rural-to-urban migration was directed to the capital or to the second largest city. In Jordan, most of the migrants moved to the capital city of Amman; in the case of Egypt, to Cairo, and to a lesser extent to Alexandria; and in the case of Iraq, to the capital city of Baghdad and to Basra.

As a result of this process, the proportion of the population of the capitals within the total population of these countries gradually increased. The percentage of Amman's population within the total Jordanian population, for example, increased from 18.5 percent in 1952 to 31.8 percent in 1994.[20] In Egypt one can find the same trend. Thus, according to the 1986 population census, more than 20 percent of the total Egyptian population were living in Cairo, as compared with 12 percent in 1947.[21] Also in Iraq, as a result of the concentration of a large number of rural migrants in the capital city of Baghdad, by 1987 23.5 percent of the total Iraqi population were living in the city,[22] as compared with 17.4 percent in 1957.[23] Thus, in this regard, the pattern of rural-to-urban migration in Syria is a unique case in the entire Middle Eastern countries.

Tables 3.2 and 3.3 clearly illustrate the unique pattern of the rural-to-urban migration movement in Syria. While the proportion of the urban population within the total Syrian population gradually increased from the late 1950s onward, the distribution of the population among the various provinces of the country remained more or less stable with very limited changes. In contrast to most other Middle Eastern and North African capital cities, the percentage of

Table 3.3 Syria: Distribution of the population, according to provinces, 1960–95 (in percentages)

Year Province	1960	1970	1981	1990	1995
Damascus city	11.6	13.2	12.3	11.5	10.5
Damascus rural areas	10.4	9.8	10.1	10.3	12.2
Aleppo	21.0	20.9	20.8	20.7	21.4
Homs	8.8	8.7	9.0	9.3	8.8
Hama	7.1	8.2	8.1	8.1	7.9
Ladhaqiya	11.5	6.2	6.1	6.1	5.4
Deir Al-Zur	4.8	4.7	4.5	4.4	5.1
Idlib	7.3	6.1	6.4	6.6	6.5
Al-Hasakah	7.7	7.4	7.4	7.4	7.4
Al-Raqqa	3.9	3.9	3.9	3.8	4.0
Al-Suwayda	2.2	2.2	2.2	2.2	1.9
Dar'a	3.7	3.7	4.0	4.3	4.4
Tartus	–	4.8	4.9	5.0	4.2
Quneitra	–	0.3	0.3	0.3	0.3
Total	100	100	100	100	100

Sources: Data taken from table 3.2.

the Damascus population within the total Syrian population remained stable during the last three and a half decades: 11.6 percent according to the 1960 census, increasing slightly to 12.3 percent in 1981, and then decreasing to 10.5 percent in 1995, according to official Syrian figures. The same trend was also found in the other major provinces. The population of Homs province, for example, constituted 8.8 percent within the total Syrian population, both in 1960 and in 1995 (see table 3.3).

In the provinces themselves the percentage of the urban population increased steadily. For example, in the province of al-Hasakah, while in 1960 the percentage of the urban population within the total province population was 16.4, this figure increased to 40.4 percent in 1994. In the province of al-Raqqa, the increase was even higher: from 8.4 percent in 1960 to 69.7 percent in 1994 (see table 3.2).

While there are many reasons for this unique pattern of rural-to-urban migration in Syria, the two most important of them are as follows:

1   **The spatial distribution policies of the Syrian authorities.** Since the early 1960s, after the Ba'thi revolution, the Syrian authorities have gener-

ated more emphasis on the socioeconomic development of the rural areas and remote provinces. Apart from their socioeconomic aims, these development plans, which include the establishment of industrial factories and other governmental facilities and public services, also have a political role: to intensify the identification of the inhabitants of these areas with the regime and its policies, especially in the remote provinces where opposition movements have emerged.[24] Thus, for example, during the late 1960s and early 1970s, the province of al-Raqqa, including the town of al-Raqqa itself, attracted a large number of migrants as a result of the implementation of the Euphrates Development Project.[25] The sharp increase in work opportunities in this region constituted the main reason for the migration movement to the city of al-Raqqa, both from the countryside of al-Raqqa province, as well as from areas outside the borders of the province.

2   **The geographical structure of the country.** In contrast to Egypt and Jordan, and similar to Iraq, in Syria the parts most suitable for human settlement on a large scale are not concentrated in small areas. In Jordan, for example, more than 80 percent of the land area is desert, and almost the entire Jordanian population is concentrated in the northern and central highlands, where rainfall is sufficient for agriculture.[26] In Egypt, about 96 percent of the total country's area is desert, and almost the entire population is concentrated in the Nile Valley and the Delta. However, in Syria

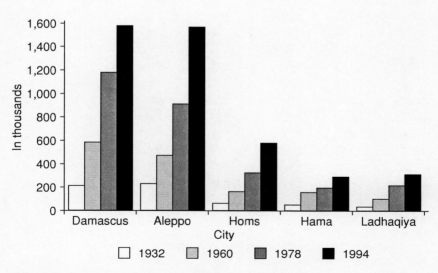

Figure 3.2   The population of the major Syrian cities, 1932–94 (in thousands)

Table 3.4   The population of the major Syrian cities, 1932–94 (in thousands)

City Year	Damascus	Aleppo	Hama	Homs	Ladhaqiya	Total
1932	216	232	50	65	24	587
1942	276	299	66	95	nd	nd
1943	286	320	71	100	36	813
1950	303	339	75	106	nd	nd
1957	440	428	161	140	56	1,225
1958	455	451	104	146	59	1,225
1960	530	425	110	136	68	1,269
1961	508	496	116	164	68	1,352
1963	545	529	126	175	75	1,450
1964	563	547	132	182	78	1,502
1965	600	563	136	190	nd	nd
1966	618	579	199	143	nd	nd
1967	579	522	148	190	87	1,526
1968	790	567	196	231	nd	nd
1969	813	589	157	198	98	1,855
1970	834	639	137	215	126	2,005
1975	1,042	779	162	267	157	2,407
1977	1,097	843	173	292	191	2,596
1978	1,142	878	180	306	204	2,710
1979	1,156	919	198	326	204	2,803
1981	1,251	977	177	355	197	2,957
1982	1,112	985	177	355	197	2,826
1985	1,197	1,145	193	409	229	3,173
1986	1,216	1,191	198	428	240	3,273
1987	1,292	1,216	214	431	241	3,394
1988	1,326	1,261	222	447	249	3,505
1989	1,343	1,308	229	464	258	3,602
1990	1,378	1,355	237	481	267	3,718
1994	1,549	1,542	273	558	303	4,225

nd = no data available

Sources:

1932: David Jean-Claude, "Alep," in André Raymond (ed.), *La Syrie D'Aujourd'hui* (Paris: Centre National de la Reacherche Scientifique, 1980), p. 391.

1942: Great Britain, Naval Intelligence Division, *Syria* (London: H.M. Stationery Office, April 1943), pp. 211, 213, 215.

1943: De-Vaumas, "La Population de la Syrie," p. 78.

1950: *The Middle East and North Africa – 1953*, p. 300.

Table 3.4 Sources *(continued)*

1957–58: Syria, *Statistical Abstract – 1958*, p. 24, table 2.

1960: Damascus, Aleppo, Homs, Hama: UN, *Demographic Yearbook – 1963*, p. 248.
Ladhaqiya: UN, *Demographic Yearbook – 1970*, p. 457.

1961: *The Middle East and North Africa – 1963*, p. 375.

1963: *The Middle East and North Africa – 1965/6*, p. 572.

1964: UN, *Demographic Yearbook – 1965*, p. 154.

1965: UN, *Demographic Yearbook – 1966*, p. 190.

1966: UN, *Demographic Yearbook – 1967*, p. 222.

1967: Damascus, Aleppo, Homs, Hama: UN, *Demographic Yearbook – 1968*, p. 181
Ladhaqiya: *The Middle East and North Africa – 1969/70*, p. 689.

1968: UN, *Demographic Yearbook – 1969*, p. 202.

1969: *The Middle East and North Africa – 1971/2*, p. 584.

1970: UN, *Demographic Yearbook – 1975*, p. 245.

1975: UN, *Demographic Yearbook – 1976*, p. 268.

1977: UN, *Demographic Yearbook – 1977*, p. 266.

1978: UN, *Demographic Yearbook – 1979*, p. 280.

1979: UN, *Demographic Yearbook – 1981*, p. 279.

1981: UN, *Demographic Yearbook – 1982*, p. 255.

1982: UN, *Demographic Yearbook – 1984*, p. 272.

1985: UN, *Demographic Yearbook – 1985*, p. 270.

1986: UN, *Demographic Yearbook – 1986*, p. 285.

1987: UN, *Demographic Yearbook – 1987*, p. 311.

1988: UN, *Demographic Yearbook – 1988*, p. 320.

1989: UN, *Demographic Yearbook – 1989*, p. 266.

1990: UN, *Demographic Yearbook – 1991*, p. 246

1994: UN, *Demographic Yearbook – 1994*, p. 285.

there are many and varied regions which are suitable for human settlement, both in the south, where the capital city of Damascus is located, and in the north and the northeast regions, where there is enough water, as well as large quantities of cultivable land for intensive agriculture.[27]

Reasons for Rural-to-Urban Migration

There are a variety of factors accounting for the large-scale migration from the rural areas to the urban centers in Syria. However, similar to many other Middle Eastern and North African countries, in Syria the "push" factors constituted the dominant reasons, while the "pull" factors served only as secondary reasons.[28]

The "Push" Factors

1 **Scarcity of cultivated land.** The scarcity of cultivated land was the result of the rapid population growth in the rural areas, which outpaced the increase in cultivated land. Thus, while in 1960 the per capita cropped area among the rural population was 1.21 hectares, it dropped by 40 percent to only 0.72 hectares in 1994 (see table 2.18). This, combined with the introduction of modern agricultural cultivation methods within the framework of the Agrarian Reform, including large-scale mechanization, constituted the most important reasons for the rural-to-urban migration in Syria, as in many other Middle Eastern countries. As a result, the percentage of those employed in the agricultural sector within the total Syrian labor force steadily declined from the late 1950s onward. While in 1960, according to the census results conducted that year, the percentage of employees in the agricultural sector within the total civilian labor force was more than 50 percent,[29] two and a half decades later, in 1986, their percentage sharply dropped to only 30 (745,550 out of 2.488 million).[30]

   During the second half of the 1980s, as a result of the massive development plans in the agricultural sector, the number of employees in this sector significantly increased, reaching almost 917,000 by 1991. However, in spite of the sharp increase, the percentage of those employed in the agricultural sector within the total civilian labor force continued to decrease to only 28.2 percent that year due to the rapid population growth.[31] As a result, the growth of the available work force in the countryside remained higher than the increase in the available work opportunities in the agricultural sector, leading to the continuing migration from the countryside to the urban centers for purposes of employment.

2 **Low level and instability of income in the rural areas.** Since most of Syrian agriculture is based on non-irrigated land (more than 80 percent), the Syrian peasants were suffering from instability of income, caused by substantial oscillations in agricultural production from one year to another, which was vulnerability to the damage of natural forces, such as drought, extreme cold weather, and flooding. Thus, for example, while in 1970 the cereal production per one hectare was only 0.4 tons, it increased to 1.3 tons two years later, in 1972, and dropped again to only 0.3 tons in 1973, and then increased again to 1.0 ton in the following year.[32] Accordingly, the income of the peasants suffered from sharp oscillations from one year to another, according to the scale of agricultural production. Thus, for example, while in 1956, the per capita income in the Syrian countryside was LS 352, it decreased to only LS 260 one year later, in 1957. The same trend also continued into the 1960s. In 1964, for example, the per capita

income in the rural areas was LS 422, while it dropped to LS 392 one year later, in 1965 (in current prices).[33]

Since the implementation of the Agrarian Reform, almost all of the cultivated land is owned by the peasants themselves, and only a small portion has remained in the hands of the state (see table 5.4). However, until recently, the peasants were required to sell all their products to state agricultural marketing companies at low fixed prices. The reason for such low prices of agricultural produce was due to the government's desire to keep the food prices as low as possible in order to minimize the government's subsidies of basic food commodities.[34] However admirable the objective of keeping consumer prices down, mainly basic food products, the result is that farmers have had little incentive to increase agricultural production.[35] In fact, this policy caused a substantial reduction in farmers' income, thus constituting a major incentive for them to leave the agricultural sector and migrate to one of the urban centers, seeking more profitable sources of income.

3   **Concentration of the rural economy almost exclusively on agriculture.** In spite of the government's ambitious plans to increase and diversify the Syrian rural economy, it continued to be based in the 1970s and 1980s almost exclusively on agriculture.[36]

4   **The gap in the standard of housing between the urban centers and the rural areas.** A major component in the rural-to-urban migration movement in Syria is the substantial gap in the standard of housing between the urban centers, especially the major cities, and the rural areas. Thus, for example, by the mid-1970s, 75 percent of the dwelling units in the urban centers enjoyed running water, as compared with only 26 percent in the countryside. Similarly, while in the urban centers 86 percent of the dwelling units benefit from electricity, in the rural areas this rate dropped to only 14 percent.[37] Just a few years earlier, in 1972, only 108 villages out of 6,121, or less than 2 percent, were supplied with electricity.[38] In other categories, such as sanitation, the same gap existed.

During the 1970s and 1980s, there was a substantial improvement in governmental services in the countryside.[39] However, the gap between the public service systems in the urban centers and the rural areas continued to prevail. During the years 1975–83, while 98 percent of the urban population enjoyed access to safe water, this percentage fell to 54 percent among the rural inhabitants.[40] This gap continued to exist even in the late 1980s and the beginning of the 1990s, albeit largely diminished. During the years 1990–95, the percentage of the urban population with access to safe water was 92 percent, as compared with 78 percent in the rural areas.[41]

In spite of the massive governmental development projects in the countryside, even by the 1980s a large number of villages continued to suffer from lack of access to basic public services. Thus, for example, in September 1980, the official daily newspaper *al-Thawra* reported that the village of *Ma'ashuq* (located in al-Hasakah province), with a total population of 3,000, was not connected to the electricity and telephone systems, and that there was not a road connecting the village to the nearest city.[42] This is only one example, but one can find other reports in the official Syrian newspapers regarding villages which continued to suffer from lack of suitable public services and infrastructure facilities even by the late 1970s and early 1980s.[43]

5   **The gap in health-care and educational services between the urban centers and the rural areas.** Another major "push" factor was the large gap in health services and educational facilities between the rural areas and the urban centers, as well as between the various provinces of the country. The Foreign Areas Studies Division described the health-care system in the Syrian rural areas in the mid-1960s as follows:

> Rural health and sanitation conditions are poor, medical facilities are limited, particularly in the northern villages along the Turkish border. Rural medical personnel are few, and the ill can obtain medical services only by making long and expensive trips to the larger towns and cities.[44]

One can also find a similar picture in an official Syrian report from the late 1970s:

> The countryside in our country continued to suffer from neglect, deprived of the attention of the state and of the gifts of civilisation, as it was in want of schools and health dispensaries, clean waters, electricity, roads, etc ... This compelled many of its sons to emigrate to cities in look for the requisites of a life of dignity.[45]

In 1978, according to official Syrian figures, 89 percent of Syrian physicians worked in the urban centers, even though the proportion of the urban population within the total Syrian population at that time was approximately 40 percent. As a result, in the urban areas the ratio of population per physician was 1:1,120, while in the rural areas the ratio was 1:13,470.[46]

This gap in the health-care system, both in quality and quantity, between the urban centers and the rural areas, also found its expression in large differences in health services between the various provinces of the country. Thus, the higher the rate of the province's urban population, the lower the ratio between population and medical services. For example, in 1982, the ratio of population per physician in Damascus (including the rural province) was 1:1,095, as compared

Table 3.5 Syria: Distribution of physicians, according to provinces, 1958–93

Province	1958 Number of physicians	1958 Average number of persons per physician	1970 Number of physicians	1970 Average number of persons per physician	1982 Number of physicians	1982 Average number of persons per physician	1990 Number of physicians	1990 Average number of persons per physician	1993 Number of physicians	1993 Average number of persons per physician
Damascus (two provinces)	482	1,893	844	1,712	1,900	1,095	3,270	811	3,779	771
Aleppo	202	6,402	314	4,159	1,055	1,827	2,537	986	3,241	853
Homs	53	5,985	102	5,314	381	2,194	1,177	955	1,509	831
Hama	43	7,377	58	8,759	185	4,086	690	1,422	819	1,320
Ladhaqiya	70	7,288	65	5,938	364	1,563	590	1,245	881	917
Deir al-Zur	30	12,284	48	6,042	118	3,551	339	1,572	386	1,508
Idlib	–		30	12,667	118	5,059	534	1,511	513	1,760
Al-Hasakah	37	7,639	44	10,545	115	5,983	318	2,811	446	2,235
Al-Raqqa	–		29	8,310	86	4,163	291	1,598	370	1,354
Al-Suwayda	9	15,000	18	7,667	62	3,290	231	1,143	317	915
Dara	16	11,095	24	9,625	85	4,412	385	1,351	488	1,211
Tartus	–		38	7,895	148	3,081	543	1,109	920	724
Quneitra	–		9	1,778	16	1,694	122	320	194	222
Total	942	4,693	1,623	3,849	4,633	2,006	11,682	1,037	13,863	966

Sources:

1958: Population: Syria, *Statistical Abstract – 1958*, p. 25, table 3,
Physicians: Ibid., p. 63, table 9.

1970: Syria, *Statistical Abstract – 1971*, p. 359, table 202.

1982: Syria, *Statistical Abstract – 1983*, p. 331, table 2/11.

1990: Syria, *Statistical Abstract – 1991*, p. 352, table 1/11.

1993: Syria, *Statistical Abstract – 1994*, p. 360, table 1/11.

Table 3.6 Number of hospital-beds in Syria, according to provinces, 1958–93

Year Province	1958		1970		1982		1990		1993	
	Number of hospital beds	Average number of persons per hospital-bed	Number of hospital beds	Average number of persons per hospital-bed	Number of hospital beds	Average number of persons per hospital-bed	Number of hospital beds	Average number of persons per hospital-bed	Number of hospital beds	Average number of persons per hospital-bed
Damascus (two provinces)	1,713	533	3,076	407	4,337	480	5,228	507	5,509	529
Aleppo	1,239	1,044	1,231	1,077	2,655	726	3,105	805	3,342	827
Homs	282	794	401	1,352	676	1,237	927	1,213	1,054	1,190
Hama	153	2,073	174	2,920	483	1,565	735	1,335	903	1,191
Ladhaqiya	222	2,298	200	1,930	562	1,012	946	777	998	810
Deir Al-Zur	232	1,588	315	921	342	1,225	390	1,367	505	1,152
Idlib	–	–	176	2,159	276	2,163	304	2,655	347	2,602
Al-Hasakah	115	2,458	73	6,359	212	3,245	457	1,956	604	1,615
Al-Raqqa	–	–	26	9,269	252	1,421	362	1,284	439	1,141
Al-Suwayda	49	2,755	194	708	288	708	466	567	284	1,021
Dar'a	85	2,088	100	2,310	271	1,384	334	1,557	336	1,759
Tartus	–	–	267	1,124	416	1,096	409	1,472	372	1,709
Quneitra	–	–	–	–	–	–	–	–	–	–
Total	4,090	1,081	6,216	1,005	10,770	863	13,663	887	14,698	911

Sources:

1958: Population: Syria, *Statistical Abstract – 1958*, p. 25, table 3.
Number of hospital-beds: Ibid., p. 62, table 8.

1970: Syria, *Statistical Abstract – 1971* p. 358, table 201.

1982: Syria, *Statistical Abstract – 1983* p. 333, table 4/11.

1990: Syria: *Statistical Abstract – 1991*, p. 353, table 2/11.

1993: Syria: *Statistical Abstract – 1994*, p. 361, table 2/11.

with 1:5,059 in Idlib province and 1:5,983 in al-Hasakah province (see table 3.5). Similarly, in the same year, the ratio between population and hospital beds in Damascus was 1:480, while this ratio increased to 1:2,163 in Idlib province and 1:3,245 in al-Hasakah province (see table 3.6).

During the late 1980s and early 1990s, in spite of massive governmental investments to improve the level of health-care services in the countryside and in the remote provinces, a substantial gap in the health-care facilities between the various provinces of the country continued to prevail. By 1993, the ratio of population per physician was 1:771 in Damascus and 1:853 in Aleppo provinces, while it increased to 1:1,508 in Deir al-Zur province and 1:2,235 in al-Hasakah province (see table 3.5). The same differences are also evident in the ratio between population and hospital beds (see table 3.6). This gap in the quality as well as the quantity of health services between the urban centers and the countryside is one of the most important factors accounting for the higher mortality rates and lower life expectancy in the rural areas than in the urban centers, especially the largest cities.

In the field of education, there was also a substantial gap in the level of services provided to the main urban centers and the countryside. While in 1960 the rate of illiteracy in the urban centers was 31.9 percent among males and 65.4 among females, these rates increased to 58.7 percent and 93.9 percent, respectively, in the rural areas. Ten years later, in 1970, this gap continued to exist, and the total illiteracy rate (of both sexes) in the urban centers was 38.3 percent, as compared with 65.6 percent in the countryside. During the 1970s and 1980s, however, impressive improvements were made in the field of educational facilities in the rural areas, resulting in a drop in 1989 in the illiteracy rate (of both sexes) in the rural areas to 28.4 percent, as compared with 17.6 percent in the urban centers (see table 2.7).

The "Pull" Factors

1   **Desire for acquisition of higher education.** One of the most important "pull" factors was the tendency of large numbers of students from the countryside to stay in the urban centers after graduation, partly as a result of the greater number and variety of work opportunities available in the urban centers, especially in the largest cities of Damascus and Aleppo. In contrast, work opportunities in the rural areas suitable to their level of education were scarce due to the absence of industry in these areas. Another important factor accounting for the tendency of large numbers of students to stay in the major cities after graduation was the attraction of city life. According to a survey conducted by the Syrian Ministry of Planning in 1989, the education factor was the second most important reason for the

migration from rural areas to urban centers (after the economic factor), with 27.6 percent among the males and 30.1 percent among the females considering the education factor as the main reason for their migration.[47]

2   Industrial development in the urban centers. Another important "pull" factor, although less important than the others, was the industrial development that was concentrated almost solely in the urban centers, and attracted manpower from the countryside, mainly to the two largest cities, Damascus and Aleppo. Regarding the Syrian industrial distribution during the first half of the 1980s, Elisabeth Longuenesse wrote:

> Regional distribution [of the industrial sector] is still characterized by the predominance of Damascus and Aleppo, despite the policy of industrial decentralization, particularly in the food processing and cement industries. These two main cities together encompass half the workers counted by the unions, whereas their respective populations in 1982 amounted to 18 percent of the total Syrian population.[48]

The beginning of modern industry in Syria dates back to 1930, with the establishment of a cement factory near Damascus. However, during the 1930s and 1940s the rate of industrial development in Syria was very slow, mainly as a result of the French Mandate policy. Thus, until the World War II, Syrian industry remained dependent primarily on manual production methods and had to compete with imported machine-made consumer goods, a situation that seriously hampered its development.[49] Even after independence, in the 1950s and the 1960s, as we saw earlier, the pace of industrial development remained slow.

It seems that the year 1970 marked a turning point in industrial development in Syria. The political stability in the country after Asad's *coup d'état* of that year, combined with the changing economic policy, which became more liberal under Asad's regime as compared with the previous regime of Salah Jadid, fueled the acceleration of industrial development in Syria during the 1970s, especially after the "oil boom" of October 1973. Within the framework of the Fourth Five-Year Development Plan for the years 1976–80, the industrial sector was to get $2.872 billion, representing 20.8 percent of the total investments in the plan.[50] By 1981, the industrial sector constituted 31 percent of the total Syrian GDP,[51] as compared with only 22 percent in 1965.[52] However, as a result of economic hardship during the latter part of the 1980s,[53] the percentage of the industrial sector of the total GDP decreased to 23 percent in 1992.[54]

The development of the industrial sector also created large number of work opportunities in related services. However, it must be emphasized that while in the industrialized western European countries the development of industry in the urban centers, in parallel to mechanization of agricultural production, were the main reason for the rural-to-urban migration, in Syria, as in most of the other Middle Eastern and North African countries, the major incentives for the urbanization process were the "push" factors.

All of these factors, both the "push" and the "pull," brought about the massive rural-to-urban migration in Syria from the late 1950s and early 1960s onward. A very similar trend can be found in many other Middle Eastern and North African countries, except for the Gulf oil-exporting countries where the incentives for rapid urbanization process were different from those in Syria and the other Middle Eastern and North African non-oil countries.[55]

Economic Consequences of the Rapid Urbanization Process

In spite of the fact that "urbanization complements modernization" in many developing countries, the rapid urbanization process led to overcrowding; a rise in open unemployment and disguised unemployment, particularly in the public sector; increased crime; housing problems; pollution; water and electricity shortages; transportation problems; and other social problems.[56]

Following the publication of the 1970 census results, the CBS reported:

Continuous migration into towns and cities from the countryside has caused numerous problems in towns and cities with regard to quantitative and qualitative shortage in housing, transport and communications, water, electricity, education and health. Migration from rural areas brought about seasonal scarcity of workers, particularly during harvest time.[57]

In the following pages the economic problems caused by the rapid urbanization process in Syria are traced and analyzed.

It seems that the most negative consequence of the rapid urbanization process in Syria was the creation of housing and infrastructure problems, which were more drastic in the capital city of Damascus than in any other urban centers. The creation of a severe housing and infrastructure problem in the capital is not unique to Syria alone, but is also evident in most other capitals of the Middle East region. The reason for this phenomenon is that the capitals attract a large proportion of the rural migrants with their large number and variety of available work opportunities, and when combined with the high natural increase rates of the city populations themselves, a very rapid population increase is the end result.

In an interview on the city of Damascus with the official daily newspaper

Tishrin in 1976, the Governor of Damascus examined the unique reasons for the housing problem in the city, which was more severe than anywhere else in the country. According to the Governor, the main reason was that the infrastructure facilities of the city were suitable for serving only 800,000 inhabitants, while at that time the total population of the city was almost twice this number. A second important reason was the concentration of the Palestinian refugees in refugee camps around the city. (By 1990, these camps hosted more than 200,000 Palestinian refugees.)[58] In addition, the city had been forced to absorb a large number of refugees from the villages of the Golan Heights, which were occupied by Israel during the June 1967 War. Another reason was the concentration of the governmental ministries and other official establishments, as well as foreign embassies, in the city.[59]

One of the basic reasons for the overall housing problem in the major Syrian urban centers was the delay in the implementation of the planned housing programs and projects. According to the sample surveys conducted by the Ministry of Municipal and Rural Affairs, 183,000 dwelling units were required during the years 1960–70 to alleviate the housing shortage in the 12 major Syrian cities. This number included: 81,000 units to compensate for the natural increase, 60,000 units to replace destroyed property, 9,000 units to replace those destroyed as a result of implementation of public infrastructure projects, and 33,000 units to accommodate the existing population living in substandard conditions. In addition, another 40,000 units were needed in the provincial towns. Thus, the total dwelling units required in the Syrian urban centers during the years 1960–70 was estimated to be 223,000.[60]

Within the framework of the First Five-Year Development Plan for the years 1960–65, it had been decided to build 60,000 dwelling units in the major urban centers in order to diminish the housing shortage, for which an investment of LS 260 million was envisaged, LS 245 million in the private sector, and LS 15 million in the public sector. The planned investment in the housing sector constituted 9.5 percent of the total investments within the five-year plan. The actual investment in the housing sector during the five-year plan has far exceeded this amount, totaling LS 682 million, more than twice the amount planned. However, due to a miscalculation of the real amount of investment needed, the number of dwelling units built has not been much higher than the target of 12,000 units per annum.

Within the framework of the Second Five-Year Development Plan for the years 1965–70, a target of 163,900 dwelling units was proposed by the Housing Institute. However, the actual target set in the plan for the public sector was only 14,480, assuming that the rest of the dwelling units needed would be built by the private and cooperative sectors. In practice, what was actually achieved during the five-year plan fell far below the expectation, and only 41,804 dwelling units were actually built: 1,740 by the public sector and 40,064 by the private and cooperative sectors.[61] The private sector refrained from large-scale investments in the housing sector because of the meager economic returns of such investments, which were fixed by the regulations according to the rental value.[62] As a result, by the end of 1977, the shortage of dwelling units in the Syrian urban centers was estimated to be 159,000.[63]

The housing crisis in the major cities was due not only to the shortage of dwelling units, but also to their high prices, which from the early 1960s were far beyond the capacity of the lower stratums of urban society, particularly the rural migrants. While in 1967 the average cost of a dwelling unit in one of the major Syrian cities was LS 17,600, and the average saving period for an average income family to acquire such an apartment was 4.2 years, only eight years later, by 1975, the cost of such an apartment increased to LS 84,000 (in current prices), and the saving period needed for an average income family to buy it rose to 14 years.[64] This rapid increase in housing prices was due to the fact that the supply of dwelling units was far below the demand.

As a result of the sharp rise in housing prices, many dwelling units were acquired not for residence, but for purposes of speculation. By the mid-1970s, according to the estimates, there were more than 10,000 unoccupied dwelling units in the Damascus city alone, owned by Arab businessmen for purposes of speculation.[65] This phenomenon was further exacerbated during the second half of the 1970s, and according to the 1981 housing census, the number of unoccupied dwelling units in Damascus city alone was 37,000. However, it must be emphasized that this problem of large numbers of unoccupied dwelling units for purposes of speculation was not unique to the capital alone, but also prevailed in the other major cities of the country. The increasing demand for housing in the major urban centers, which led to a rise in rent prices, constituted the basic reason for this phenomenon. According to the 1981 census, there were more than 302,000 unoccupied dwelling units (some of them in the process of building) throughout the Syrian urban centers, constituting approximately 18 percent of the total dwelling units in the country at that time.[66]

Another important consequence of the increasing housing prices was that informal residence areas started to be established within the boundaries of the major cities in the 1960s. By the beginning of 1977, the informal dwelling units in the capital city of Damascus constituted 25 percent of the total dwelling units in the city, most of which was built by rural migrants who worked in the city as daily workers.[67] This phenomenon of informal housing areas in the major cities, however, is not unique to Syria and can be found in most major cities in developing countries throughout the entire world, including those of the Middle East.

These informal neighborhoods constitute a serious obstacle to future development planning for these cities.[68] The Syrian authorities, like those of

Egypt or any other country with the problem of large-scale informal housing construction in the major cities, realized that they could not cope with this problem by supplying alternative housing solutions for the residents of such informal neighborhoods and were forced instead to provide them with basic public services. Thus, for example, by the beginning of 1990, the director of the National Electricity Company announced that during the year, the company would connect some of these areas to the national electricity network.[69]

The rapid urbanization process also severely affected the urban labor force. Since industrial development in the major Syrian urban centers, as in most other Middle Eastern and North African countries, was slower than the increase in the available labor force, many of the newcomers, especially the rural migrants, could not find employment in the developing industry and related services and were thus forced to base their livelihood on the informal services sector, especially those in which the productive contribution to the overall economic development is marginal, if any.

Moreover, during the nineteenth century, in western European countries, the technologies prevailing in industry did not require a very high degree of skilled labor; consequently, those who migrated from rural areas to the urban industrial centers could be absorbed in industrial production almost without any prior skill or vocational training. This, however, has not been the case in most of the Arab countries, including Syria in recent decades. Not only has the rate of industrialization been much slower than the growth of the urban labor force, but the relatively modern technology methods in industrial production have constituted a serious barrier to the absorption of rural migrants, who in most cases lack the required skills and training.[70]

The phenomenon of large numbers of breadwinners who are forced to find their income in the informal service sector is one of the common economic characteristics of the major urban centers in developing countries all over the world, including those of the Middle East. However, the acceleration of the urbanization process since the latter part of the 1950s, combined with the accelerating natural increase rates of the urban populations themselves, has created a situation in which the unemployment rates in the urban centers, especially in those forced to absorb the largest proportion of rural migration, have been gradually on the rise. While in 1967 the unemployment rate in the major Syrian urban centers was estimated to be 7.3 percent,[71] during the 1970s and 1980s this rate had increased, and by 1989, according to official Syrian figures, 56 percent of the total Syrian unemployed population were concentrated in the capital city of Damascus, and another 6.5 percent in Aleppo.[72]

At the same time, the rapid urbanization process also affected the level of rural manpower, since in many cases the migrants were the most educated and needed for further development of the countryside. Marvin Weinbaum noted in this regard as follows:

Uneconomical farming and more attractive employment opportunities in industry have created in many countries acute shortages of skilled and even unskilled farm workers . . . Perhaps most significant, the loss by the rural areas of their most ambitious and enterprising sons deprives them of some of the very people who are best qualified to lead agricultural sector development.[73]

This description, however, particularly fits the situation in Syria, which, in contrast to other Middle Eastern countries, such as Egypt and Jordan, does not suffer from severe water shortages and limited cultivable lands. The massive rural-to-urban migration movement has created a shortage of skilled and professional agricultural workers, which constitutes one of the major barriers to the introduction of developed and modern agricultural methods. At the same time, the continued use of traditional and ineffective agricultural technologies has caused underemployment and low per capita income in the rural areas, which are among the most important factors accounting for the continued of the rural-to-urban migration movement.[74]

4

Syrian Migration Abroad

Permanent Migration

Emigration, or permanent migration, from the Syrian region is not a new phenomenon, and residents from the Syrian area have emigrated abroad, mostly for trade purposes, for hundreds of years. From the middle of the nineteenth century onward, the emigration trend from Syria sharply increased.[1] It seems that there are two main obstacles to determining, or even estimating, the exact number of emigrants from the Syrian region during the late Ottoman period. First, there was a lack of registration of entrances and exits over the Ottoman Empire borders. The second obstacle was the fact that present-day Syria never constituted one administrative unit under the Ottoman rule, and thus, it is almost impossible to determine the number of emigrants from the areas that eventually became present-day Syria. As a result, most of the data regarding the number of emigrants from Syria during the late Ottoman period also included the emigrants from the areas which developed into present-day Lebanon, the Hashemite Kingdom of Jordan, and northern Israel.[2]

Nevertheless, according to various estimates, the number of emigrants from the Syrian region during the last four decades of the nineteenth century was about 120,000. At the beginning of the twentieth century, the migration trend from the Syrian region substantially increased, and prior to World War I, the number of emigrants from the areas of present-day Syria and Lebanon was estimated to be 15,000 annually.[3]

There were many and varied reasons accounting for the large-scale emigration from Syria and Lebanon during the late Ottoman period, some of them political and others economic. From the political point of view, the events of 1860 made life and property insecure, and many sought to escape from this insecurity through emigration. In the meantime, travel was becoming cheaper and safer with the introduction of steamboats in the Middle East. The encouragement from relatives and friends who had emigrated earlier also contributed to the increase in emigration. Another major impetus for emigration was the institution in 1909 of compulsory military service for all subjects of the Ottoman

Empire, and not only for Muslims, as it had been previously. Due to the many wars in which the Ottoman Empire was engaged at the beginning of the twentieth century, many youth sought to escape from military service via emigration.[4] This emigration was mostly permanent, and only a tiny percentage of the emigrants ever returned to live in their homeland.

The first destination for the Syrian emigrants during the second half of the nineteenth century and the beginning of the twentieth century was Egypt, especially after the British occupation in 1882. On the eve of World War I, the Syrian community in Egypt was estimated to be more than 30,000.[5] The second major destination was North America and after that South America, especially from the beginning of the twentieth century.[6] During the period following World War I, the flow of emigration from Syria continued, but to a much smaller extent than during the period prior to the war. The most common destination of Syrian emigrants after the war was South America. In 1953, the number of Syrian and Lebanese emigrants, together with their offspring, in both North and South America, was estimated at over 810,000, of whom about 650,000 were in Brazil and Argentina alone.[7]

After independence, the emigration trend from Syria continued and was even strengthened following the adoption of a socialist economic policy in the early 1960s.[8] This emigration involved many businessmen and professional workers who resented the nationalization measures taken by the new regime.[9] According to semi-official data published in 1985, during the years 1958–68, about 350,000 Syrian citizens emigrated abroad.[10] From the early 1970s onward, emigration from Syria to areas outside the Middle East continued, albeit in relatively small numbers as compared with the late 1950s and throughout most of the 1960s.

The tremendous economic opportunities which were opened in the Gulf oil-exporting countries changed the wave of the overall Middle Eastern migration trend, including Syria. Since then, almost the entire Syrian migration trend has been concentrated within the boundaries of the Middle East, mainly in the GCC (Gulf Cooperation Council) countries. However, since the Syrian authorities did not annually publish official data regarding the number of emigrants, it seems that the only way to determine the number of Syrians living abroad is to compare the number holding Syrian citizenship with the total Syrian population. This is due to the fact that the number of foreigners living permanently in Syria (except the Palestinian refugees for which the Syrian authorities are publishing data on regular basis in their official publications) is relatively very small. According to this comparison, at the beginning of the 1990s, almost two million Syrian citizens were living outside their homeland.[11]

Temporary Migration for Employment Purposes: Syrian Workers in Other Middle Eastern Countries

Migration within the boundaries of the Middle East region for purposes of employment is a relatively new phenomenon. It began in the late 1940s, following World War II, as a result of the development of the oil industry in the Gulf region, and reached a peak in the late 1970s and early 1980s, with the sharp rise in oil prices due to the Iran–Iraq War. The source of this migration lay in the enormous increase in income via oil export on the part of the Middle Eastern oil-exporting countries. The dramatic increase in oil prices following the "oil boom" of October 1973, transformed the Gulf oil-exporting countries into the wealthiest nations in the Arab world.

The change in the amount of money streaming into the Middle Eastern oil-exporting countries was not just extreme in its scope, but developed rapidly over a short period of time, during the first half of the 1970s. The total revenues from oil export among the seven Middle Eastern members of OPEC jumped from $10 billion in 1972 to a peak of $217 billion in 1980 (in current prices).[12] The revenues of Saudi Arabia alone increased from $3.1 billion to $102 billion (in current prices) during the same years.[13] As a result, the per capita GNP in Saudi Arabia jumped from $500 in 1968 to $15,270, 14 years later, in 1982, and from $3,650 to $19,320 in Kuwait during the same period.[14]

Following the "oil boom," the authorities of the Gulf states had to deal with the complicated dilemma of what to do with the enormous revenues from oil export. Because oil is a depletable resource and the price for it can fluctuate substantially, the creation of alternative sources of income and employment opportunities through economic diversification became a major target for the authorities of these countries. Thus, for example, one of the three major objectives of Saudi Arabia's first five-year development plan covering the years 1970–75 was: "Diversifying sources of national income and reducing dependence on oil . . . "[15] The same objective also appeared in the first Omani five-year development plan.[16] It seems that they eventually decided to invest in three major fields.

The first field was the development of the infrastructure system: from roads, highways, and airports, through telecommunication systems and power stations, to the building of other governmental services. The main reason for the vast investment in infrastructure was that it constitutes the first and most critical stage in the transformation process from a developing to a developed country. The second field was the development of the industrial sector in order to ensure a long-term high level of per capita GNP and income, due to the high instability of the oil prices.[17] The third field was the improvement of social services, including health-care and education, as well as housing facilities. In addition, the declaration of oil as a national asset led to a partial distribution of the oil wealth to the national populations of these countries through the supply of comprehensive social services free of charge.[18]

However, these development plans required an extensive work force of a quality and quantity which could not be supplied by local sources for three main reasons: The first was the very small size of the national populations. In 1975, the total national population of the GCC countries was estimated to be 6.059 million,[19] while the total national labor forces of these countries amounted to only 1.31 million.[20] The second reason was the low skill level of the national work forces due to high illiteracy rates among the local populations, as well as the lack of professional education and training. The third, and perhaps the most important, factor was the relatively low rates of labor force participation, caused mainly by the high rates of natural increase, in parallel to extremely low rates of female labor force participation.[21]

As a result of these basic limitations, in order to implement the various socioeconomic development plans, the capital rich Gulf countries were forced to substantially increase the size of their foreign work force. From an economic point of view, the enlistment of large-scale foreign labor did not require any incentive campaigns, since the wages offered to foreign workers by the Gulf countries were several times higher than those paid at home for the same work.[22]

One of the distribution characteristics of the proven oil reserves in the Arab world is that they are greatest in the countries with relatively small populations. As a result, those countries with the larger populations and the greatest need for additional work opportunities have little, if any, oil.[23] From the early 1970s, the authorities of the labor-exporting countries realized the benefits that could be reaped from the inter-Arab labor movement, the main benefit deriving from the financial remittances transferred by workers to their home countries, which amounted to billions of dollars annually from the mid-1970s until the Iraqi invasion of Kuwait in August 1990. Such substantial amounts of income allowed the labor-exporting countries to meet part of their chronic balance of trade deficits, eased their foreign exchange shortage, and financed construction and industrial projects.[24]

From a political point of view, it was the growth of pragmatism in the Arab world that enabled the large-scale movement of workers between the Arab countries. The period of the 1950s and the 1960s was characterized by ideological struggles between two major forces in the Arab world: Nasserism that sought to change the prevailing regimes in the Arab world, and Monarchism that sought to protect those regimes. During the 1970s, a new stability appeared in the Arab balance of power: On the one hand, the radical regimes were eager to share in the benefits of the huge oil revenues; and on the other hand, the conservative regimes recognized the chance to convert their economic power into political influence.[25] Consequently, the extensive economic and employment opportunities in the oil-exporting countries, combined with the tight economic and employment situations in most of the "radical" countries, together facilitated pragmatism in the Arab world, thereby enabling the relatively liberal movement of workers between the Arab countries.

The migration trend in the Middle East differs from those in western Europe in several ways. First, the migration trend in Europe is from the less advanced to the more industrialized countries. Second, labor migration in the Middle East has been largely characterized by temporary sojourns followed by a return to the homeland after the expiration of work permits and contracts.[26] Only a tiny percentage of the migrants eventually become citizens in the labor-importing countries of the Middle East.

The Scope of Syrian Migrants in Other Middle Eastern Countries

According to one estimate, by A. M. Farrag, the number of the Syrian migrant workers in the Middle Eastern oil-exporting countries circa 1970 was 58,821, in addition to another 33,800 who worked at that time in Lebanon.[27] However, this estimate seems to be too high due to an overestimate regarding the number of Syrian migrant workers in Saudi Arabia at that time, said to be about 40,000 (see below).

As a result of the implementation of the large-scale socioeconomic development plans, the number of migrant workers in the Middle Eastern oil-exporting countries increased rapidly, including those from Syria. In 1975, according to a Birks and Sinclair estimate, there were 50,265 Syrian workers in these countries, accompanied by 86,505 family members. Thus, altogether there were 136,770 Syrian citizens in these countries in 1975 (see table 4.1). In addition, there were approximately 22,000 Syrian citizens in Jordan, and another 200,000–400,000 temporary and seasonal Syrian workers in Lebanon (see below).

During the second half of the 1970s, the number of Syrian workers in the Middle Eastern oil-exporting countries increased sharply. Birks and others estimated that in 1980, about 89,000 Syrian citizens were working in these countries, representing an increase of almost 80 percent in only five years.[28] Richards and Waterbury estimated the number of Syrian migrant workers in the Middle Eastern oil-exporting countries to be only 67,150 in that particular year.[29] Nazli Choucri estimated their number in the early 1980s to be 80,000,[30] much closer to the estimate of Birks and others than the estimate of Richards and Waterbury. Furthermore, another 60,000 Syrians were working at that time in Lebanon and Jordan. All in all, it seems that at the early 1980s, approximately 140,000 Syrians were working in other Middle Eastern countries, the vast majority of them in the Gulf states.

During the 1980s, the number of Syrian migrants in other Middle Eastern countries remained more or less stable. According to the HRD base estimates, in 1985 there were 173,444 Syrian citizens in the GCC countries and Libya (67,896 workers accompanied by 105,548 family members – see table 4.1). In addition, about 22,000 others were working in Jordan that particular year (see below). During the second half of the 1980s, the number of Syrian migrant workers in the Middle Eastern oil-exporting countries remained more or less stable. The 1990 figures are not complete, since official figures or even estimates regarding the number of Syrian migrants in Libya at that time are not available. However, there are no reports regarding a massive return of Syrian migrants from Libya during the second half of the 1980s. Hence, if the number of Syrian migrants in Libya remained more or less stable during the second half of the 1980s (almost 9,000 workers accompanied by 8,000 family members), then we can assume that by mid-1990, on the eve of the Iraqi invasion of Kuwait, there were approximately 200,000 Syrians, including workers and accompanying family members altogether, living and working in the Middle Eastern oil-exporting countries.

The Iraqi invasion of Kuwait in August 1990 brought about dramatic changes in the scale of migration for purposes of employment in the GCC countries, mainly in Kuwait and Saudi Arabia. Following the invasion, about two million Arab migrants returned to their homelands, including about 100,000–110,000 Syrians.[31] However, with the beginning of the reconstruction programs after the war, mainly in Kuwait, there was a massive movement of foreign workers back to the GCC countries, including Syrian workers. During the second half of 1991 and the beginning of 1992, Syrian workers started to return to the GCC states, but in relatively small numbers as compared with those prior to the Iraqi invasion. By mid-1992, the number of Syrians in the GCC countries was estimated at little more than 110,000. Thus, it appears from these data that the number of Syrians in these countries in mid-1992 reverted back to the level present at the beginning of the 1970s (see table 4.1).

The Incentives for Syrian Labor Migration

The main, and perhaps the only, reason for migration of Syrian workers to other Middle Eastern countries from the late 1960s onward was economic, namely, a huge difference between the wages in Syria and those paid for the same work in the Gulf countries, Libya, and even in Lebanon and Jordan. For example, at the beginning of 1977, an unskilled construction worker in Damascus might earn LS 250 a month ($68 at that time), while in Saudi Arabia he would probably earn at least five-fold this amount for the same work.[32] Regarding income differences in the agricultural sector, the average annual income of a Syrian

Table 4.1 Syrian migrants in the major labor-receiving countries of the Middle East, 1970–92

Year	1970			1975			1980		
Country	W	F.M	T	W	F.M	T	W	F.M	T
Bahrain	17	35	52 (a)	68	140	208	103	213	316 (b)
Kuwait	12,659	14,558	27,217	16,547	24,415	40,962	35,000		
Saudi Arabia			30,000 40,000 (c)	15,000	28,500	43,500	24,600 (d)		
UAE			7,000 (e)	4,500	6,800	11,300	6,000		
Oman				400	700	1,100			
Qatar				750	1,150	1,900	1,000		
Libya	4,812 (f)			13,000	24,000	37,800	17,653 (g)		
Total				50,265	86,505	136,770	68,446		

Year Country	1985			1990			1992
	W	F.M	T	W	F.M	T	T
Bahrain	50	59	109	60	50	110	110
Kuwait	24,850	65,611	90,461		107,496		21,000
Saudi Arabia	27,000	17,444	44,444	18,730	15,320	34,050	48,088
UAE	4,790	7,292	12,082	7,336	11,176	18,512	20,800
Oman	160	454	614	50	68	118	
Qatar	2,298	6,680	8,978	1,963	5,705	7,668	21,680
Libya	8,748	8,008	16,756				
Total	67,896	105,548	173,444		184,712		111,678

Notes:

a. Related to 1971.

b. Related to 1977.

c. Related to the end of the 1960s

d. Related to the beginning of the 1980s.

e. Related to 1968.

f. Related to 1972.

g. Related to 1981.

Sources for table 4.1:

J. S. Birks and C. A. Sinclair, *International Migration Project, Country Case Study: The State of Bahrain* (Durham: The University of Durham, Department of Economics, May 1978); idem, *International Migration and Development in the Arab Region* (Geneva: ILO, 1980); J. S. Birks, I. Serageldin, and J. A. Socknat, "Who is Migrating Where? An Overview of International Labor Migration in the Arab World," in Alan Richards and Phillip L. Martin (eds), *Migration, Mechanization and Agricultural Labor Markets in Egypt* (Boulder: Westview Press, and Cairo: The American University in Cairo Press, 1983), pp. 113–14, table 1; J. S. Birks, and C. A. Sinclair, "The Libyan Arab Jamahirya: Labour Migration Sustain Dualistic Development," *Maghreb Review*, Vol. 4, No. 3 (May/June 1979), p. 99; Nazli Choucri, "Migration in the Middle East: Transformation and Change," *Middle East Review*, Vol. 16, No. 2 (Winter 1983/4), p. 18; R. J. Ward, "The Long-Run Employment Prospects for the Middle East Labor," *The Middle East Journal*, Vol. 24 (Spring 1970), p. 153; Saad Eddin Ibrahim, *The New Social Order: A Study of the Social Impact of Oil Wealth* (Boulder: Westview press, 1982), p. 33, table 3.3; A. Richards and J. Waterbury, *A Political Economy of the Middle East* (Boulder: Westview Press, 1990); *al-Muntagun*, 12 December 1981; HRD base Ltd, Lloyds Bank Chambers, *Socio-Demographic Profiles of Key Arab Countries* (Newcastle, May 1987); State of Kuwait, The Planning Board, Central Statistical Office, *Annual Statistical Abstract*, Various Issues (Kuwait: Government Printing Press); State of Bahrain, Central Statistical Organisation, Directorate of Statistics, *Statistical Abstract*, Various Issues (Manama: Government Printing Press); Birks & Sinclair Ltd, *GCC Market Report – 1990 and 1992* (Durham: Mountjoy Research Centre).

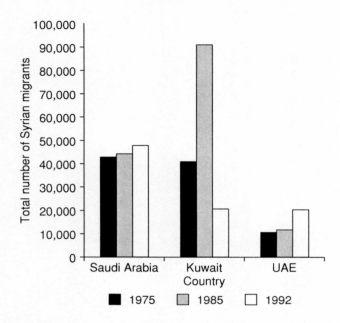

Figure 4.1 Syrian migrants in the major labor-receiving countries of the Middle East, 1970–92

peasant in 1978 was LS 1,500–2,000, as compared with LS 1,000 per month in one of the Gulf countries.[33]

Another reason for migration to the Gulf region was the high cost of the *Mahr* (a gift that the groom gives to the bride's father), which reached about LS 5,000–6,000 by the end of the 1970s.[34] It seems that the only way for the lower strata of Syrian society to earn this sum was to work for several years in one of the Gulf countries. In her anthropological research work on the Euphrates Valley, Annika Rabo describes the reason for migration from the Raqqa province:

> Young men may see migration to the Gulf as the only rapid means of gaining money to get married, to build a house, to buy a car or to invest in some business . . . The proclaimed success of others acts as a stimulus. Admittedly, those who have migrated, and return home on vacation, talk of the hardships in the Gulf . . . But they all say it is worthwhile since the pay is good.[35]

In contrast to the migration trends outside the Middle East, the migration of Syrian workers to the Middle Eastern countries for purposes of employment was basically temporary. The only aim of the migrants was to work in one of the Gulf states for several years in order to save some money and then return to Syria and improve their socioeconomic condition. Rabo depicts the situation among the migrant workers from the Raqqa province:

> Migration is strictly for work, and many people say they work more or less day and night. The move is never permanent, even though some have worked more or less continuously for the past decade.[36]

The distribution of the migrants from the various districts of Syria is not equal. During the second half of the 1970s, the highest rate of migration to the oil-exporting countries was from the Dar'a province. In late 1979, according to Syrian sources, 35 percent of the labor force in the province were working outside the country, most of them in the Gulf countries. This high rate of labor migration from the Dar'a province was not accidental, since the heavy drought suffered by the region during that time caused a substantial decrease in the income and standard of living of the population, pushing many of them to migrate to the Gulf countries.[37]

Distribution of Syrian Migrants in the Host Countries

Syrian Migrants in Lebanon

Until the mid-1970s, the main destination of migrant workers from Syria for purposes of employment in the Middle East was Lebanon. According to a sample survey conducted in Lebanon, in late 1970 about 100,000 Syrians were working in the country,[38] while according to an unofficial estimate, their number at that time was only 33,800.[39] However, this estimate seems to be too low in comparison with other estimates for the same period, as well as estimates for the coming years.

While no official data or estimates regarding the number of Syrian workers in Lebanon during the first half of the 1970s are available, it appears from various unofficial sources that in the early 1970s their number was about 200,000–400,000.[40] According to a Syrian semi-official estimate, on the eve of the outbreak of the Civil War in 1975 about 600,000 Syrians were working in the country.[41] This figure seems to be too high, since it is not reasonable that almost one-third of the Syrian civilian labor force was working in Lebanon at that time. One explanation for the considerable differences among the various estimates regarding the number of Syrian workers in Lebanon during the first half of the 1970s was that during the winter there was a sizable seasonal migration of agricultural workers from Syria to Lebanon. Some of the Syrians

were employed by companies and establishments owned by Syrian businessmen, while the vast majority were employed in the construction and
agricultural sectors.[42]

The outbreak of the Civil War and the Israeli invasion seven years later, in
1982, brought about an end to Lebanon serving as a major employment destination for Syrian workers for the following one and a half decades. By
mid-1980, the number of Syrian workers in Lebanon was estimated to be
30,000,[43] representing only 10 to 20 percent of their number prior to the Civil
War. During the second half of the 1980s, the number of Syrians in Lebanon
continued to decrease.

The signing of the Ta'if agreement (1989) and the Treaty of Friendship and
Cooperation between Syria and Lebanon (May 1991)[44] granted Syria a direct,
at least *de facto,* control over many aspects of Lebanese life. As a result of the
reconstruction of the country that followed, there was a rapid increase in the
number of Syrian workers in Lebanon, especially in the construction and
infrastructure sectors. However, neither the Lebanese government nor the
Syrian authorities are publishing official data regarding the number of Syrian
citizens living and working in Lebanon. Despite the fact that many of the
workers are seasonal migrants, making accurate estimates all the more difficult, unofficial sources estimate their number at the beginning of the 1990s to
be very high. According to one source, an estimated 500,000 to one million
Syrians were working in Lebanon by mid-1995.[45] Another source estimated
their number to be almost a million in mid-1997,[46] including about
35,000–40,000 Syrian troops.[47] At the beginning of 1998, Lebanese sources
estimated the number of Syrian workers in Lebanon to be approximately one
million, while according to another source, their number at that time was
much lower, only 800,000.[48] By mid-1998, according to an official Lebanese
source, the number of Syrian workers in the country was more than 1.25
million, while according to an unofficial Lebanese source, their number was
much lower, amounting to approximately 300,000, in addition to about 40,000
Syrian troops.[49]

Economists claim that by the early 1990s the remittances of the Syrian
workers in Lebanon amounted to $1 to $3 billion annually.[50] However, a
comparison between the scale of the workers' remittances of Syrian migrants
in Lebanon and their estimated numbers would indicate that the average remittances of one Syrian worker in Lebanon by the mid-1990s was only a few
hundred dollars annually. This amount is very low even in comparison to the
average salaries in Syria at that time. Thus, either the estimates of the scale of
Syrian workers' remittances from Lebanon were too low, or the estimates of
the numbers of Syrian workers in the country were too high. In addition,
according to the above-mentioned estimates, it appears that approximately
35–40 percent of the labor force in Lebanon during the mid-1990s were Syrians,

which is not at all reasonable. Thus, the highest number of Syrians working permanently in Lebanon during the mid-1990s could not be more than 300,000–400,000.

Syrians Migrants in Jordan

In parallel to the sharp decrease in the demand for workers in Lebanon after the outbreak of the Civil War, the demand for workers in Jordan increased dramatically due to the migration of hundreds of thousands of Jordanian workers to the Gulf, mainly to Kuwait, from the early 1970s onward. Many of these Jordanian workers were replaced by Syrians, in essence creating a phenomenon of "immigrant workers replacing emigrant workers." A large number of the Syrians who migrated to Jordan had worked earlier in Lebanon. Thus, from the mid-1970s onward, the second largest community of foreign workers in Jordan, after the Egyptians, were the Syrians.

According to a Birks and Sinclair estimate, in 1975, of 70,150 Syrians who were working in various Middle Eastern countries, 20,000 were working in Jordan, accompanied by 2,000 family members, thereby bringing the total Syrian community in Jordan in that particular year to 22,000.[51] However, the Jordanian Ministry of Labor estimated the number of Syrian workers in the Kingdom in that year to be closer to 25,000.[52] Four years later, in 1979, the same source estimated that there were up to 30,000 Syrians working in the country, many of them staying for only a few weeks or months at a time.[53]

During the first half of the 1980s, the number of Syrian workers in Jordan somewhat decreased, and by 1985 their number was estimated to be 18,549, accompanied by 3,405 family members.[54] During the second half of the decade, the number of Syrian workers in Jordan continued to remain stable, and according to Jordanian official figures, by the end of December 1988 there were 18,736 Syrian workers in the country.[55] According to the latest Jordanian figures, by 1996 the Jordanian Ministry of Labor had issued 1,286 work permits to Syrian workers in the Kingdom.[56] However, this figure represents only the legal workers and therefore does not include those who were working without work permits.

The main reason for the relatively large number of Syrian workers in Jordan was economic. Although Jordan is not an oil-exporting country, there was still a large difference in salaries between Jordan and Syria. In the late 1980s, a Syrian manual laborer in Jordan could earn five times as much as a government clerk in Damascus, partly because of the strength of the Jordanian Dinar (JD) as compared with the declining LS.[57] This disparity in currency values was due to the high inflation rates in Syria during the second half of the 1980s.[58] Besides the economic factor, the two main factors accounting for the relatively large number of Syrian workers in Jordan during the latter part of the 1970s and throughout most of the 1980s were the close distance between the two countries, as well as the waiver of visas and work permits for Syrians, due to the informal agreement between the two countries.[59]

Syrian Migrants in the Libyan Arab Jamahiriya

The Libyan Arab Jamahiriya has made more use of bilateral agreements than most other Middle Eastern labor-receiving countries. In this case, the Libyan–Syrian agreement is of particular importance insofar as several military aid package deals also include the provision of Syrian workers to Libya.[60] Syrians were working in Libya even before the "oil boom," and by 1972, according to the Libyan Ministry of Labor figures, their number was 4,812, representing 5.3 percent of the total number of non-Libyan Arab workers in the country at that time.[61] One year later, in 1973, their number was estimated by the same source to be 6,000.[62]

After the "oil boom," the number of foreign workers in Libya increased sharply, including that of Syrians. By 1976, the number of Syrian workers was estimated by the Libyan Ministry of Labor to be 13,029, representing an increase of 170 percent over their number four years earlier, in 1972.[63] During the second half of the 1970s, the number of Syrian workers in the country continued to increase, and by 1981, according to Libyan sources, their number was 17,653, many of whom had migrated under the auspices of the Syrian–Libyan intergovernmental agreements (see table 4.1).

As a result of the financial problems caused by the drop in oil prices, the Libyan authorities sharply cut the level of public spending, and reports published in mid-1982 noted large-scale layoffs of foreign workers.[64] However, workers from countries which enjoyed close relations with Libya, including Syria, were largely untouched by the expulsions. Thus, at the beginning of the 1980s, the number of Syrian workers in Libya further increased, and by 1983 their number was estimated at 24,000.[65] According to ILO figures, by July 1985 there were 583,900 foreign workers in Libya, of whom 30,000 were Syrians, representing 5.1 percent of total foreign workers in the country at that time.[66] According to the HRD base figures for that particular year, Syrian migrants in the country totaled 16,756, of whom only 8,748 were workers and the rest were accompanying family members (see table 4.1). Regarding the number of Syrian workers in the country during the second half of the 1980s, no official or even unofficial estimates are available.

Syrian Migrants in Saudi Arabia

One of the major destinations for Syrian migrant workers from the 1960s onward was Saudi Arabia. During the late 1960s, the number of Syrian migrants (including dependents) in the Kingdom was estimated by Richard Ward to be 30,000–40,000, most of them professional, skilled, and semi-skilled workers.[67] According to Farrag's estimate, which was also adopted by Nazli Choucri, the number of the Syrian workers was approximately 40,000 in circa 1970.[68] However, this estimate seems to be too high, since five years later, in 1975, after the "oil boom," the number of Syrian workers in Saudi Arabia was estimated by Birks and Sinclair to be only 15,000, accompanied by 28,500 family members (see table 4.1). According to official Saudi figures, the number of Syrian workers in the Kingdom was less than 4,000 in 1973, and then increased to 20,878 in 1978.[69] It seems that during the first half of the 1970s, the number of Syrian workers in the Kingdom never exceeded 20,000–21,000. If there were 40,000 Syrian workers in the country during that period, as some sources indicated, then the total Syrian population in the Kingdom, including both workers and accompanying family members, would have reached about 60,000–70,000, which is too high in comparison with the various sources.

By the beginning of the 1980s, the number of Syrian workers in Saudi Arabia was estimated to be 24,600. Their number continued to increase during the first half of the 1980s, and in 1985 the total Syrian community in the Kingdom was estimated at 44,444, of whom 27,000 were workers and 17,444 were accompanying family members (see table 4.1). According to another estimate, the number of Syrian workers in the Kingdom in that year was lower, only 22,190, accompanied by 18,090 family members.[70] During the second half of the 1980s, the number of Syrian migrants in Saudi Arabia decreased steadily, and by mid-1990, on the eve of the Iraqi invasion of Kuwait, their number was estimated to be 34,050, of whom 18,730 were workers and 15,320 were accompanying family members (see table 4.1).

The Iraqi invasion of Kuwait caused a massive departure of foreign workers from Saudi Arabia.[71] But, during the early 1990s the number of foreign workers in the Kingdom increased again, and by mid-1992 the Syrian community in Saudi Arabia was estimated to be 48,088, including workers and accompanying family members altogether (see table 4.1).

Syrian Migrants in Kuwait

The most important pull factor for the foreign workers in Kuwait was economic. Kuwait offered higher salaries than did most countries in the Middle East, including the other Arab oil-exporting countries. Moreover, consumer goods were relatively inexpensive, since VAT (value-added tax) was not imposed in Kuwait. Consequently, Kuwait attracted large numbers of workers from other Arab countries, as well as from Southeast Asian countries, who were seeking employment in Kuwait in order to acquire consumer goods. Another major pull factor was the free health-care and education services available to all residents in the country, including the accompanying family members of the foreign workers.[72]

The earliest data regarding the scale of Syrian migration to Kuwait is from the 1965 census, which reported a total of 16,849 Syrian citizens in the country.[73] At the time of the former population census, which was conducted in Kuwait in 1961, the Syrians and the Egyptians were merged together in the UAR.[74] During the second half of the 1960s, the number of foreigners in Kuwait increased rapidly, in fact more so than in any other Gulf states at that time. As a part of this trend, the number of Syrian workers in Kuwait also increased significantly during this period, and according to the 1970 census there were 27,217 Syrian citizens in the country, including both workers and accompanying family members (see table 4.1).

During the 1970s, the foreign population of Kuwait continued to increase rapidly, and according to the 1975 census, the total foreign population of Kuwait numbered 522,749, including 40,962 Syrian citizens.[75] The 1975 census was the last one that provided the distribution of the foreign population according to country of origin. Since then, we only have data regarding the distribution of the foreign population according to their nationalities (Arabs, Asians, etc.). During the second half of the 1970s, as a result of the implementation of large-scale socioeconomic development plans, the total number of foreign workers in Kuwait increased more rapidly than in any other previous periods. The number of Syrian workers in the country also increased accordingly, reaching an estimated 35,000 in 1980 (see table 4.1).

During the 1980s, the growth of Syrian migration to Kuwait outpaced that of any other GCC countries. By 1985, there were an estimated 90,461 Syrian citizens in Kuwait, of whom 24,850 were workers and 65,611 were accompanying family members. During the latter half of the decade, the number of Syrian migrants in the country continued to increase, but by lower rates compared with previous years. In mid-1990, on the eve of the Iraqi invasion, the number of Syrian migrants in the country was estimated to be 107,496, including both workers and accompanying family members (see table 4.1).

The Iraqi invasion of Kuwait brought about a dramatic demographic change in both the national and foreign populations. Within a few weeks after the invasion, over 90 percent of the foreign population left the country. Of about 500,000 Asians, only 12,500 remained at the time of the withdrawal of Iraqi forces in February 1991. It seems that the entire Syrian population, which was estimated at 107,000, left the country, in addition to about 250,000 Egyptians.[76]

As a result of the reconstruction projects, which required a large-scale work force, both in terms of quality and quantity, the foreign population of Kuwait started to increase rapidly once again in mid-1991. One year later, by mid-1992, the total Syrian population in the country, including workers and accompanying family members altogether, was estimated at 21,000 (see table 4.1). By the end of the year, the number of Syrian workers in Kuwait was estimated to be 40,000,[77] increasing to 43,000 by mid-1993.[78]

Syrian Migrants in Bahrain

Bahrain has the longest history of population censuses among the GCC countries. The population of Bahrain has grown steadily since oil was discovered in 1932, but not at the same pace as in Kuwait, Qatar, or the UAE. Throughout the period under discussion, the number of Syrian migrants in Bahrain was the smallest among the GCC countries. According to the 1959 population census, there were only 43 Syrian citizens in the country, increasing to 53, according to the 1965 census, and 52, according to the 1971 census.[79]

The "oil boom" and the implementation of wide-ranging socioeconomic development plans brought about a rapid increase in the number of foreign workers in the country. In contrast to Kuwait, Qatar, and the UAE, the nationals in Bahrain continued to constitute the majority of the total population. According to the 1981 census, foreigners constituted 32.0 percent of the total Bahraini population.[80] By 1975, the number of Syrian migrants, including workers and accompanying family members, has risen to 208, but declined back to 109 in 1985 and 110 in mid-1990 and mid-1992 (see table 4.1).

Syrian Migrants in Qatar

While there are no official or even unofficial estimates regarding the number of Syrian migrants in Qatar prior to the mid-1970s, it seems that their number did not exceed a few hundred. According to an estimate by Birks and Sinclair, in 1975 there were 1,900 Syrian citizens in Qatar, of whom 750 were workers and the rest were accompanying family members. During the second half of the 1970s, the number of Syrian workers in the country increased, but not to a large extent, and by 1980 their number was estimated to be 1,000 (see table 4.1).

During the first half of the 1980s, the total number of foreign workers in Qatar increased sharply. According to the 1986 population census, there were 369,000 foreigners in the country, constituting 77 percent of the total population.[81] This represents a significant increase over the 59.5 percent reported in the 1970 population census.[82] During this period, the number of Syrian migrants also substantially increased, reaching almost 9,000 in 1985, of whom 2,300 were workers and the rest were accompanying family members (see table 4.1).

During the second half of the 1980s, the foreign population of Qatar continued to increase, although at a slower pace than in the earlier years of the 1980s. In 1991, the number of foreigners in the country was estimated at 350,000, representing 78 percent of Qatar's total population.[83] In mid-1990, on the eve of the Iraqi invasion of Kuwait, the Syrian community in the country was estimated to be 7,668, of whom 1,963 were workers. According to these estimates, during the second half of the 1980s, the number of Syrian migrants in Qatar declined by 15 percent (see table 4.1).

The Iraqi invasion of Kuwait did not substantially affect the size of the foreign population in Qatar, which the IMF estimated at 413,000 in 1993,[84] representing an increase of 18 percent as compared with their number two years earlier, in 1991. After the Gulf crisis, the number of Syrian migrants in Qatar increased sharply, and by mid-1992, their number was estimated to be 21,680, representing an increase of almost three-fold as compared with their number only two years earlier, in mid-1990 (see table 4.1).

Syrian Migrants in Oman

The most difficult obstacle to researching demographic developments in Oman is that the first, and so far the only, population census was conducted in 1993. During the period under discussion, the number of Syrian migrants in Oman was relatively very small. There are no official data or even unofficial estimates available regarding the number of Syrian migrants in Oman prior to the mid-1970s. According to an estimate by Birks and Sinclair, in 1975 there were approximately 132,500 foreigners in Oman,[85] of whom 1,100 were Syrians, including 400 workers and 700 accompanying family members. This figure represents less than one percent of the total number of foreigners in the country at that time (see tables 4.1).

During the latter half of the 1970s and the early 1980s, in parallel to the other GCC countries, the total foreign population of Oman increased by high rates. In 1985, the number of foreigners in the country was estimated to be 391,000, representing more than 30 percent of the total population,[86] of whom only 614 were Syrians. During the second half of the 1980s, the number of Syrian migrants in Oman further declined, dropping to an estimated total of 118 by mid-1990. After the Gulf crisis, it seems that all the Syrian migrants had left the country, so that by mid-1992, there were no more Syrians reported to be working in Oman (see tables 4.1).

Syrian Migrants in the United Arab Emirates (UAE)

Even before the "oil boom," there were Syrian migrants in the UAE. According to the 1968 census, there were 43,000 foreign workers in the country, of whom about 7,000 were Syrians, representing more than 16 percent of the total foreign work force.[87] Since then, in parallel with the other Gulf countries, the foreign population of the UAE increased sharply. According to the 1975 census, the total foreign population in the country reached 387,700,[88] of whom 11,300 were Syrians (2.9 percent), including 4,500 workers and 6,800 accompanying family members (see table 4.1).

During the latter half of the 1970s, the total foreign population of the UAE almost doubled, reaching 746,000 by 1980,[89] of whom 470,800 were workers.[90] However, the number of Syrian workers in the UAE did not increase during this period, and even somewhat decreased, so that by 1980, their number was estimated to be only 6,000 (see table 4.1). During the first half of the 1980s, although the foreign population of the UAE rose rapidly,[91] the number of Syrian migrants continued to decline. By 1985, the Syrian community in the country was estimated to be 12,082, of whom only 4,790 were workers (see table 4.1).

During the second half of the 1980s, in spite of the reduction in oil prices, the number of foreign workers in the country continued to increase, even by relatively high rates. By mid-1990, the total foreign work force in the UAE was estimated to be 805,000, as compared with 612,000 in 1985, representing an increase of more than 30 percent in just five years.[92] During that period, the number of Syrian migrants in the country also increased, reaching 18,512 in 1985, of whom 7,336 were workers and 11,176 were accompanying family members (see table 4.1).

During the early 1990s, the UAE population of the United Arab Emirates sustained its high growth rates, more than 4 percent annually. By 1993, the total population of the UAE was estimated by the Ministry of Planning to be 2.09 million, of whom only 20 percent were nationals, while the remaining 80 percent were foreigners.[93] The Syrian population in the country also continued to increase in the early 1990s, reaching 20,800 in mid-1992, as compared with 18,512 in mid-1990, representing an increase of 12.4 percent in just two years (see table 4.1).

Economic Consequences of Labor Migration

The Labor Market

Both the permanent Syrian migration to the West and the temporary migration to other Middle Eastern countries caused a severe shortage of skilled and professional workers in Syria. Despite the relatively small number of Syrian migrant workers, from the mid-1960s onward, the shortage of skilled workers was considerable, due to the imbalance in the distribution of migrants among the various skilled professions.

Many of the migrants were skilled and professional workers in the industrial, construction, and related services, which caused a substantial shortage of manpower in these particular sectors.[94] The data show that until 1970 more than 14,000 university graduates were living and working abroad. This figure represents about 31 percent of the total number of university graduates, estimated at that time to be 46,000. During that period, more than 1,400 women graduates, representing 23 percent of the total number of women graduates, had emigrated abroad. During the 1960s, Syria lost about one-fifth of its total number of engineers and more than one-third of its physicians;[95] this, in turn, caused severe damage to the Syrian economy.[96] In September 1973, the Syrian Minister of Industry, Hussain Mohammed al-Khatib, stated that one of the major problems facing Syrian industry was the shortage of expert and professional manpower, caused mainly by the drain of engineers and technicians who emigrated abroad.[97] As a result, many factories during the 1970s were running below capacity by as much as 50 percent.[98] A 1975 ECWA report noted that:

> The Syrian Arab Republic . . . has been a net exporter of manpower; this factor has recently begun to have an impact on such activities as the building industry.[99]

In addition, those who remained to work in Syria in the sectors which suffered from a labor shortage demanded much higher salaries.[100] In an interview conducted at the beginning of 1977, the Syrian Deputy Minister of State for Planning, Riad Abrash, noted:

> We were hit by workers being attracted to the Gulf states, Saudi Arabia and West Germany, and our economy just cannot possibly compete at present with wages offered by Arab petroleum-producing and European countries.[101]

The large-scale migration of skilled and professional workers turned the Middle Eastern labor-exporting countries, including Syria, into virtual "training schools" for the capital rich Arab countries, as well as for the western industrialized countries. In all the Middle Eastern labor-exporting countries, education is provided at every level either free of charge or subsidized to a large extent. This created a situation in which these countries invested a large amount of money in education and professional training without receiving direct and sufficient returns from the capital rich Arab oil-exporting countries that were benefiting from the influx of labor.[102] Mostafa Nagi has observed:

Not only is the productive capacity of the migrants lost during their most active years, but, also, the process is selective and tends to draw away many of the most able members within each skill level of the labor force. Countries of origin are losing manpower from the very sectors that are most crucial to their development.[103]

Crown Prince El-Hassan bin-Talal of Jordan proposed at the 63rd Conference of the ILO (1977) that an International Labor Compensatory should be established so that labor-exporting countries suffering from the so-called "brain drain," including the Arab labor-exporting countries, could be compensated. Such a facility would operate with resources provided by the labor-importing countries that stood to benefit from the "brain drain."[104]

Workers' Remittances

The most positive outcome of the migration of workers from the poorer countries to the rich Arab oil-exporting countries was that of the workers' remittances, which constituted a major component in the balance of payments of the labor-exporting countries. During the late 1970s and early 1980s, when migration reached its peak, the official workers' remittances alone were much higher in many of the labor-exporting countries than their total export of goods and services. In Jordan and Egypt, for example, the official workers' remittances in 1980 reached $715 million and $2.7 billion, respectively,[105] exceeding to a great extent the traditional sources for foreign exchange of these countries (cotton exports and tolls from the Suez Canal, in the case of Egypt; and phosphates exports from the Dead Sea, foreign financial aid, and tourism, in the case of Jordan). A very similar picture also appeared in YAR, where in 1980 and 1985 workers' remittances were worth almost five-fold the value of the total export of goods and services.[106] In the case of Syria, the official figure for workers' remittances in 1980 was $773.5 million. Although they never constituted the major component for foreign exchange, they certainly represented one of its major components during the late 1970s and early 1980s.[107]

It seems that there are not any surveys or other sources of data regarding the use of the Syrian workers' remittances. According to a sample survey conducted in 1984 by Allan Findlay and Musa Samha among returned and current Jordanian migrant workers, it appeared that the most common use for workers' remittances was for housing; the second priority was for purchasing a car; and the third priority was for purchasing land. Only less than 10 percent of the migrants used the remittances for investment in industrial or agricultural projects.[108] At the beginning of the 1980s, Roger Owen noted that "only a small proportion of the migrants' remittances is used directly for productive investment."[109] There is no reason to believe that the Syrian workers were using their remittances in other forms than did the Egyptian or the Jordanian migrant workers.

In addition, Syria was forced to deal with the problem of large-scale unofficial workers' remittances, that is, "black market" remittances. The reason for such transfer through unofficial channels was due to the wide gap between the official rate of the LS and the unofficial rate on the "black market." By 1990, for example, while the official rate was LS 11.2 to one US dollar, the unofficial rate available in Lebanon and Jordan was more than four times that of the official rate.[110] During the years 1993–94, the "neighboring countries" rate held steady at about LS 50 to one US dollar.[111]

It seems that the most prominent manifestation of the extent of the transfer of remittances via unofficial channels is the sharp oscillation from one year to another in the scale of the official workers' remittances. For example, in 1978 the official workers' remittances of the Syrian workers abroad amounted to $635.7 million, and then increased to $901.4 million in 1979. One year later, in 1980, the scale of the workers' remittances was sharply reduced to only $773.5 million and continued to decline to $436 million in 1981.[112] However, according to the various sources, the number of Syrian migrant workers abroad during those years was more or less the same, and there is no information indicating a sharp reduction in the salaries of the migrant workers in the Gulf countries or in Libya at that time. Hence, it seems that the only logical explanation for these sharp oscillations in the scale of the official workers' remittances is the large-scale transfer through unofficial channels.

Other Middle Eastern labor-exporting countries also suffered from the same problem. In 1983, for example, the documented workers' remittances of the Jordanian migrants totaled $1.1 billion, while it was estimated that undocumented remittances could account for as much as one-third of this amount.[113] Regarding the Sudanese migrant workers in the Gulf countries, Nazli Choucri estimated that only 10 to 15 percent of earnings were transferred through the official channels, and the remaining 85 to 90 percent through unofficial channels.[114]

Iamail Serageldin and others claimed that:

A case is also made that the countries supplying manpower have trained labor at considerable cost in the skills which the oil-rich countries attract. Remittances, it is asserted, do not make up for this investment in labor which the poorer country has lost. Remittances tend to be spent on consumer goods and are not used as a source of investment funds. Moreover, the remittances received are highly unpredictable . . . Such vagaries make it more difficult for governments of labor-supplying countries to utilize remittance flows effectively. In particular, the future level of remittances is difficult to determine by any single labor-exporting country in isolation.[115]

This approach was also shared by Mostafa Nagi:

> Remittances, it is asserted, do not make up for this investment in labor which the poorer country has lost; and countries of origin find themselves facing the added problem of reabsorption of erstwhile migrants. Finally, the demand for labor is highly volatile, and, hence, it is difficult for the labor-exporting countries to plan ahead effectively for stable economic gains to be accrued from immigrant labor.[116]

However, in spite of these problems, the workers' remittances in all of the Arab labor-exporting countries fulfilled a very important role, not only as a major source for foreign exchange, but also in the overall economic development. Even in Syria, where the number and the percentage of migrant workers were relatively small compared with other Middle Eastern labor-exporting countries, the official workers' remittances alone constituted a major source for foreign exchange, as well as an important component in the balance of payment from the mid-1970s onward.

Moreover, except in the case of Jordan, and to a lesser extent that of YAR, which were at the same time a labor-exporting and a labor-importing country,[117] it seems that the only alternative to large-scale migration in the other Middle Eastern labor-exporting countries was massive unemployment. Thus, in spite of the negative consequences resulting from the loss of skilled and professional manpower, the workers' remittances, both the official and the undocumented, combined with the diminished employment pressures, accounted for a substantial contribution to the economies of the Middle Eastern labor-exporting countries.

In the case of Egypt, in 1983, there were 2.5–3.0 million Egyptian workers in the GCC countries, Iraq, Jordan, and Libya, representing 20–24 percent of the total Egyptian labor force at that time.[118] The official remittances of these workers amounted to $3.2 billion.[119] However, their total remittances, including the undocumented remittances, reached approximately $20 billion.[120] Although the vast majority of these remittances were not invested in industrial or agricultural projects, they created a vast number of work opportunities, mainly in the construction sector and its related services and industries. In addition, these remittances substantially improved the standard of living of the migrants and their families, thus increasing private consumption.

There is no doubt that the huge labor migration caused substantial damage to the Egyptian economy, while the amount of the official remittances did not compensate the resources invested by the state in education and vocational training of these migrant workers. The main question is: What were the alternatives to liberal migration policy[121] that were open to the Egyptian authorities? Was it possible for the Egyptian economy at that time to produce an extra 2.5–3.0 million work opportunities in addition to providing employment to the one million who were already unemployed at that time,[122] not to mention the huge disguised unemployment rates which prevailed in the Egyptian economy? It seems that the answer to this question is clear. Without the extensive labor migration the unemployment rate in Egypt would have been much higher, maybe even more than 20 percent. Moreover, the documented remittances alone constituted one of the most important sources of foreign exchange, without which the deficit of the balance of payments would have been much higher.[123] One can also find a similar case in YAR, as well as Sudan, during the second part of 1970s and throughout the 1980s. Thus, in spite of the various negative consequences of the massive labor migration, it seems that it was the only possible way for the Egyptian authorities to diminish the huge demographic and employment pressures caused by the rapid population growth, and at the same time to improve the balance of payments.

Regarding Syria and Jordan, which both suffered from economic recession during the latter part of the 1980s, particularly from a severe shortage of foreign exchange, the importance of the workers' remittances in the balance of payments was further strengthened. In addition, without the massive labor migration, the unemployment rate in these countries was even higher, particularly in the case of Jordan. Thus, in conclusion, it seems that in spite of all the severe problems caused by the massive labor migration, it was one of the most prominent factors accounting for economic development during the second half of the 1970s and the early 1980s, when migration reached its peak in most Middle Eastern labor-exporting countries.

5

Demographic Policies of the Syrian Authorities

The aim of this chapter is two-fold. First, to examine and analyze the Syrian authorities' attitudes from the late 1940s onward towards the three demographic fields discussed earlier, namely: the natural increase of the population; the spatial distribution of the population; and the migration of Syrian workers to other Arab countries, especially from the early 1970s onward. The second part of the chapter evaluates the authorities' polices regarding each of these three fields.

Family Planning

At the beginning of the process of accelerating population growth in the late 1940s and the early 1950s, many leaders in developing countries, including those of the Middle East, saw a blessing in the rapid population growth and therefore made no attempt to limit it. Rather, they adopted pro-natalist policies, based on the concept that a large nation is a strong nation.[1]

However, during the late 1950s and even more so throughout the 1960s, leaders of developing countries started to become aware of the direct link between rapid population growth and the various socioeconomic problems which were emerging in their countries. These problems included high urbanization rates with all its attendant problems, including increasing unemployment rates in the larger urban centers which were forced to absorb the majority of the rural migration. This rise in unemployment was due to the fact that the increase in the labor force far outpaced the increase of available work opportunities in the major urban centers. Another major problem was the increasing housing shortage, which created an uncontrolled sprawl of slum neighborhoods. In many cases, the capacity of the authorities to integrate and service these new neighborhoods was grossly inadequate relative to the rate of expansion.[2] In addition, the rapid population growth caused a rise in government expenditures on public services, especially health-care and education, as well as subsidies of basic food items.

The governments of many developing countries then realized that the only solution to the severe problems caused by rapid population growth involved a reduction in the natural increase rates of the population. Accordingly, these governments started to implement various family planning programs. It was natural that they looked to the UN for advice, as well as financial and technical assistance in order to implement these programs.[3] From the second half of the 1960s onward, the population question became a key issue for the various UN agencies.

The first two Arab countries to adopt official anti-natalist policy were Egypt and Tunisia in the mid-1960s. During the late 1960s and throughout the 1970s and 1980s, many other Arab countries adopted anti-natalist policies, including Morocco, Algeria, Sudan, Yemen Arab Republic, Yemen Democratic Republic, and Jordan.[4] At present, it seems that all the Arab countries, with the exception of the Gulf countries, are implementing at least some anti-natalist policies.[5]

The attitude of the Syrian authorities towards family planning can be divided into three main periods. During the first period (1949–74), the authorities supported increasing fertility rates through pro-natalist policies. In the intermediate period (1974–87), they activated direct and indirect means to reduce fertility levels; however, at the same time, the pro-natalist regulations were not cancelled. In the third stage, which began in 1987, the pro-natalist regulations were cancelled and the Syrian authorities enhanced their efforts to achieve a substantial reduction in the fertility levels by implementing both direct and indirect means.

The First Period: 1949–1974

During this stage, the Syrian authorities did not advocate a family planning policy but, on the contrary, strove to increase the fertility rates. It seems that the concept behind this pro-natalist policy was that the Syrian population was too small in comparison with economic and especially military needs. Thus, the Syrian authorities aspired to increase the total Syrian population by operating pro-natalist policy in several areas:

1   In 1949, a law was enacted forbidding the propaganda, distribution, or use of contraception. Transgressors were subject to imprisonment from one month to one year, as well as to a fine of LS 25–100.
2   Two further regulations were ratified in 1952: The first determined that families with more than three children would be granted tax reductions and

discounts on public transport; the second was that these families would receive a special government award.

3   Another decree entitled state employees to a government allowance in addition to their salary, according to the number of children they had. Originally, this allowance was meant to subsidize education costs for families with many children, but it soon became an instrument for encouraging higher fertility rates among state employees.[6]

The Second Period: 1974–1987

At the beginning of the 1970s, particularly after the results of the 1970 population census became known, the attitudes of the Syrian authorities towards family planning and rapid population growth began to change, and they began to advocate a reduction in fertility levels. The main reason for this change, it appears, was the surfacing of social and economic problems whose origin lay in the high fertility levels, namely: a reduction in the labor force participation rate; a rapid increase in public spending on food subsidies; and a rise in public expenditures for providing health-care and educational services for the burgeoning population.

As reported by the CBS in 1973:

It seems that high population growth rates have adversely affected the efforts exerted for securing [a] better life for all members of the population. Despite the high economic development rates which were achieved during the last decade, such rates are still not sufficient to meet basic population needs, and especially in the fields of education, health, housing and transportation. The high percentages of dependent children have led to increased consumer expenditure and a decreased volume of savings which are supposed to be invested in capital goods and irrigation and land reclamation projects to meet high entrance rates into the labor force and for creating new employment opportunities and diminishing the value of pure and disguised unemployment.[7]

Thus, the CBS, which painted a clear picture of the socioeconomic consequences of rapid population growth, started to lead a campaign in order to draw the attention of both the authorities and the public to the necessity of adopting a new attitude to the subject of population growth and family planning. The CBS also expressed its point of view on several occasions in the press, as well as in seminars held by specialist UN bodies in Damascus during 1972. This resulted in the establishment of a committee composed of the Minister of State for Planning Affairs, the Director General of the CBS, a number of other specialists from the CBS, representatives of the Ministries of Education, Health,

Information, and Social Affairs and Labor, as well as representatives of major public organizations, including the General Confederation of Trade Unions, the Peasants Unions, and the General Women's Union. The major aim of the committee was to prepare the necessary recommendations for the formulation of a population policy for the country.[8]

This change in attitude in population policy was gradual and slow and did not lead to an overall state policy for encouraging family planning. The Syrian authorities adopted the approach that socioeconomic development, including a substantial rise in the standard of living and, most importantly, an improvement in the level of education for the entire population, but particularly for women, would lead eventually to a reduction in fertility rates. In addition, during the "oil decade" (1973–82), Syria benefited from economic prosperity and a considerable increase in the per capita income. Thus, although the negative consequences of rapid population growth became clear, the Syrian authorities felt that they did not have to adopt any emergency measures in order to diminish the high fertility rates within a short period of time. They assumed that through the adoption of indirect means, mainly increasing women's educational level and increasing their participation in the labor force, the fertility levels would naturally decrease, albeit gradually.

A petition for aid submitted by the Syrian government to the UNFPA in July 1974 clearly illustrates this approach. The petition included a governmental statement that a correlation had been established between fertility rates and the level of education. In this way, the authorities acknowledged that education constituted an important social policy with respect to its effect on fertility trends and that the government intended to invest larger resources in this area, especially in women's education.

This approach was voiced publicly by the head of the Syrian delegation to the 1974 International Population Conference, held in Bucharest, where it was reported that the Syrian government believed that a reduction in the illiteracy rate among the population and an increase in participation by women in economic activities would eventually be followed by a decrease in the fertility levels.[9] A similar approach also found expression in the letter sent by Asad to the International Population Conference held in Mexico in 1984, where he emphasized that the population problem had to be addressed within the framework of the overall socioeconomic development strategy.[10]

Related to the new fertility approach of the Syrian authorities, Hamed Abou-Gamrah wrote in the early 1980s that while the Syrian government had no explicit policy for fertility reduction, "several measures which indirectly affect fertility are being taken, such as improvements in educational level and woman status, and increasing work opportunities for women."[11]

In 1974, a family branch of the Ministry of Health was established in order to coordinate activities in the field of family planning within the framework of the mother and child clinics that had been operating in Syria since the 1950s. In February of the same year, the Syrian Family Planning Association was established with financial support by the Ministry of Health.[12] The main targets of the Association included improving health-care for both mothers and children; supplying contraceptives and providing training on their proper use; as well as conducting research in the areas of fertility and family planning and other demographic issues. In addition, the Association conducted workshops and lectures on the subject of the importance of family planning.[13] The Association maintained close connections with youth movements and women's organizations, as well as parallel associations in other Arab countries and the International Association for Family Planning.[14] By 1982, the Association was operating ten centers for family planning services within the framework of the mother and child clinics in six large cities: Damascus, Aleppo, Ladhaqiya, Deir al-Zur, al-Hasakah, and Idlib.[15]

From the early 1980s, the Syrian press began to publish reports and articles about the socioeconomic consequences of rapid population growth, not only at the national level, but also at the family level, emphasizing the need to take family planning steps. Since the Syrian mass media are under strict governmental control, these reports clearly reflected the authorities' changing attitude towards family planning. Through the mass media, the Syrian authorities consistently stressed the close connection between family planning activities and the health of the mother and child. They also emphasized that the number of children and the timing of births should be in line with the economic condition of the family in order to avoid poverty, especially among young families.

In all their official statements, the authorities tried to hide their intentions to reduce the fertility levels by such means and showed no inclination to implement a national family planning program. The reason for this approach, it seems, was the desire of the Syrian authorities to avoid confrontation with the Muslim Brotherhood, as well as to emphasize the benefits of family planning for the citizens themselves, rather than for the nation as a whole. By taking this kind of approach, they hoped to achieve more cooperation among the general populace. For example, a typical article in the official government daily newspaper, *Tishrin*, in mid-1980, emphasized that the aim of distributing methods of birth control was not to reduce the fertility levels, but simply to maintain the health of both the mother and child by increasing the birth intervals, as well as to align the size of the family with its social and economic condition.[16]

Following publication of the 1981 census results, the official Syrian press started to devote more attention to demographic issues. Since then, a large number of articles advocating the importance of family planning and highlighting the negative projections of rapid population growth appeared in the official newspapers.[17] In one article from mid-1985, it was advised that family planning was the most effective way of preserving the health of the mother and child, and that the size of the family should be determined in accordance with the economic situation of the family. Furthermore, bringing children into the world without previous planning would result in these children not being able to go to school, since they would have to work in order to contribute to the family income.[18]

Another approach was the use of caricatures in the newspapers illustrating the consequences of bringing a large number of children without first taking the family income into consideration. Illustration 5.1 shows a very poor family with a large number of children. Illustration 5.2 shows a large family with a pregnant mother "threatening" the head of the family. The aim of these caricatures was to illustrate to the population the severe socioeconomic consequences of continued high fertility rates without taking into consideration the family income. Similar methods have also been extensively employed by the Egyptian authorities, mainly from the mid-1980s onward.[19] However, it should be noted that despite the direct and indirect governmental activities in the area of family planning, the pro-natalist regulations had not yet been cancelled at that stage.

The Third Period: 1987 Onwards

The year 1987 marked a turning point in the official demographic policy of the Syrian authorities. The financial benefits given to large families were finally cancelled. At the same time, the Ministry of Health appealed to young families through the mass media to take family planning steps, while the range of activities of the Family Planning Association was expanded.[20] From the beginning of the 1990s, the Syrian authorities started to deal with the problem of rapid population growth by conducting conferences on various demographic issues, including family planning. These conferences received broad press coverage and were therefore designed to highlight to the whole of Syrian society the dangers of uncontrolled rapid population growth, as well as the methods which had to be implemented in order to reduce the high fertility levels.[21]

Similar to other Middle Eastern countries facing the problem of rapid population growth, it seems that the Syrian authorities also came to the conclusion that in order to get the population to use contraceptive methods, they would have to convince them first that there was no religious instruction prohibiting the use of birth control methods.[22] During the Sixth National Conference for Population Problems and Development, conducted in March 1994 in al-Raqqa, all of the religious aspects of birth control were explored, and it was emphasized that there were no Islamic prohibitions against the use of contraceptives. In addition, during the conference, the Assistant to the Minister of Information, Adib Ghanem, emphasized the important role of information and mass communication in the areas of population policy and family planning.[23]

From the late 1980s onward, but especially since the early 1990s, the Syrian authorities devoted much more attention to the problem of rapid population growth than ever before. They affirmed the urgent need to substantially narrow the crude birth rate, which, as we saw in chapter two, was one of the highest until the mid-1980s, not only among the Middle Eastern and North African countries, but all over the entire world.

Overall, the means that the Syrian authorities adopted during the third stage were very similar to those which they used in the second stage (1974–87), in addition to the use of *'ulama* in order to convince the Muslim population that there were no Islamic restrictions against the use of contraceptives. Another difference between the two stages is that while in the second stage the Syrian authorities acted more through indirect means, in the third stage, they operated more directly by conducting large numbers of demographic conferences and appealing to the populace, particularly young couples, to adopt methods of family planning. In addition, during the third stage, the Syrian authorities increased the use of mass media in order to raise awareness of the population about the devastating consequences of continued high natural increase rate.[24]

A joint conference conducted by the Family Planning Association in collaboration with the Ministry of Health in August 1982 raised the following question: What are the reasons for delaying the enactment of family planning in the Arab countries in general, and in Syria in particular, and what is the solution for this delay? The conclusions reached were that the low socioeconomic status of women, together with the absence of a clear and sustained policy by the central authorities, were the main factors underlying the lack of success in implementing family planning programs in the Arab world. The key to success in this area, the experts claimed, was to introduce a more explicit demographic policy; increase awareness of the population about the demographic issue; and implement the family planning program within the overall socioeconomic development strategy and not as a separate activity.[25]

It can be said that this strategy has been adopted by the Syrian authorities, who are striving to reduce fertility levels with a two-pronged approach, namely, through the widening of activities in the distribution of birth control methods to the population, and in parallel, through an increase of propaganda in the mass media emphasizing the advantages of small families. However, the Syrian authorities are also operating at the same time through indirect measures, that is, supporting activities aimed at social and economic changes whose main focus is not anti-natalist policies but which, nevertheless, have an extensive influence on determining fertility trends. This approach applies mainly to raising the educational level of the whole population, especially that of women, and to increasing the rates of women's labor force participation. These two areas, according to the demographic surveys and censuses conducted in Syria and in other Arab countries during the last three decades, have been shown, more than any other factor, to have the greatest influence on fertility trends. The higher the women's educational level, the lower the fertility rates; likewise, the fertility rates among women working outside the home are much lower than those of housewives.

Hence, since the 1970s, the Syrian authorities have encouraged women to work outside the home so as to increase labor force participation rates and reduce the ratio between breadwinners and dependents. Within the framework of this policy, one of the major aims of the Fifth Five-Year Development Plan for the years 1981–85 was: "Giving attention to Syrian woman and prompting her to work in order to enable her to play her full role in building the motherland."[26] While the main factor in encouraging women to work outside the house is economic, by increasing the overall labor force participation rates, it also serves, at the same time, the aim of reducing fertility rates.

In this particular area, however, the activities of the Syrian authorities cannot be considered successful. In 1988, the crude economically active rate among Syrian women (15 years and over) was only 4.12 percent,[27] one of the lowest all over the Middle Eastern countries. In Jordan, which until the mid-1980s had a very similar demographic characteristics to those of Syria, this rate was 5.3 percent in the same year,[28] while in Egypt, two years earlier, according to the results of the 1986 population census, this rate was 6.2 percent.[29]

The second area of the indirect measures was education. Since the 1960s, and even more so during the 1970s, the Syrian authorities have made extensive efforts to eradicate illiteracy and increase the level of education of the whole population. In this area, in contrast to women's employment, the authorities have shown considerable success. In 1993, the illiteracy rate among Syrian women was 30.6 percent as compared with 83.2 percent in 1960 (see table 2.7).

Also in the field of secondary education, a substantial improvement has taken place since the early 1970s, especially regarding women. In 1970, the percentage of females within the total student population at the secondary educational level was 25.4. The highest proportion of female pupils was registered in the capital, Damascus (34.1 percent), and the lowest in the Idlib province (14.5 percent).[30] During the 1970s and 1980s, the ratio of female pupils in secondary education increased, reaching 41.5 percent by 1990. However, even in 1990, the percentage of female students in the rural provinces was substantially lower than the national average. In general, it can be said that there was a high degree of correlation between the proportion of the urban population in a given province and the proportion of females within the total student

Source: *al-Thawra*, 28 May 1987.

Source: *al-Thawra*, 26 July 1984.

Illustrations 5.1 and 5.2: Caricatures from the Syrian press about the consequences of a large number of children

population at the secondary educational level in Syria.

One can also find substantial improvement in the field of higher education. While in 1975 the number of students per 100,000 inhabitants in Syria was 990,[31] it increased to 1,695 in 1992.[32] The increase in the number of female students was higher than the average increase: from 512 to 1,415 per 100,000 people during that period.[33]

Despite the substantial success in the field of education, it cannot be ignored that in the late 1980s, one-quarter of the urban women and almost half of the rural women did not receive even an elementary level education and remained illiterate (see table 2.7). This fact, beyond any other, constitutes the main reason for the continued high fertility levels, even in the early 1990s, despite the increasing involvement of the Syrian authorities in the field of family planning. The relatively wide gap in the educational level between urban women and rural women also explains the higher fertility levels in the countryside as compared with the urban centers.

The Spatial Distribution of the Population

The Changing Attitude of the Syrian Authorities towards the Rural Areas

In spite of the major role of the agricultural sector in the economies of all Middle Eastern countries, including Syria, the rural populations of these countries remained far outside the main priorities of the authorities until the late 1940s and the early 1950s, when the revolutionary regimes came to power, first in Syria and afterwards in other Middle Eastern countries. Since then, the rural population and the agricultural sector have begun to constitute a major factor and political force in many Middle Eastern countries, including Syria.

The reasons accounting for this substantial change in the authorities' attitude towards the countryside were varied, some of them political-ideological and others socioeconomic. From the political-ideological point of view, the revolutionary regimes adopted socialist models of socioeconomic development, striving to diminish the huge gap, both economic as well as political, between the major cities and the countryside. From the economic point of view, the rapid population growth, which vastly increased food demands, and the scarcity of arable lands in the rural areas, which led to massive rural-to-urban migration movement, in parallel to relatively low agricultural productivity levels, all emphasized the importance of the rural areas for continuing socio-economic development.[34]

The revolutionary regimes, for the first time in the modern history of the Middle East, seized the political power from the traditional urban leaders, many of whom were landlords and therefore held the economic power in their hands. Thus, as long as they constituted the political elite, it was impossible to implement any rural or land reforms, simply because any redistribution of the agricultural lands or implementation of any other rural reforms, such as social labor laws, would be against their own interest.

However, the *coups d' état* regimes changed this state of affairs, and the new revolutionary regimes in Syria, as well as in other countries in the region (such as Egypt and Iraq), were able to initiate rural and other social reforms. The Syrian Constitution of 1950 under the Shishakli *coup d' état* regime, which laid down the principles on which land reform legislation could be based,[35] underscored the changing attitude of the revolutionary regimes towards the countryside and the rural population. However, the political instability in Syria from early 1949 until the establishment of the UAR in February 1958, constituted a major barrier to implementing any socioeconomic reforms, including rural reforms.

Thus, the drive to institute rural reforms began in Syria only with the formation of the UAR. The new regime, in contrast to the earlier revolutionary regimes, had the necessary political power and stability to begin with the process of major rural reforms. Within a short period of time after the unification, Abd al-Nasser, the President of the UAR, started to implement the socialist policy in the northern part of the UAR, namely, Syria. The first act within this policy was the introduction of the Agrarian Reform Law in September 1958.[36]

The trend of rural reforms accelerated, both in scope and magnitude, under the Ba'th regime. The Ba'th party, from its formation, recruited its main support from the rural population, the minorities, and the urban educated middle-classes. Raymond Hinnebusch noted in this regard that: "The Ba'th recruited all those who were outside the system of connections, patronage and kin on which the old regime was built."[37] Many, particularly the rural lower-middle class and young minorities (including Asad himself),[38] were attracted to the Ba'th party due to its ideology: "Unity, Freedom, and Socialism." As for Ba'thi socialism, articles 26 and 27 of the party Constitution, adopted in April 1947, established that: "The Party of the Arab Ba'th is a socialist party. It believes that the economic wealth of the fatherland belongs to the nation. The present distribution of wealth in the Arab fatherland is unjust. Therefore a review and a just redistribution will become necessary."[39]

Indeed, since March 1963, these principles, whose implementation started under the UAR regime, accelerated in a wide variety of socioeconomic fields. Under the regime of the radical wing of the party, during the years 1966–70, the rural reforms progressed even further, and by the end of 1969, the implementation of the agrarian reform was completed.[40] The next stage of the rural reforms, which took place during the 1970s and 1980s, was the rapid expansion of public services in the countryside, including the development of health-care and educational services, as well as public infrastructure.

The new regime also reflected significant changes in the composition of the Syrian political elite. The traditional elite, which was composed primarily of Sunni-Muslims from Damascus and Aleppo, was replaced by a new elite, which included the educated lower-middle class, minorities, villagers, and residents of the provincial towns. This transformation was clearly reflected in the composition of the Syrian cabinets during that time. During the years 1942–58, 63.3 percent of the Syrian cabinet members originated from the two major provinces, Damascus and Aleppo. However, their percentage was sharply reduced to less than 30 percent in the cabinets which ruled in Syria during the period between March 1963 and October 1976, even less than the relative percentage of the population of these two provinces within the total Syrian population.[41]

Thus, in the following pages we will examine and analyze the attitude of the Syrian regime towards the rural areas mainly through three prisms: the agrarian reform; the expansion of irrigation areas; and the development of public services in the countryside, not only by a nominal index, but also as compared with the rate of development of these services in the urban centers.

Prior to examining and analyzing the policies and measures which were taken by the Syrian regime in the field of spatial distribution of the population, it must be emphasized that the regime's policies were not directly intended to deal with this particular issue, as was the case in the fields of family planning and migration of Syrian workers to other Arab countries. In contrast, in the area of spatial distribution of the population, the measures which were taken by the authorities were primarily a result of the regime's ideology and its socioeconomic policies, as well as a means to gain a political advantage and support from the rural population. The purpose of achieving more balance in the spatial distribution of the population was only secondary in terms of priorities.

Thus, the agrarian reform was undertaken, first and foremost, in order to break down the "feudal system" in the Syrian countryside and to rapidly develop agricultural production, as well as to sharply improve the standard of living in the rural areas. Paradoxically, as we shall see below, the implementation of agrarian reform was one of the main catalysts for the acceleration of the rural-to-urban migration movement during the late 1950s and throughout the 1960s.

In the same way, the first and the most important factor in the implementation of the various irrigation projects was to increase agricultural production. It was only of secondary importance to transfer peasants from the southern provinces, where the population density was high, to the northern provinces of the country, where the main irrigation projects were being conducted, but where the population density was very low. Furthermore, the improvement and expansion of public services in the countryside and the provincial towns was due to the Ba'th ideology of regional equalization, no less than to the regime's intention to regulate and diminish the rapid urbanization process.

The Syrian Agrarian Reform (1958–1969)

Land reform was not a necessary precondition for further development of the Syrian agricultural sector. In fact, during the decade following World War II, the agricultural sector in Syria developed at a rapid pace. During the years 1945–58, the Syrian total cultivated area more than double – from 2.290 million hectares to 5.452 million hectares (see Appendix 2). This expansion of cultivated area, especially irrigated land, was concentrated in three main regions: the first was in the north of the country, along the Turkish border; the second was located east from Aleppo up to the Iraqi border, across the provinces of the Euphrates and the Jezira; and the third area was in the provinces of Aleppo and Ladhaqiya, as well as in the Homs-Hama plain.[42] The high prices for agricultural products at that time also attracted large-scale private investments in the agricultural sector.[43]

However, the rapid expansion of cultivated land and agricultural production was not accompanied by a major change either in the standard of living of the rural population or in the distribution of ownership of agricultural lands, which continued to be highly unequal. According to estimates, prior to the implementation of the agrarian reform, about half of the cultivated land in Syria was in individual holdings of more than 100 hectares, another 37 percent in holdings of 10–100 hectares, and only 13 percent in holdings of less than 10 hectares. Moreover, at that time, about 60–70 percent of the rural population

Table 5.1 Pre-reform distribution of land ownership in Syria

Area (in hectares)	Percent of agricultural population	Percent of agricultural land
Large holdings (100 hectares and over)	Less than 1	50
Medium holdings (10–100 hectares)	9	37
Small holdings (less than 10 hectares)	30	13
Landless	60	0

Source: Raymond A. Hinnebusch, *Peasant and Bureaucracy in Ba'thist Syria: The Political Economy of Rural Development* (Boulder: Westview Press, 1989), p. 88, table 5.1 [hereafter: Hinnebusch, *Peasant and Bureaucracy*].

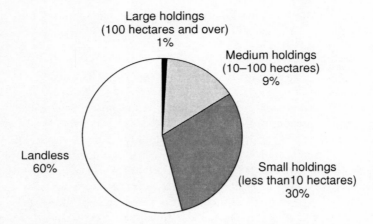

Figure 5.1   Pre-reform distribution of land ownership in Syria

remained landless (see table 5.1),[44] meaning that they were forced to find employment as agricultural daily workers or as sharecroppers. Eva Garzouzi noted that: "As regards the social aspect, the agrarian structure in Syria had, until 1958, very much of a 'feudal' pattern," considering that only 2.5 percent of the landlords owned 45 percent of the irrigated land and 30 percent of the non-irrigated land.[45]

Obviously, the landless were in the worst socioeconomic situation, since they were exploited by both landlords and middlemen. In addition, harsh measures were taken against peasants who wanted to leave their landlord by denying them employment elsewhere, especially if they had any obligation to the landlord.[46] The direct result of the highly unequal distribution of agricultural lands among the owners was the highly unequal distribution of agricultural income. Hence, the most important factors in the Syrian agrarian reform were the social and political aspects, which were intended to bring about major changes in the countryside, both to increase the standard of living of the peasants, and to intensify the identification of the rural population with the regime and, after the Ba'thi revolution, with the party and its ideology.[47]

Regarding the reasons underlying the conduct of land reform in Syria, a report of the UNESOB from 1971 noted:

Motives for land reform in the Syrian Arab Republic were mixed, and there was apparently no single compelling argument applicable to the country as a whole. There was no demographic pressure since the density of settled agricultural population per square kilometre of arable land was quite low, and even in 1964 stood at only 41, which is the lowest for any of the Arab countries in the UNESOB region . . . From a sociological point of view, it could be argued that the agrarian structure, as it existed, and infused as parts of it were with merchant capital, tended to concentrate economic power in a segment of the population, and to create a widening social gulf between that segment and the peasantry.[48]

Syria was the first country in the Middle East to introduce agrarian reform law. Under Shishakli's regime, the Syrian Constitution of 1950 outlined the principles on which land reform legislation could be based, and certain legislation to this end was even passed in January 1952 (Law No. 96/1952). However, this law was not carried out since it had many defects which made it impossible to implement,[49] besides the political instability in Syria at that time.

By September 1958, under the banner of Arab Socialism, the first comprehensive agrarian reform law (Law No. 161) was introduced in Syria, almost eight months after the establishment of the UAR. According to the law, no person was allowed to own more than 80 hectares of irrigated land and 300 hectares of rainfed land. In addition, the owner was entitled to give as a gift 10 hectares of irrigated land or 40 hectares of rainfed land to his wife and each of his children, provided that the total area given as gifts to family members did not exceed 40 hectares of irrigated land or 160 hectares of rainfed land.

The total area which was subject to be expropriated amounted to 1.37 million hectares, of which 254,700 were constituted irrigated land and the rest rainfed land. Also in September 1958, a second law was passed (Law No. 134) regulating the conditions and wages of agricultural workers, as well as the relations between landlords and tenants.[50] The law set the period of tenure for a minimum of three years.[51] From a socioeconomic point of view, the main aims of these two laws were: first, to redistribute the ownership of the means of agricultural production; second, to regulate the relationship between landlords and tenants; and third, to improve the cultivation methods through the system of agricultural cooperatives.[52]

However, there were many difficulties and obstacles in the way of carrying out the Syrian agrarian reform, the most important of which were: First, during the three years following the September 1958 agrarian reform law, there was a severe drought in Syria, which sharply reduced the overall agricultural production to less than half of the 1957 agricultural production level. Second, the Syrian agrarian reform law was copied from the Egyptian law (1952), without taking into consideration that while the former is characterized by extensive agriculture, the latter is based on intensive agriculture. Third, the resistance of the large landlords to the reform also severely hindered its implementation. Fourth, while most of the agricultural land subject to expropriation was located in the northeastern part of the country, the population was heavily concentrated

Table 5.2 Changes in the Syrian agrarian reform regulations, 1958–63

Aspect of the Agrarian Reform law	Original 1958 law (hectares)	20 February 1962 (hectares)	30 April 1962 (hectares)	23 June 1963 (hectares)
1. Retention of land				
Irrigated land	80	200	80	15–45*
Non-irrigated land	300	600	300	80–200*
Non-irrigated land in certain areas	450	1,200	450	300
2. Distribution of land to peasants				
Irrigated land	10	10	8	8
Non-irrigated land	30	15	30–45	30–45

* Depending on the area

Source: Ziad Keilany, "Land Reform in Syria," *Middle Eastern Studies*, Vol. 16, No. 3 (October 1980), pp. 214–15, table 2.

in the south and the western parts of the country, resulting in serious difficulties in distribution of the expropriated land.[53]

In addition, the political instability following the break-up of the UAR, in September 1961, led to frequent changes in the agrarian reform law (see table 5.2), which caused delays in actual implementation of the reform.[54] After the Ba'thi revolution, the acceleration in the conduct of the agrarian reform became a major governmental priority. The new regime reinstated the original reform law of September 1958, albeit with some changes in accordance with Syrian agricultural characteristics. By the end of 1969, the implementation of the Syrian agrarian reform was totally complete.

In order to measure the success of the Syrian agrarian reform, it is necessary to first examine the scale of the expropriation and distribution of agricultural land to farmers within the framework of the reform, and then to examine the changes in the socioeconomic conditions of the landless, who had constituted the majority of the rural population during the period prior to agrarian reform. By the end of 1969, according to official Syrian figures, 1.374 million hectares had been expropriated, constituting about 25 percent of the total cultivated area in Syria at that time (see Appendix 2). Most of the expropriations were conducted in the northern provinces of the country, mainly in al-Hasakah (462,200 hectares), Aleppo (289,900 hectares), al-Raqqa (164,000 hectares), and Homs (147,700 hectares). In addition, the vast majority of the expropriated land was non-irrigated, and only 66,200 hectares, or less than 5 percent, of irrigated land were expropriated (see table 5.3).

The expropriated land was to be distributed within the rural population such that the property of the beneficiaries would not exceed eight hectares of irrigated land or 45 hectares of non-irrigated land. Among the total expropriated land, 780,762 hectares were redistributed while the remaining area which was not redistributed became state domain. In addition, another 38,076 hectares were sold to farmers, and 432,666 hectares of state domain land and reclaimed land from the various irrigation projects[55] were also distributed to peasants. All in all, 1,251,504 hectares were redistributed to 102,238 families in the countryside.[56] The land which was redistributed within the framework of the agrarian reform was heritable; however, it could not be sold or rented. Beneficiaries were obliged to work their land by themselves and to become members in the agrarian cooperatives.[57]

As a result of implementing agrarian reform, the percentage of the landless within the total rural population decreased from 60–70 percent prior to the reform to about 38 percent.[58] Hence, in this respect, it seems that the success of agrarian reform was quite marginal, as more than one-third of the rural

Table 5.3 Area of land expropriated, according to the Syrian agrarian reform (1,000 hectares)

Mohafazat (province)	Irrigated land	Non-irrigated land	Uncultivated land	Total expropriated area
Damascus	6.3	55.7	–	62.0
Aleppo	6.2	223.5	60.2	289.9
Homs	5.7	85.1	56.9	147.7
Hama	2.4	86.1	21.8	110.3
Ladhaqiya	3.0	2.3	1.0	6.3
Deir al-Zur	9.8	7.7	–	17.5
Idlib	3.9	61.1	18.6	83.6
Al-Hasakah	9.3	449.8	3.1	462.2
Al-Raqqa	16.4	129.5	18.1	164.0
Al-Suwayda	–	2.9	–	2.9
Dar'a	0.3	8.3	–	8.6
Tartus	2.5	6.4	1.6	10.5
Quneitra	0.4	7.7	–	8.1
Total	66.2	1,126.1	181.3	1,373.6

Source: Syria, *Statistical Abstract – 1973*, p. 159, table 11/4.

population remained landless, even after implementation. One of the main reasons for this shortcoming was that while almost all of the expropriated land was located in the northern provinces, most of the landless and the small farmers, who were entitled to receive land within the framework of the agrarian reform, were concentrated in the southern provinces.

In spite of this limitation, the Syrian agrarian reform dramatically changed the distribution of ownership of agricultural land and agricultural income, and was successful in breaking up the large estates. According to the 1970 Agricultural Census, only 18 percent of the area surveyed was in holdings of more than 100 hectares, as compared with 49 percent in 1952, while approximately 70 percent of the total cultivated area was in holdings of less than 50 hectares, as compared with only 41 percent in 1952.[59]

Those who received sufficient irrigated land, or even non-irrigated land in rainfall areas, no doubt benefited from the reform, since they could now enjoy all the profits from their crops without sharing with the landlords as previously required. However, many beneficiaries obtained only a few hectares of non-irrigated land, which was not sufficient to secure the subsistence of a family and made it necessary to secure alternative income and employment. In any

Table 5.4   Cultivated lands in Syria, according to sectors, 1972 (1,000 hectares)

Mohafazat (province)	Total	Cultivated Lands Private	Cooperatives	Public
Damascus	118.0	97.6	20.1	0.3
Aleppo	672.5	542.8	129.4	0.3
Homs	252.9	185.8	67.1	–
Hama	334.8	251.9	82.7	0.2
Ladhaqiya	80.4	62.4	17.6	0.4
Deir al-Zur	99.1	68.1	30.1	0.9
Idlib	267.2	203.6	63.4	0.2
Al-Hasakah	712.9	649.2	13.1	50.6
Al-Raqqa	167.4	138.9	24.3	4.2
Al-Suwayda	107.2	100.5	6.7	–
Dar'a	165.6	149.3	15.9	0.4
Tartus	114.2	94.1	20.1	–
Quneitra	11.9	10.5	1.4	–
Total	3,104.1	2,554.7	491.9	57.5

Source: Syria, *Statistical Abstract – 1973*, p. 158, table 10/4.

case, agricultural workers remained among the poorest and least protected classes of Syrian society even after the implementation of agrarian reform.[60]

Although agrarian reform dramatically changed the distribution of ownership of agricultural land, and thus also had a great influence on the socioeconomic stratification in the Syrian countryside, it seems that, at the same time, it had a negative effect on the overall agricultural production. The unstable political situation, which led to frequent changes, both in the government and the agrarian reform law (see table 5.2), caused serious delays in the implementation of the reform. This, in turn, brought about prolonged periods of uncertainty, which led to a sharp decline in the net capital formation of the agricultural sector during the 1960s.[61]

In a special report of the monthly *The Arab Economist* (October 1979), the following statement appeared with regard to the effect of the agrarian reform on the overall Syrian agricultural production:

> The fluctuation in the level of agricultural production and the low rate of growth in the level of agricultural production are not due only to the fluctuation in the level of rainfall but also to the land reform measures introduced in the 1960s which disturbed the economy and led to caution as regards investment by the private sector.[62]

While the effect of agrarian reform on the overall agricultural production was negative, it nevertheless accomplished a clear and important political advantage – a reduction in the dependency of the landless and small farmers on the landlords. At the same time, the reform clearly mobilized the support of the small peasants and the wide-based landless class for the central regime. The failure of agrarian reform to provide sufficient land to the entitled population in the countryside, combined with the sharp reduction of investments in the agricultural sector by the private sector and the overall reduction in agricultural production during the period following the implementation of agrarian reform, led to an increase in rural-to-urban migration movement during the 1960s. This was one of the most important factors leading the Syrian authorities to conclude that the solution of the socioeconomic problems in the rural areas was not the redistribution of existing agricultural land, but rather a substantial expansion of the total area of cultivated land and the transfer of rainfed land to irrigated land to the furthest extent possible.

The Expansion of Irrigation Areas

One of the main priorities of Syrian agricultural policy was to rapidly and substantially expand the cultivated area, especially that of irrigated land, in order to achieve three main aims: First, to substantially increase agricultural production for supplying the increasing food demands due to the rapid population growth. Second, since most of the Syrian agricultural land was non-irrigated, there were considerable oscillations in agricultural production from one year to another in accordance with the changes in weather. Third, while in the southern provinces the population density in the rural areas was very high, in the northeastern provinces, vast quantities of land suitable for agricultural purposes were available. Development of this land would enable the transfer of a substantial number of landless from the southern to the northeastern provinces in order to achieve a more equitable balance in the spatial distribution of the population. The irrigation projects were useful insofar as "the Syrian government endeavored to bring about a lowering of the rate of migration of rural people to the cities," according to the UNFPA report from 1980.[63]

Until the late 1950s, the implementation of new irrigation projects, like other areas of economic development, was in the hands of the private sector under the capitalist approach of the Syrian economy at that time. Following the formation of the UAR, and especially after the Ba'thi revolution, within the framework of the socialist economic policy established by the new regime, the public sector took the leading role in directing the socioeconomic development plans, including the implementation of the new irrigation projects. The first irrigation project implemented by the central government was the *Ghab–Asharneh* project, located in the Middle Orontes Basin, which took place during the period from 1954 to 1970 and was intended to cover 134,000 hectares.[64]

The most prominent Syrian irrigation project was the Euphrates Development Project. Plans to increase the area of irrigated land in the *Jezira* region by increasing the use of the Euphrates water were first initiated after World War I by the French Mandate. However, these development plans were never actually implemented. During the late 1950s, a Dutch consulting company (NEDECO) carried out a study regarding the feasibility of the plans. At the same time, a British consulting company (Sir Alexander Gibb and Partners) conducted another study regarding the irrigation possibilities in the Euphrates Basin. As a result of these investigations, plans were drawn up to build a dam across the Euphrates River, at a place known as al-Tabqa, the name of which was later changed to al-Thawra.[65]

The Euphrates Development Project had two main aims: The first aim was to irrigate 640,000 hectares so as to double the total Syrian irrigation area by the end of the century. This project included the establishment of new villages and towns in order to redress the rapid urbanization process taking place in Syria at that time. The second aim was to provide an electricity-generating capacity of 800 MW through the construction of eight turbines, each providing 100 MW. An additional aim was to regulate the flow of the Euphrates River in order to prevent flooding.[66] By March 1978 the second and final phase of building the Euphrates Dam and the hydroelectric power stations was completed. The total cost of the project was about $400 million, much of it provided by the Soviet Union.[67]

Soon after the completion of the dam and the power stations, the scheme began to face serious difficulties. First, the original ambitious plan to irrigate 640,000 hectares had to be abandoned because much of the land was riddled with large gypsum deposits and as many as 300,000 hectares which were scheduled to be irrigated with the Euphrates water would be left dry. As a result, priority was given to the irrigation of land where the main problem was salinity, for which solutions, albeit expensive ones, were tested.[68]

After completion of the irrigation facilities, the total area under irrigation in 1986 was planned to be 240,000 hectares, a figure which seems rather low when compared with the 150,000 hectares that were irrigated in this area prior to the construction of the dam. By 1986, the area of land irrigated under the original project comprised only about 10 percent of the long-term goal, meaning only 64,000 hectares, and representing less than half of the total irrigated land in the area prior to the construction of the dam. Moreover, Lake Asad covers an area of 300 villages which once had 72,000 inhabitants, who were forced to leave their homes.[69]

The second aim of the project, that is, to solve the country's power shortage, was also only partially achieved. Of the total energy produced in 1982, 52 percent originated from hydroelectric sources. Two years later, in 1984, hydroelectric power accounted for only 26 percent of the total energy production. This decline resulted from chronic problems with the eight turbines of the dam, as well as a reduction in the water level of Lake Asad, caused both by the increasing use of the Euphrates water by Turkey after the construction of the Keban dam and by two years of drought. This badly affected industrial output and the pumping of water for irrigation.

By 1987, the 800 MW power station on the dam was operating at only one-third of its capacity.[70] The completion of the Ataturk Dam on the Euphrates River by Turkey in early 1990 also caused a further reduction in the water level of Lake Asad, according to official Syrian sources.[71] As a result, massive food imports became necessary to meet the local demand which increased considerably during the 1980s due to the rapid population growth.[72]

Expanding and Improving Public Services in the Rural Areas

Another step taken by the Syrian authorities in order to restrain the rate and pace of urbanization was the improvement and expansion of public services in the rural areas, including infrastructure facilities, educational services, health-care, electricity, and safe water, as the gap in the quantity and quality of public services between the main urban centers and the countryside was one of the major reasons for the rapid urbanization process in Syria during the 1960s and 1970s.

The development of the countryside and the remote provinces, as well as the achievement of regional equalization, were explicit aims of the Ba'th party since its formation, as we saw earlier. Thus, within the framework of the Second Five-Year Economic and Social Development Plan for the years 1966–70, two of the general targets were: "Developing the rural community and raising its standard by means of an increase in social services, opportunities for work, and the abolition of illiteracy;" and "improving the regional distribution of factors of production."[73]

This policy of rapid development of the countryside and equalization of the standard of living in the rural areas to that prevailing in the major cities continued into the 1970s. One of the major objectives of the Third Five-Year Economic and Social Development Plan, covering the years 1971–75 was:

> To pay great concern to the countryside especially in remote *Muhafazat* [provinces], for the improvement of the standard of living and the productive potentialities through the provision of fundamental public services, the intro-duction on a wider scale of rural industries to increase the opportunities of employment and to lessen the immigration of villages to [the] city (aim no. 10).[74]

In the Fourth Five-Year Economic and Social Development Plan for the years 1976–80, very similar objectives can be found. Two of the general aims of the plan were:

1 To achieve an optimal geographical distribution of projects among the various regions of the country so as to make available suitable work opportunities to the rural manpower, and to improve the rural living conditions and provide them with the main services (aim no. 3).
2 To provide optimal full employment for the available manpower and mobilize the rural manpower for the exploitation of idle agricultural resources, and to develop the countryside in general (aim no. 5).[75]

Expanding Educational Services
Since the Ba'thi revolution, the overall educational services in Syria, including the countryside and the remote provinces, have been radically improved. The reason behind the expansion and improvement of educational services in the remote areas and the countryside under the Ba'th regime was not just ideo-logical, but political as well. According to Delwin Roy and Thomas Naff, because of the heterogeneous nature of Syrian society, one of the fundamental targets of the educational system was:

To produce an average Syrian male with loyalties to the state and party and to Arabism rather than to his region, group or sect. A fairly distributed national education system is seen as one way to achieve this aim.[76]

In contrast to health-care services, where there are a wide range of activities initiated by the private sector, the educational system is almost solely controlled by the government. All pre-university education falls under the supervision of the Ministry of Education, except for the secondary agricultural schools, which are controlled by the Ministry of Agriculture. The higher education institutes come under the responsibility of the Ministry of Higher Education. Thus, by controlling the curriculum of the students at all levels, from the first grade through university level, the authorities can produce among the students loyalty to and ideological identification with the regime and the party.

The success of the Syrian authorities in promoting education, especially in the remote provinces and the rural areas, is impressive. According to the 1960 census data, the illiteracy rate among the rural population was 76.2 percent (58.7 percent among males and as high as 93.9 percent among females), compared with 48.3 percent among the urban population; this gap was substantially reduced during the following three decades, especially among females. By 1989, the illiteracy rate among the rural population dropped to 28.4 percent (14.7 percent among males and 42.2 percent among females), compared with 17.6 percent among the urban population (see table 2.7).

Despite the rapid population growth, the ratio between teachers and students in the educational system has declined substantially over the past three decades. In Dar'a province, for example, the average number of students per teacher at the primary school level dropped from 31 in 1970 to 27 in 1990, and in Quneitra province from 33 to only 24 during the same period.[77] A similar phenomenon can be found in the other remote provinces as well. Consequently, the illiteracy rates have been dramatically cut all over the country during the last three decades, but especially in the countryside and the remote provinces. By 1991, the illiteracy rate (10 years and over) was 17.1 percent in Quneitra province, 29.8 percent in al-Hasakah province, and 17.9 percent in Ladhaqiya province.[78]

There was also massive improvement in intermediate and secondary education, and the gap between the main urban centers and the rural areas and remote areas was also substantially reduced in the period following the Ba'thi revolution.[79] One of the main means of supplying the necessary educational services to the countryside and the remote provinces was through the requirement that graduates of teachers' colleges serve a period of three years in the rural areas after graduation. However, the need to enforce such a regulation only underscores the extent to which employment in these areas is still regarded as unattractive.[80]

In the area of higher education, in particular, the urban centers enjoyed a considerable advantage over the countryside. By 1989, among 203,000 people with higher education and over, only 61,000 were from rural areas (30 percent), as compared with 142,000 from the urban centers (70 percent),[81] while the proportion of the urban population within the total Syrian population that year was only 50 percent (see table 3.1). Hence, in spite of the massive efforts of the Syrian authorities to equalize the educational services between the various regions of the country, by the early 1990s the educational facilities in the major cities continued to be substantially better and wider in scope than in the remote provinces and the rural areas.

Health Services
In almost all developing countries one can find a large difference in both the quality and availability of health services between the various areas of the country. Typically, when health-care remains largely in the hands of the private sector, physicians and other medical personnel tend to converge in the main urban centers, especially in the capital cities, rather than in the remote areas or the countryside, where there are "too few patients with too little money."[82]

Prior to the Ba'thi revolution, the health-care system in Syria was very similar to those of other developing countries, where the provision of health services was highly inequitable among the various provinces of the country. In 1958, while the per capita physician ratio in Damascus province was 1:1,893, this ratio sharply increased to 1:12,284 in Deir al-Zur province, and 1:15,000 in al-Suwayda province (see table 3.5). Similarly, the ratio of population per hospital-bed was much higher in the remote provinces: 1:2,088 in Dar'a province, for example, compared with 1:533 and 1:1,044 in Damascus and Aleppo provinces, respectively (see table 3.6).

Within the framework of the socialist policy adopted by the Ba'th regime, similar to the area of education, the authorities started to invest considerable effort in order to develop health services in the rural areas. In order to achieve this goal, the Syrian authorities implemented the following two measures:

1 Since 1963, more medical students from the remote provinces and the countryside have been recruited to the medical faculties, assuming that they are more likely to return to their place of birth to work after graduation. Indeed, following the Ba'thi revolution, the proportion of medical students from Damascus and Aleppo has declined in favor of students from the peripheral provinces and the rural areas.[83]

2 In 1951, a new regulation was enacted which prohibited medical graduates from practicing in the five main cities for the first two years after graduation. However, only after the Ba'th took power was the regulation effectively enforced by the authorities.[84] In any case, this policy continued throughout the 1970s and 1980s, and according to an ESCWA report from

1992: " . . . young physicians are urged to stay in the countryside at least at the beginning of their career life."[85]

Three decades after the Ba'thi revolution, one can find a substantial improvement in health services in the remote areas, as well as in the countryside. Although there is no general health insurance in Syria, services in the governmental clinics and health centers are free to the entire rural population, while in the urban centers they are available only to those with low income.[86] However, even in the early 1990s, there was still a considerable gap in both the quality and availability of health services between the major cities and the other areas of the country, albeit a dramatically lower gap than existed in 1963. The sharp reduction in the crude death rates and, in particular, the infant and child mortality rates, both in the remote provinces and the rural areas, is a direct result of the Ba'thi health policy. According to UNDP data, by the late 1980s, 99 percent of the Syrian rural population had access to health services, compared with 80 percent in Tunisia and only 30 percent in Morocco, for example.[87]

Electricity Supply in the Rural Areas

Another area of improvement in public services in the Syrian rural areas was their connection to the national electricity system. By the beginning of the 1970s, only less than 2 percent of the total Syrian villages were supplied with electric power.[88] Within the framework of the Third Five-Year Economic and Social Development Plan for the years 1971–75, the following aims were set:

1   To connect all neighboring villages' networks to the main network by 20 KV distribution lines with a view to dispense gradually with diesel engines which will be installed in other villages far from the network.
2   To illuminate all villages whose inhabitants exceed 2,000 . . . tourist villages, summer resort villages and border villages.[89]

During the second half of the 1970s, countryside electrification was a top priority of the Ministry of Electricity. During the years 1973–75, 424 villages were supplied with electric power, and in 1979 alone, 408 villages were electrified. Eastern European countries were particularly active in helping with the rural electrification program. In early 1976, East Germany signed an agreement to give a $51 million credit to Syria in order to expand rural and urban electric power. In December 1979, a second agreement was signed with East Germany to build six electric substations,[90] and in the same year the Czechoslovakian company, Pragoinvest, signed an agreement to supply 195 generator sets worth $4.8 million for installation in the rural areas.[91]

International financial organizations were also involved with the Syrian rural electrification program. In March 1978, the World Bank approved a $40 million loan to Syria in order to help in financing a ten-year countryside electricity program aimed to supply electric power to the entire Syrian countryside by 1987.[92] Within the framework of the program, the Minister of Economy, Muhammad al-Atrash, stated that: "One village a day has been supplied with electricity."[93]

The feasibility study for the program was prepared by France's Sofrelec. The first stage included the supply of electric power to villages with more than 100 households, for an estimated total of 1,200–1,700 villages with approximately 900,000 inhabitants. The electric power for these villages would be generated by the Euphrates Dam hydroelectric station, which began operation in 1974; the existing power station at Mehardeh, located west of Hama;[94] as well as new electric power stations located in Damascus and Banias, which were scheduled to begin operation in 1984 and 1981, respectively.[95] In early 1981, Syrian officials announced that during 1980, another 366 villages were provided with electricity, bringing the total to 1,947 villages with electric power.[96]

During the 1980s, the rural electrification program continued. At the same time, power demands were rapidly expanded as a result of both increasing demand on the part of industry and the rapid population growth. Yet, in parallel, electricity supplies fell far below expectations since the 800 MW power station on the Euphrates Dam was working much below its original capacity. In addition, the economic crisis of the late 1980s, which included an acute foreign exchange shortage, also hindered increasing electricity supply. The result was a delay in the implementation of the rural electrification program, which was supposed to be completed in 1990 according to the plan. New power projects were also planned, but their implementation was delayed as well.[97]

Despite these obstacles, the rural electrification program was completed in some provinces during the second half of the 1980s. In early March 1989, the daily newspaper *Tishrin* reported that all the households of al-Suwayda province, both in the urban centers and in the rural areas, were being connected to the electricity system.[98] By the end of 1990, within the framework of celebrating 20 years of *al-Harakat al-Tashihiyya* ("The Corrective Movement"), indicating the rise of Asad to power, the newspaper reported that in the Aleppo province, 944 villages were connecting to the electricity system, compared with only 13 in 1970.[99] By the beginning of March 1991, the daily newspaper *al-Ba'th* reported that every household in Quneitra province was connected to the national electricity network.[100]

All in all, during the 1980s, the number of customers of the National Power Company had more than doubled, from 1,057,258 in 1980 to 2,146,130 in 1990.[101] Regarding the number of customers in the rural areas, Patrick Seale noted that: "By the late 1980s, all but 2 percent of the rural population watched television and listened to the radio while refrigerators and washing machines were coming fast."[102] However, despite the increase in the number of electricity customers, Syria's power sector faced substantial difficulties during the late 1980s and even in the early 1990s, with lengthy power cuts virtually every day, both in the main urban centers as well as in the rural areas.[103]

Syrian participation in the anti-Iraqi coalition during the Gulf crisis paved the way for a major expansion of Arab and international development aid.[104] During the early 1990s, many of the infrastructure projects which were supposed to be implemented during the 1980s, but were delayed as a result of the economic crisis, now began to be carried out, including those in the area of electricity supply. In September 1993, when the power to villages near the capital city of Damascus was being cut for 10 days at a time, Asad declared that regular supplies of electricity were "nothing less than a right for every Syrian."[105]

From the mid-1990s onward, the Syrian power sector has been in reasonable shape, due to a rapid expansion of electricity production, financed mainly by Kuwait, Saudi Arabia, and Japan. Kuwait provided the financing for gas turbine generators, mostly supplied by Fiat Avio of Italy. In 1995, Mitsubishi Heavy Industries (MHI) completed one major power project, financed by Japan's Overseas Economic Cooperation Fund (OECF), and began work on a second, financed by the Saudi Fund for Development and scheduled for completion in 1997. According to the plan, installed capacity would rise to 7,500 MW by the year 2003, as compared with 4,000 MW in 1996.[106]

Labor Migration to Other Arab Countries

When the authorities of the Middle Eastern labor-exporting countries started to consider how to cope with the "brain drain" during the mid-1970s, caused by migration of labor to the oil-exporting countries of the Middle East following the "oil boom," two principal approaches were formulated:

1   An "open door" policy would be implemented by which the decision to emigrate would be left up to the individual without coercion exerted by the authorities to influence this decision. Such a policy was enacted by Jordan and Egypt. From the beginning of the 1950s, the Jordanian authorities demonstrated a liberal attitude towards labor migration, and even encouraged it by sending advisers to the Jordanian embassies in the Gulf in order to protect the interests of those already employed, as well as to promote the employment of other Jordanian workers.[107]

    Despite the loss of skilled and professional workers, the Jordanian government was not inclined to revise its "open-door" migration policy due to the large role played by workers' remittances in the Jordanian economy as a whole, particularly in the balance of payments.[108] However, in parallel, the Jordanian authorities also took measures in order to bring labor migration under some control. The Egyptian authorities also encouraged the migration of labor to the Arab oil-exporting countries in order to reduce the pressures on the Egyptian labor market and the high unemployment rates caused by rapid population growth, as well as to benefit from the workers' remittances, which, by the mid-1980s, constituted the major foreign exchange earner in the Egyptian economy.[109]

2   The "brain drain" would be prevented by means of coercion and by denying exit visas to those who were important to the economy. This was the approach adopted by the Syrian authorities from the early 1970s onward.[110]

The Syrian authorities did not allow public sector employees to migrate abroad for purposes of employment without approval. Those who emigrated without an approved permit from the authorities were subject to severe penalties.[111] These restrictions, however, were not absolute; and in some cases, the authorities enabled scientists to leave the country and to work in one of the Gulf countries for about four years.[112] In addition, the migration of unskilled and semi-skilled workers was almost completely unregulated by the authorities.[113]

Another measure taken by the Syrian authorities in order to reduce the scale of migration of needed professional and skilled workers was to directly approach the labor-receiving countries, asking them not to employ Syrian citizens in certain occupations. In 1979, the Syrian Ministry of Education approached Saudi Arabian authorities with the request not to renew the work contracts of Syrian teachers after they expired.[114]

Another approach used was to secure employment in Syria for skilled and professional workers. In 1988, a regulation was passed according to which graduates, especially engineers, would be employed for five years in the public sector if they could not find work for themselves in the private sector. In practice, following this regulation, many engineers were employed in the public sector in secretarial and managerial positions.[115]

Similar to other Middle Eastern labor-exporting countries, Syria also suffered from the large-scale transfer of workers' remittances via unofficial channels, as noted earlier in chapter 4. In order to minimize this phenomenon as much as possible, the Syrian authorities decided in April 1981 to conduct a reform in the exchange rate.[116] The Syrian Minister of Economy and Foreign Trade, Muhhamad al-Atrash noted:

> We expect around $1,000 million a year in remittances from Syrian expatriate workers . . . Previously, a Syrian working abroad was not going to sell his dollars or pound sterling at the official rate; he would go to Beirut [to change it on the open market].[117]

However, that reform and others conducted in the following years did not succeed in narrowing the gap between the official rate of the LS and the "black market" rate, as noted earlier in chapter 4. Thus, the percentage of workers' remittances transferred by unofficial channels continued to be high throughout the 1980s.

On the surface, it seems that Syria should also have operated a liberal migration policy, like Jordan, Egypt and YAR, since Syria was also a relatively poor country. In 1974, with the beginning of the mass migration from the poorer countries to the capital rich Arab oil-exporting countries, the per capita GNP in Syria was as low as $650, and the total export of goods and services amounted to only $1.1 billion.[118] Considering the economic situation in Syria during the first half of the 1970s, the main question that arises is: Why did the Syrian authorities not operate a liberal migration policy, similar to other Middle Eastern countries with its high potential for improving the balance of payments and raising the standard of living and the per capita income through the workers' remittances?

Apparently, neither Asad nor any other high official in the Syrian government ever publicly considered this question directly. It seems that three main factors guided the Syrian authorities in their operation of a restrictive migration policy during the second half of the 1970s and throughout the 1980s. The first factor was the combined result of the relatively small civilian work force due to a relatively small population; the high natural increase rates, which brought about very low rates of labor force participation; and the high demand for workers in the security forces (the army, the police, etc.). In 1989, the total economically active population in Syria was only 3,068,832 (2,595,576 males and 473,256 females).[119]

In contrast to Jordan and Egypt, unemployment rates in Syria at the beginning of the 1970s were quite low, and in some occupations there was even a substantial shortage of workers, mainly due to the large-scale migration of skilled and professional workers to western countries. It seems that the Syrian authorities realized that extensive labor migration to the rich Arab oil-exporting countries would bring about the import of foreign workers, as has been the case particularly in Jordan, but also in the YAR since the mid-1970s. The Syrian authorities preferred to avoid this situation because of potential economic and even political consequences, in both the short and the long term.

The second factor, it seems, was that the Syrian authorities did not want to rely on workers' remittances as the main source for foreign exchange. This was particularly due to the sharp and frequent oscillations in oil prices, which directly influenced the extent of the foreign workers and their salaries in the labor-receiving countries, as well as, in turn, the scale of their remittances.

The third and most important factor lay in the nature of Asad's regime, which was characterized by caution in all its actions. Liberal migration policy could lead to oscillations in the scale of migration not only as the results of changes in oil prices, but also in case of war or other unexpected political events. In this case, the Syrian regime would be forced to deal with creating a large number of work opportunities for the returnees within a very short period of time, as well as with ameliorating the marked decrease in the standard of living among the migrants themselves and their dependents. It seems that these three factors led Asad's regime to implement a very careful policy towards the migration of Syrian labor to the Middle Eastern oil-exporting countries.

Evaluation of Syrian Demographic Policies

Family Planning

The most important question regarding the Syrian natalist policy from the mid-1970s onward is: Why did the Syrian authorities, who were aware of the negative consequences of the high natural increase rates, fail to enact a more comprehensive and energetic national policy for family planning?

One reason seems to be that the economic and social pressures in Syria caused by the rapid population growth were not so severe as in Egypt, for example. Second, the communal factor has great importance in this regard. The Alawi regime which was considered, at least by part of Syrian society, as non-Muslim, would find it difficult to implement a national family planning policy in what is essentially a religious, traditional Muslim society, many of whose members would see such policies as contrary to the Islamic faith. Therefore, in order to bring about a substantial reduction in the fertility rates, the Syrian authorities have concentrated on indirect steps, mainly improving the educational level of women and encouraging them to work outside the home.

While these steps serve economic and social aims, they are not directly associated with the sensitive issue of birth control and thus do not arouse opposition within the population. However, since the late 1980s and the early 1990s, after the sharp recovery in the Syrian economy and, at the same time, an improvement in the relationship between Asad's regime and the Sunni-Muslim majority, the Syrian authorities have also given religious legitimacy to their anti-natalist propaganda, as part of the overall increasing governmental involvement in the field of family planning.

If the results of the SMCHS and the data published by ESCWA in 1997 regarding fertility levels in Syria in 1996 are accurate and reliable, then the success of the Syrian authorities in the reduction of the crude birth and total fertility rates during the last few years is without parallel in the entire Middle East region. According to these data, by 1993–96 the fertility levels in Syria were among the lowest in the entire Middle East region, undoubtedly representing a great success for the regime.

The most astonishing point is that the sharp reduction in the fertility rates has occurred precisely at a time when there were almost no incentives for sharp reduction of fertility levels in Syria. On the contrary, since health-care and education at all levels are either provided to the entire population free of charge or are highly subsidized, as are basic foodstuffs, these serve, in effect, as positive incentives to increase fertility rates. In addition, in spite of the increasing governmental involvement in the area of family planning, still, Asad himself is not as active in the anti-natalist propaganda as is Egypt's President Husni Mubarak, who has emphasized the importance of reducing the fertility rates in most of his public speeches since the mid-1980s. In any case, it is clear that from the late 1980s onward, the crude birth and total fertility rates in Syria have been sharply reduced. The credit for this is at least partly due to the Syrian government.

Spatial Distribution of the Population

In comparison to other Middle Eastern countries which also experienced a rapid urbanization process, the spatial distribution of the Syrian population, not only among urban centers and rural areas, but also among the various provinces of the country, is much more balanced, as can be seen in table 3.3. In spite of the steadily increasing percentage of the urban population within the total Syrian population, the distribution of the population among the various provinces has remained in the mid-1990s more or less the same as it was during the early 1960s. This is, it must be emphasized, a unique phenomenon among the Middle Eastern and North African countries, in almost all of which the vast majority of the rural migrants are concentrated in the capital or in the second largest city. In Syria, as we saw earlier, most of the rural-to-urban migration movement has been concentrated in the capitals of the provinces themselves.

Although it was more or less balanced, the Syrian urbanization process has had various negative socioeconomic consequences, as was discussed earlier in chapter 3. In a conference on the urbanization process in Syria, which was conducted in Damascus in September 1990, it was recommended that in order to diminish the pace of the urbanization process, the Syrian authorities should take the following measures:

1   Increase the available work opportunities in the rural areas, not only in the agricultural sector, but also in the industrial sector. This would be achieved by the establishment of factories for processing agricultural products.

2   Improve public services in the rural areas.
3   Diminish the income gap between the major cities and the rural areas.[120]

By adopting these measures, the Syrian authorities would succeed in slowing the pace of the urbanization process and thus avoid at least some of its negative socioeconomic consequences. It seems that in the coming years, the factor which will have the most influence in shaping the rate of the urbanization process in Syria will be the development of the agricultural sector and the number of available work opportunities in the rural areas.

The experience of the last three and a half decades teaches us that in spite of the tremendous effort and the considerable investment on the part of the Syrian authorities to increase the agricultural area, especially the irrigated area, the achievements were not impressive. While in 1960, the total cropped area was 3.480 million hectares and the irrigated area was 527,000 hectares, 34 years later, in 1994, the total cropped area was 4.852 million hectares, representing an increase of less than 40 percent. The total irrigated cropped area that year was 1.082 million hectares, representing an increase of approximately 105 percent (see Appendix 2). The number of employees in the agricultural sector also did not increase substantially during that period as a result of the continuous urbanization process.

On the surface, it seems that during the period under discussion in this book, in comparison with the heavy investment, the increase in agricultural land was relatively low. Nevertheless, from the late 1980s onward, the overall increase in agricultural land, particularly the irrigated area, was rapid. While in 1988 the total irrigated area was 650,000 hectares, it steadily increased to 1.082 million hectares in 1994, representing an increase of 66.5 percent during a period of only eight years (see Appendix 2). During that period, agricultural production also substantially increased accordingly. In fact, the dramatic improvement in agricultural production, brought about by a combination of good weather and price liberalization, was one of the most important contributors to the overall boost in the Syrian economy in the early 1990s.[121]

In light of the massive investment in agricultural projects in Syria during the last three decades, the most important question is: Was it worth it? Are the tremendous sums of money invested in agricultural development projects, mainly that of the Euphrates basin, justified from an economic point of view? Would it not be more beneficial to invest such sums of money in other economic sectors, such as to develop light industry in the rural areas, and by so doing, to create vast numbers of work opportunities in the countryside and thereby, to reduce the rapid urbanization process?

This question is particularly relevant with regard to the ambitious Euphrates Development Project which, in spite of the tremendous financial investment, did not succeed in fulfilling the initial expectations. According to the official

Syrian line, the Euphrates Development Project, in spite of the obstacles involved, justified itself from an economic point of view, since the money saved on other sources of electricity almost covered the cost of the building of the dam until 1979. Moreover, the surplus of electricity production was exported to Lebanon, Jordan, and even Turkey.[122]

The combination of rapid population growth, which caused a steady and rapid increase in food demands, on the one hand, and increased use of the Euphrates water by Turkey, mainly after the completion of the Ataturk Dam in 1990, on the other hand, led to a gradual reduction in the per capita water availability in Syria. In 1989, experts predicted that Syria will face an annual water deficit of 1,000 million cubic meters (mcm) by the year 2000, and even now, Damascus and Aleppo frequently suffer from water shortages in the summer months.[123] According to projections, the per capita water availability in Syria will be sharply reduced from 2,914 cubic meters in 1990 to only 1,021 in the year 2025. Although Syria has other water resources, the Euphrates is the only major river crossing the country with reliable annual flows.[124] Thus, the construction of the Euphrates Dam, as well as other water projects, are undertaken not only for agricultural purposes, but also for water storage to benefit the residents of the major cities, which will continue to grow at a rapid pace, at least in the foreseeable future.

In addition, the irrigation projects conducted by the Syrian authorities have to be judged not only by pure cost-benefit analysis, but also from other aspects. The concentration of a large percentage of the rural-to-urban migration movement within the provinces themselves, and not solely in the capital city of Damascus or other major cities, as is the case in almost all other developing countries worldwide, including those of the Middle East, must be attributed, at least partially, to these development projects. The construction of the Euphrates Dam resulted in the development of al-Raqqa city, to which many of the employees in the project were moved. While according to the 1960 census, the city's population numbered 15,554, by 1981 the number of the city's dwellers reached 87,138, representing an increase of almost five-fold during only 21 years. This rapid increase was a direct result of the Euphrates Development Project.

Moreover, within the framework of the project, a new city was built, al-Thawra (for the name of the dam), whose population numbered 44,782, according to the 1981 census.[125] In 1995, according to official Syrian figures, the total population of al-Raqqa province numbered 566,000, compared with 178,000 in 1960, representing an increase of more than three-fold during that period (see table 3.3). The rapid increase of these cities was one of the most significant results of the Euphrates Development Project.

Indeed, the aim of achieving a more balanced spatial distribution of the population among the various provinces, particularly by moving population from the heavy-density provinces in the south to those with a sparse population in the northeast of the country, has so far not achieved much success. At the same time, however, the authorities' success in keeping a large percentage of the rural-to-urban migration movement within the provinces themselves constituted a major achievement in itself. The failure of almost the entire Middle Eastern countries in achieving this aim makes the Syrian success all the more pronounced.

Labor Migration to other Arab Countries

The Iraqi invasion of Kuwait in August 1990 came as a complete surprise. The Middle Eastern labor-exporting countries were not prepared, in terms of their labor markets and public infrastructures, to absorb hundreds of thousands of returnees in the space of only a few months. The return of 350,000 Jordanians and Palestinians to Jordan, for example, changed the Jordanian labor market dramatically. Within a few months, Jordan's population increased by more than 10 percent. If we also take into account the natural increase rates, then Jordan's population increased by almost 14 percent between August 1990 and August 1991.

The large skilled work force, previously regarded as the most valuable asset for the Jordanian economy, turned into a heavy burden to the Jordanian authorities. In September 1991, the Jordanian Minister of Planning, Ziad Fariz, estimated the cost of absorbing the returnees from the Gulf countries at $4.5 billion over the next three to five years only to maintain the current level of services,[126] while the total Jordanian GDP in that year was only $3.52 billion.[127] This sum was far beyond the capacity of the Jordanian economy at that time. As a result, in October 1991 the official unemployment rate was almost 23 percent, while unofficial estimates were even higher, as much as 35 percent.[128]

Similarly, the return of 800,000–850,000 Yemenis from Saudi Arabia created serious economic pressures because of the country's dependence upon the income from workers' remittances.[129] In Syria, however, the negative consequences of the return of 110,000 migrants from the Gulf countries, mainly from Kuwait, were minor. We do not have any reports from Syrian newspapers, or from any other official or unofficial sources, about serious unemployment problems or housing shortages as a result of the return of the Syrian migrants from the Gulf.

The main question is: Was Asad's policy towards labor migration wise or misguided? Would it have been better for the Syrian economy if the migration of workers was more liberal, as was the case in other Middle Eastern countries, thereby increasing the amount of workers' remittances accordingly? From a historical perspective, it seems that the Syrian policy towards labor migration was wise, since it did not fully restrict migration, and the authorities enabled the migration of unskilled and semi-skilled workers, in which the government did not invest large sums of money for education and professional training. In turn, the remittances of these workers constituted an ongoing source of revenue for the economy. At the same time, the government kept in the Syrian labor market the educated and the most professional and skilled workers, in whom they had invested large sums of money.

Therefore, while Jordan and Yemen were occupied, throughout the first half of the 1990s, in the reconstruction of their economies and absorption of hundreds of thousands of returnees from the Gulf, Syria was free to deal with the development of its economy and infrastructure systems. Whereas the per capita GNP in most of the other Arab labor-exporting countries decreased during the first years of the 1990s, as a result of the mass return of workers and the sharp decrease in workers' remittances, in Syria the per capita GNP increased due to the minor role of workers' remittances in the overall economic development.

However, from the late 1980s onward, Syria has become heavily dependent on the Lebanese labor market, similar to the dependency of Jordan on the Kuwaiti labor market and YAR on the Saudi labor market during the 1970s and 1980s. By the mid-1990s, as we saw in the previous chapter, approximately 10 to 12 percent of the total Syrian civilian labor force was employed in Lebanon, according to the lowest estimates. This, however, makes Syria quite vulnerable to any changes in the Lebanese economy, particularly in the labor market. Such dramatic changes have already occurred in the past, with the outbreak of the Civil War in 1975. While in the mid-1970s many of the Syrians who were working in Lebanon relocated for purposes of employment either to Jordan or to one of the Gulf labor-receiving countries, this option of a large-scale alternative to employment opportunities in other Middle Eastern countries no longer exists.

Thus, if the economic or the political situation in Lebanon deteriorates again due to internal events, such as increasing tension between the various religious groups and political parties, or as a result of the expansion of the war in the south to other areas of the country, then not only will the Lebanese economy suffer severe damage, but the Syrian one will be adversely affected as well. Moreover, during the last decade, the Syrian economy has become heavily dependent on the Lebanese economy, not only as a major source of employment for its citizens, but also in other economic aspects, such as the provision of financing to the Syrian business community.[130]

From the late 1980s onward, following the signing of the Ta'if agreement, the Lebanese economy has grown by very high rates due to political stability and the huge investment in the reconstruction of the country, after the long Civil War; however, this situation could change again in the future. Thus, as long as the Lebanese economy continues to grow, the Syrian authorities can continue to rely on the Lebanese labor market to absorb many Syrian workers and can thus avoid having to supply them with employment opportunities in Syria. They should nevertheless take into consideration the possibility that this convenient situation could change again sometime in the future.

6

Conclusions: Demography, Economy, and Political Changes under Asad

During the last three generations, the Syrian population has increased by very high rates. According to the 1922 population census, which was conducted by the French Mandate authorities shortly after they established control in Syria and Lebanon, the total population of the area now under Syrian sovereignty numbered 1.3 million. Throughout the Mandatory period, the Syrian population increased rapidly, reaching 3.04 million in 1947. As reported in the 1960 census, the population of Syria grew to 4.56 million, and continued its growth to 13.8 million in 1994, according to the latest census, which was conducted in September of that year. In mid-1997, according to an official estimate, the Syrian population numbered 15.1 million. With a natural increase of about 3 percent annually, by the end of 1997, it seems that the total Syrian population has reached approximately 15.3 million. These data show that during the last 75 years the Syrian population has increased almost twelve-fold, representing one of the highest rates all over the Middle East and North Africa region. A population forecast prepared by the World Bank indicates that by the year 2000, the Syrian population will reach 17 million and then more than 30 million by the year 2020.

In contrast to Jordan and the GCC countries, the only factor which has contributed to the rapid population growth in Syria has been the high rates of natural increase, which amounted to 3.8 percent annually during the mid-1980s, representing one of the highest rates not only among the Arab countries, but in the entire world. This high natural increase rate was a result of the continuously high fertility levels, in parallel to a steady reduction of the crude death rates, due both to a sharp decline in the infant and child mortality rates and a rapid increase in the average life expectancy of the population.

One of the major factors accounting for the high natural increase rates of the Syrian population from the late 1950s until the mid-1980s was the pro-natalist policies implemented by the Syrian authorities. These pro-natalist policies, it seems, were adopted in response to the belief on the part of the Syrian authorities that the population was too small to address the military and economic needs of the country at that time.

The peace agreement between Egypt and Israel, in March 1979, left Syria alone in the armed struggle against Israel. After the Camp David accord in August 1978, Asad imposed on the Syrian society and economy a high priority mission: To achieve a "strategic balance" with Israel, meaning that Syria by itself, without any other Arab countries, would succeed in conducting a military confrontation against Israel. The most important question is: Why did the Syrian authorities adopt the "strategic balance" policy? Rizkallah Hilan provides us with one set of factors that explains what led Asad to adopt such a policy:

> As is well known, Syria was the birthplace of Arab–Islamic civilization, and since the nineteenth century has been the principal source of Arab nationalism and the anti-imperialist struggle. Because of this, the Syrians see themselves charged with a historic mission of Arab nationalism, which is always evident in their discourse.[1]

Beyond the historical and cultural explanations, there were also some practical factors which led Asad to adopt the "strategic balance" policy: The first, and perhaps the most important, factor was the Egyptian–Israeli peace treaty, which removed Egypt from the war circle against Israel, at least for the time being. The second factor was the Iran–Iraq War which began in 1980, only less than a year after the signing of the Egyptian–Israeli peace treaty. The Syrian support of the Irani side, and the tension between Asad and Saddam Hussein, turned Iraq into an impossible partner in any future military confrontation between Syria and Israel. The third factor, it seems, was the close relationship between Jordan and Israel, which brought Asad to assume that in any future Syrian–Israeli military confrontation, Jordan would not support him. The token participation of Jordan in the October 1973 War only strengthened this basic assumption.

In order to achieve a strategic balance, the Syrian authorities allocated substantial resources – in fact one of the highest among the Arab countries – to military purposes. During the late 1970s and the first half of the 1980s, military expenditures constituted approximately 20 percent of the total Syrian GDP.[2] In 1979, the import of arms to Syria totaled $2 billion, as compared with $650 million only two years earlier, in 1977, the last year before the adaptation of the "strategic balance" policy. By 1980, the import of arms already amounted to $2.7 billion.[3]

By the mid-1980s, according to foreign sources, military expenditures were running between 50 and 60 percent of the total Syrian governmental budget.[4] According to one source, defense spending accounted for 58 percent of the budget in 1985.[5] One year later, in 1986, Syrian military expenditures were reported to constitute 55 percent of the total governmental outlay.[6] Indeed, within only a few years, from the late 1970s until the mid-1980s, it seems that the Syrian army achieved a quantity balance with the Israeli army. By 1986, the Syrian army had half a million soldiers in the regular service, with approximately 4,100 tanks and 650 aircraft.[7] In addition, considerable financial resources were allocated to intelligence units, employing approximately 200,000 men by the mid-1980s.[8]

At the same time, during the 1970s and until the late 1980s, the high natural increase rates had a variety of negative effects on the socioeconomic aspects of Syrian society. The first and foremost was the creation of a wide base of the age pyramid, with almost half the population in the mid-1980s under the age of 15, making them consumers rather than producers. The direct result of the disproportionately high percentage of the young population has been a very low rate of labor force participation: approximately 23 percent, compared with 50 percent, and even higher, in the industrialized countries. Thus, the ratio between breadwinners and those being supported is 1:2, or even less, in the developed countries, compared with 1:4.5 in Syria.

Moreover, children and teenagers are large consumers of public services, such as health care and education, while their productive contribution is marginal, if any, particularly in the urban areas. In a country such as Syria, where public services are largely free of charge or are heavily subsidized, the large proportion of the young population has far-reaching consequences, as well as a substantial negative impact on the rate of economic growth.

Another major devastating result of the rapid population growth in Syria, especially in the rural areas, has been the steady decline of the per capita agricultural land under cultivation. While during the years 1960–94, the cropped area in Syria increased by 40 percent, at the same time the population size more than tripled, causing a substantial net reduction in the per capita cropped area. This is extremely important in a country such as Syria where, even in the mid-1990s, the rural population constitutes almost half of the total population.

Until the early 1980s, in spite of these adverse effects of the high natural increase rates, the Syrian government was simultaneously able to allocate huge resources for military and security purposes and to achieve a rapid increase in the standard of living, due to high rates of economic growth. During the 1970s and the early 1980s, the Syrian economy enjoyed prosperity and achieved high rates of economic growth, amounting to approximately 10 percent annually. This was primarily due to a high investment rate which equaled approximately 25–30 percent of the GDP.[9]

Such prosperity was the outcome of a combination of several factors, the first and foremost being the sharp rise in oil prices during the "oil decade" (1973–82). In addition to the steady capital inflow to Syria from the Soviet Union, the increasing oil prices caused a sharp increase in the capital inflow from the rich Arab oil-exporting countries, consisting of soft loans to finance investments in socioeconomic development plans, as well as large-scale grants. By the mid-1970s, Arab aid to Syria amounted to $500–600 million annually, increasing to $1.6 billion in 1979. Moreover, until 1976, Syria also benefited from $136 million annually oil transit dues paid by Iraq.[10] No less important were the remittances sent home by the Syrian workers employed in the oil-exporting countries, as well as from Lebanon and Jordan, which were estimated at almost a billion dollars annually at the end of the 1970s and the early 1980s.[11] As a result of these developments, the per capita GNP in Syria reached $1,670 by 1982, compared with only $350 in 1970, representing an increase of more than five times in only 12 years.[12]

As a result of the end of the "oil decade" in 1982, and more importantly, the collapse of oil prices in 1986–87, the Syrian economy deteriorated to a state of severe recession, which continued until the end of the decade. Like the economic prosperity of the 1970s and the early 1980s, the economic recession of the latter half of the 1980s, was mainly the result of changes in oil prices. First, the sharp decline in oil prices caused Syrian revenues from oil exports to diminish. In addition, at the beginning of the 1980s, the capital inflow to Syria from the rich Arab oil-exporting countries started to decline sharply, mainly as a result of Syria's support for Iran in its war against Iraq.[13] Whereas in 1981, the Arab transfers to Syria amounted to $1.8 billion, transfers fell to only $500 million during the years 1986–88.[14]

Furthermore, the scale of remittances of Syrian workers in the GCC states and Libya was sharply reduced from 1983 onward.[15] This was mainly due to the massive cuts in public spending and implementation of socioeconomic development plans in these countries, which caused not only a drop in the demand for workers, but also a cut in their salaries. These developments led to a chronic shortage of foreign exchange in Syria, which also severely affected the industrial sector. As a result, during the years 1982–85, the Syrian economy grew by less than one percent annually.[16] Moreover, the total GDP in 1985 fell below the 1981 level at constant prices.[17] The result of this low economic growth was a sharp decline in the per capita GDP, simply because the annual population growth was much higher — about 3.5 percent — than the economic growth level during that period.

Another negative consequence of the wide gap between population growth and economic growth was the increase in unemployment and underemployment rates during the second half of the 1980s. While during the late 1980s the official unemployment rate was 5.8 percent, according to unofficial sources the real figure was much higher, estimated at almost 10 percent.[18] The weekly publication *MEED* described the economic situation in Syria as it appeared to outside observers in November 1987:

> A chronic shortage of foreign exchange has left Syria unable to import much more than the barest essentials: industry has been starved of raw materials and spare parts, and the economy is running at a very depressed level. President Asad's policy of financing grand strategic designs from Arab aid has faltered. The aid is no longer flowing in sufficient quantities, and there are too few alternative sources of foreign exchange to fill the gap.[19]

The increase in the governmental budgetary deficit and the severe shortage of basic products, in parallel to the sharp devaluation in the value of the LS, caused a price explosion during the years 1986–87. According to official Syrian figures, the consumer price index increased by 36 percent in 1986, and by 60 percent one year later, in 1987. However, according to unofficial estimates, the real inflation rate in each of these two years was more than 100 percent.[20]

According to an IMF study published in February 1988, Syria's foreign exchange reserves in 1986 were down to somewhere between only $10 and $62 million, and the country was about to go into foreign exchange bankruptcy and had to begin delaying payments on its debt to the World Bank. The IMF report painted a gloomy picture of the economic situation in Syria during the mid-1980s.[21] Two years later, in April 1990, a *New York Times* report described the situation in the Syrian industrial sector:

> State-owned factories run at 40 percent of capacity because there is no foreign currency to buy spare parts. Two years ago, a plant manufacturing television sets simply closed because it could not afford imported components.[22]

The severe economic recession adversely affected the level of private consumption, with a continuous drop in the level of the population's welfare. According to official figures, during the years 1981–89, the per capita GDP fell by approximately 20 percent. However, unofficial estimates indicate a much sharper decline in real per capita GDP.[23] In 1989, the per capita GNP in Syria fell to only $890,[24] compared with $1,670 (in current prices) seven years earlier, in 1982.

These developments soon found political expression in various displays of dissatisfaction with the economic deterioration, mainly the shortage of basic foodstuff in the markets and the increasing activities of the "black market," which led to escalating prices of basic consumer goods and foodstuff.[25] Regarding the economic recession of the late 1980s, one Syrian businessman said ruefully: "People in Lebanon have everything in spite of the war . . . In Syria there is no war, but we have nothing."[26]

Whereas during the 1970s and the early 1980s, the Syrian government was able to allocate immense resources to military purposes without causing a reduction in the standard of living, in the late 1980s, as a result of the steady shrinking of governmental revenues and foreign grants and loans, the negative effects of the high natural increase rates of the population came to the surface and hit the welfare level of the population. Thus, the economic crisis of the late 1980s was the combined result of the decline in oil prices after the end of the "oil decade" in the short run, and the negative consequences of the high rates of natural increase in the long run, in parallel to the huge costs of implementing the "strategic balance" policy.

In spite of the decrease in governmental revenues and the beginning of economic recession, the Syrian authorities continued to allocate sizable resources for military purposes and did not withdraw from the policy of "strategic balance." One of the major reasons for this decision was the Israeli invasion of Lebanon on June 6, 1982 and the direct confrontation between the Syrian and the Israeli armies in Lebanon a few days later, which caused severe damage to the Syrian army, including the loss of 145 tanks and 100 aircraft.[27]

Finally, by the late 1980s, the Syrian authorities were obliged to recognize that they could not continue with the policy of "strategic balance" because of its heavy socioeconomic and political costs. As a result, in June and October of 1987, the Syrian parliament forced the resignation of four ministers. In November of that year there were extensive cabinet changes, including the appointment of Mahmoud Zuabi to the office of Prime Minister. The first and most important mission of the new government was to reconstruct and revive the economy.[28]

The newly appointed government began to enact revised social and economic policies. The first change was to limit the expenditures for military purposes in real terms, a process that has continued into the 1990s. While in 1985 the Syrian military expenditure was $5.432 billion, it declined to $3.563 billion (in current prices) ten years later, in 1995. In constant prices of 1995, the decline was from $7.445 billion to $3.563 billion, representing a reduction of more than 52 percent. The per capita military expenditure declined during that period from $709 to $236 (in constant prices of 1995). Thus, the percentage of the Syrian GNP devoted to military expenditures declined from 21.8 percent to 7.2 percent during those years.[29] In 1996, according to the International Institute for Strategic Studies, Syrian military expenditure was $1.8 billion, representing approximately 11 percent of the GDP.[30]

The meaning of this policy change was clear: The delay, at least for the short run, of the implementation of the "strategic balance." From the point of view of international politics, the Syrian withdrawal from the "strategic balance" policy reflected the realization of the Syrian leadership that the Soviet Union was not prepared to support and finance such a policy, in spite of the 1980

Soviet–Syrian Treaty of Friendship and Cooperation,[31] which guaranteed Soviet military support in case of direct aggression against Syria. Furthermore, the gradual withdrawal of the Soviet Union from world politics brought the Syrian authorities to the conclusion that they would have to contend with the West, particularly the United States.[32]

The second policy change was the decision of the Syrian government to adopt more direct measures in the field of family planning in order to achieve a substantial reduction in fertility levels. In 1987, the Syrian government cancelled the financial benefits given to large families. At the same time, the Ministry of Health appealed to young families through the mass media to use family planning methods, and the range of activities of the Syrian Family Planning Association was widened. In addition, from the early 1990s, the Syrian authorities started to use official religious figures in order to convince the population that there were no Islamic restrictions against the use of contraceptives, a step that, until then, they had hesitated to take, mainly for internal political reasons.

The shift of priorities in the allocation of resources was accompanied by reforms in the economic arena, primarily in the opening of more fields to private sector investment, both domestic and foreign; conducting trade reforms; adjusting the exchange rate of Syrian currency; and reducing subsidies. It seems that the discussions and decisions of the Eighth Regional Congress of the Syrian Ba'th party, held in January 1985, constituted the first step in changing Syrian economic policy. The final communique of the congress concluded with a sharp criticism of economic performance in the public sector and a call for increasing incentives for private sector investment in the Syrian economy.[33] Specifically, the first steps in the new Syrian economic reform consisted of Decision No. 186 (1985) to encourage private sector investment in tourism, and Law No. 10 (1986) to encourage the establishment of joint-venture agricultural companies.[34]

In addition to the economic crisis, the collapse of communism in the late 1980s also influenced the decision-makers in Syria to increase the role of the private sector in overall economic activities. As Raymond Hinnebusch wrote:

> The collapse of the communism has not only accelerated the ideological crisis, but, in threatening to deprive the public sector of East European aid, technology and export markets, further undermines the viability of statism.[35]

It seems that the decision of Asad to join the anti-Iraqi coalition during the Gulf crisis of 1990–91 was also part of this new approach in policy. The crisis gave Syria the opportunity to support the West at a time when the United States needed an alliance of Arab countries against Iraq. Syria was the first Arab country to condemn the Iraqi invasion of Kuwait. From the outbreak of the crisis, the Syrian regime supported the relevant UN Resolutions, including Resolution 678, which authorized the use of force against Iraq.[36] In exchange for sending about 20,000 troops to Saudi Arabia, Syria won significant economic benefits and, at the same time, considerable political advantage, both in the international system, as well as in the Arab world.

The large sum of cash that it received from the rich Gulf states enabled Syria to re-equip its armed forces with modern aircraft, tanks and long-range missiles, as well as to build power stations, establish a working telephone network, and improve water and waste-water facilities.[37] The total sum of cash that Syria received from the Gulf states during the years 1977–94 amounted to almost $18 billion, of which more than $3 billion was during the years 1991–94.[38] The $1.15 billion surplus in the Syrian balance of payments in 1991 was entirely due to aid which Syria received from Saudi Arabia and its allies as payment for joining the anti-Iraqi coalition in the Gulf crisis.[39]

The changes in the socioeconomic priorities of the Syrian regime occurred in concert with a sharp rise in oil revenues, caused by the increasing production to 600,000 b/d (barrel per day) in early 1996, from less than 200,000 b/d at the beginning of the 1980s. This level of production is higher than that of Qatar and almost equal to that of Oman. As a result of such high productive levels, governmental financial resources skyrocketed.[40] By the beginning of the 1990s, oil export of 320,000 b/d gave Syria more than 60 percent of its export earnings.[41]

The increasing oil revenues, accompanied by the financial support of the Gulf states, brought about a renewal of economic growth in Syria. GDP growth rates during the years 1990–94 were extremely high – almost 7 percent annually.[42] By 1995, the GDP had increased by another 6 percent.[43] In that year, the per capita income was estimated at just under $1,000.[44] One year later, in 1996, the per capita GDP (at current prices) was estimated at $1,289.5, compared with $617.9 in 1988, representing an increase of more than 100 percent during a period of only eight years (see table 6.1).[45]

No less important than the renewal of economic growth, in terms of liberalization of the economy, was the rise in the rate of investment. By 1996, the total gross fixed capital formation in Syria was $5.6 billion, as compared with less than one billion in 1988.[46] Also notable in this regard was the growth of the relative share of the private sector in total investments in the Syrian economy. In 1990, for the first time after the Ba'thi revolution, private sector capital investments were higher than those of the governmental sector.[47]

Investment Law No. 10 of May 1991 was intended to encourage investment by both the domestic and foreign private sector, especially capital held by Syrians abroad. The law offers various bonuses to private investors, the most important being a tax exemption for 5–9 years, and exemptions from other taxes related to projects which have been approved within the framework of the law.

Table 6.1   Syria: per capita Gross Domestic Product, 1988–97
(current prices, US$)

Year	Per capita GDP (US$)
1988	617.9
1989	645.0
1990	775.7
1991	845.8
1992	951.5
1993	1,020.2
1994	1,177.4
1995	1,229.4
1996*	1,289.5
1997*	1,370.5

* According to ESCWA estimates

Source: ESCWA, *National Accounts Studies of the ESCWA Region*, Bulletin No. 17
(New York, 1997), p. 9.

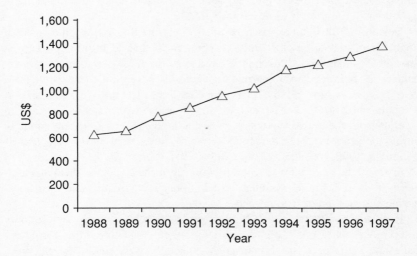

Figure 6.1   Syria: Per capita Gross Domestic Product, 1988–97
(current prices, US$)

Project applications must follow the overall development plan and incorporate a large local component. Furthermore, the applications have to be export-oriented or promote import substitution industries. The law also allows the formation of private joint stock companies for the first time in Syria since the "socialist rules" of July 1961. In addition, investors under Law No. 10 are exempted from Foreign Exchange Law No. 24 of 1986, which imposes severe penalties for its violation. Accordingly, investors can open foreign exchange accounts and can also retain 75 percent of their export earnings for their own import or reinvestment requirements. The remaining 25 percent must be turned over to the Commercial Bank of Syria at the rate of "neighboring countries."[48]

By September 1995, a total number of 1,251 projects had been approved at a planned investment of about $5.5 billion. These projects would provide almost 90,000 new jobs.[49] By the end of November 1996, the Higher Council of Investment had approved 1,457 projects at a planned investment of $8.65 billion.[50] Almost half of these projects were in the production and processing of chemicals, and another 30 percent were in the storing, packing, and processing of agricultural and other food products.[51]

Despite these incentives, the United States Embassy Investment Climate Statement noted that at the beginning of 1996 only a small percentage of approved projects had even begun construction, much less operation.[52] The banking sector, however, which was nationalized during the early 1960s along with many other private companies, still remains as a state monopoly, and it is likely to remain so, at least in the foreseeable future. A reopening of private banks would enable the smaller and middle entrepreneurs to gain financing in Syria, which is currently almost impossible.[53]

Despite the difficulties, as a result of the Investment Law, the scale of imports to Syria increased sharply, reaching more than $5 billion, for the first time, in 1995. However, despite the rapid increase in imports, Syria's account balance has not reflected concurrent high deficits. This is due to the parallel rise in the scale of exports, primarily based in three areas. The first was the oil export of about 400,000 b/d.[54] The second was comprised of a steady increase in receipts from the tourism industry, growing an average of 7 percent annually during the years 1985–95. The total Syrian revenues from tourism reached $1 billion in 1995,[55] compared with only $204 million in 1987.[56] The third consisted of the remittances of Syrians working abroad, many of them in neighboring Lebanon. These provided the additional funds required to meet local businesses' foreign exchange needs.[57]

It must be noted that in spite of the liberalization steps, the Syrian economy still remains state-controlled. Nevertheless, there is unanimity that the potential of the Syrian economy is enormous, especially in the fields of agriculture, light industry, oil, transport, and, in particular, tourism. The Syrian business community is now pressing for the abolition of Syria's multi-tiered exchange rate system, under which many import items are priced at LS 11.2 to one $US, while the rate in the "neighboring countries" is more than four times this amount.[58] In addition, they are pushing the government to establish private banking and to create a local stock exchange.[59] However, the government is insisting on the initial establishment of more shareholder-owned companies.[60]

According to the EIU, perhaps the most damaging Syrian economic problem is widespread corruption. Government employees are paid low salaries compared with the cost of living, and therefore many of them are forced to look beyond their salaries in order to supplement their income. Another major problem is large-scale smuggling, mainly from Lebanon, although this has eased following a crackdown in 1992 in which the Lebanese government cooperated.[61] The cement industry, which is a state monopoly affiliated to the Ministry of Industry, can be used as one example. While in late 1995, the official fixed price for cement was $20 per ton, the price on the "black market," which constituted approximately 60 percent of national production, was $40 per ton, twice that of the official price.[62]

It seems that one of the greatest dilemmas facing the Syrian leadership since the mid-1980s has been how to continue to uphold economic growth and privatization while simultaneously adhering to the fundamentals of the political regime, which has hardly undergone any reforms since late 1970, when Asad came to power, and which continues to sustain its autocratic characteristics. Are economic liberalization and democratization simply two sides of the same coin? Is it possible to manage economic liberalization and privatization, including a private banking system and establishment of a stock exchange, in parallel to opening the country for millions of tourists every year, and at the same time to sustain the autocratic characteristics of the regime, without any changes in or participation by the private sector?

Volker Perthes has noted that "Economic liberalization and private sector growth will not necessarily bring about democratization."[63] This is true, as Perthes has shown, but to a limited extent. It is possible to increase the role, as well as the share of the private sector in the economy, without introducing fundamental changes in `the basic autocratic characteristics of the regime, as was proved in the Syrian case during the last decade. However, beyond a certain point (which changes according to the given socioeconomic and political conditions of each country), economic liberalization also requires taking some steps towards democratization, as evidenced by the experience of other Arab countries, such as Egypt. This is seemingly one of, if not the, major reason for Syria's slow steps towards economic reform, since the government fears that rapid economic reforms could lead to social consequences which might threaten the continued stability of the current regime.

Similar to other countries in the region, Syria has a substantial external debt, which amounted to approximately $16 billion at the end of 1994.[64] The largest component of the debt, more than 80 percent, is owed to the former Soviet Union. While this is unlikely to ever be paid in full, efforts are being made to reach an agreement on part of the debt. As one observer notes: "The many billions of dollars owed [by Syria] to the former Soviet Union are somewhat academic."[65]

In 1994, the Russian government offered to write off $9 billion of this debt if Syria repaid $3 billion. However, the Syrian government rejected the Russian proposal. It seems that the Syrian government is waiting for an offer of a complete write-off, either through the Middle East peace process, or through the advent of time.[66] One Syrian analyst wonders: "Why should Egypt and Jordan have their debts written off and Syria be expected to pay theirs? It will be part and package of the deal."[67] However, more contentious is the $1.5 billion in arrears on Syria's debts to its main trading partners, namely, Japan, Germany, France, and other EU (European Union) countries. The Syrian government has held discussions with its creditors regarding this problem, but no solution has been reached.[68] The largest single creditor is Germany, which is owed approximately $900 million. Germany has taken over $500 million in principal from former East Germany. However, the Syrian government contests Germany's claim on it, as is the case with the Russian debt.[69]

The failure of the Syrian government to fulfill its debt obligation means that its ability to secure future credit from sources other than the Gulf countries is limited. One senior European diplomat described the situation at the beginning of 1996:

> Most countries go to the Paris Club (of OECD creditor nations) because they cannot pay their debts. Syria is the only state I know of that has started talking to the Paris Club because it does not want to pay its debts.[70]

However, Syria's debt deal repayment with France in late 1996 will boost its credibility, and relations with the World Bank and the IMF are set to improve after Syria begins to pay off its $562 million debt to the World Bank in September 1997.[71] A lump of $270 million has already been paid, and the rest of the debt is to be paid in small monthly installments.[72] In the meantime, however, Syria does not have to allocate large sums of money for repayment of its external debt. Therefore, Syria is able to allocate higher proportions of the governmental budget to socioeconomic development plans.

Moreover, in comparison to such countries as Jordan and Yemen, Syria adopted a wise labor migration policy during the 1970s and the 1980s. Temporary migration for employment purposes was allowed for unskilled and semi-skilled workers, in whom the government did not invest large sums of money for their education and professional training. At the same time, heavy restrictions were placed on the migration of the most professional and skilled workers, in whose education and professional training the government invested large sums of money. Thus, their skills were put to work in the Syrian labor market for the implementation of socioeconomic development plans.

Consequently, after the Gulf crisis, the Syrian authorities did not have to deal with absorbing large numbers of returning workers and their accompanying family members from the Gulf. While Jordan and Yemen were occupied throughout the first half of the 1990s with the reconstruction of their economies and absorption of hundreds of thousands of returnees, Syria was free to deal with the development of its economy and infrastructure systems. As a result of the mass return of workers and the sharp decrease in receipt of workers' remittances, the GNP per capita in Jordan decreased during the first years of the 1990s. In contrast, the per capita GNP in Syria increased due to the relatively minor role of workers' remittances in the economy.

During the mid-1990s, this set of developments engendered several economic and social outcomes. First and foremost, the level of private income and expenditure on consumption began to rise. Imports of durable consumer goods increased by tens of percent. Moreover, an improvement in public services became clearly discernible. The population of Syria now seems to expect the amelioration in its standard of living to continue.[73] The realization of such expectations demands a broader and more comprehensive application of the central government's liberalization policy – in other words, opening the door to investment by the domestic and foreign private sectors.[74]

The peace process between Syria and Israel touches on most of the economic and social variables mentioned above. It was, on the one hand, one of the outcomes of the dismantling of the "strategic balance" policy and the public pressure to bring about an improvement in the standard of living, and on the other hand, one of the major levers for returning the Syrian economy to steady and rapid growth. The rapid economic growth in Syria during the first half of the 1990s has affected both the shape and pace of the Syrian–Israeli peace negotiations. Egypt, the Palestinians, and Jordan all entered into peace negotiations with Israel when their economies were in such a severe situation that the economic recession clearly constituted a real danger to the continuation of the existing regimes.[75] This forced them not only to conclude an agreement with Israel within a short period of time, but also to withdraw some of their basic demands.

In contrast, Syria, as a result of its improved economic situation at the beginning of the 1990s, is able to manage slow negotiations and to insist on all its basic demands, simply because there is no economic pressure to conclude an agreement within a short period of time. Moreover, in the previous peace negotiations between Israel and other Arab countries, the former was in a better position, due mainly to its superior economic situation which provided increased leverage. In contrast, within the framework of the peace negotiations between Israel and Syria, the former is under great pressure to conclude a final agreement within a relatively short period of time. This is primarily because of the war in south Lebanon, which demands a very high price in man life, combined with the wide recognition that this problem cannot be solved without Syria – the real authority in Lebanon.

Considering the demographic-economic factors and the scale of available natural resources, it seems that Syria has a better chance to overcome its socio-economic problems than do either Egypt or Jordan. The core of Syria's problems in this arena lies in its misguided allocation of resources and the wide base of its age pyramid, which has led to low rates of labor force participation and, thus, low per capita income. However, due to the steady reduction of fertility levels during the last decade, the wide base of the age pyramid is gradually narrowing, while the percentage of the population in the working age groups within the total Syrian population is increasing. This process, which seems likely to continue in the coming decades, combined with the steady improvement in women's education, will eventually bring about an increase in the overall rate of Syrian labor force participation, along with an increase in per capita income. In contrast, both Egypt and Jordan suffer from more fundamental problems, the most acute being the growing pressure of the population on the available natural resources.

In conclusion, it is expected that the slow but steady improvement in the Syrian economy will continue at least in the coming decade mainly due to: the reduction in the crude birth and total fertility rates, and the increasing rates of labor force participation; the ongoing liberalization reforms in the economy; as well as the decrease in military expenditures. Beyond that point it is impossible, at least at the present time, to forecast the Syrian economic situation.

Today, it seems that there is no longer any doubt that during the last decade the Syrian economy has succeeded in implementing substantial structural changes, although limited in comparison to those that took place in Egypt during the latter part of the 1970s and throughout the 1980s. It remains to be seen whether the Syrian regime will be able to utilize the country's economic potential in the coming years.

Notes

_____

Introduction: The Middle Eastern Demographic Transition

1   John D. Durand, "Historical Estimates of World Population: An Evaluation," *Population and Development Review*, Vol. 3, No. 3 (1977), p. 259, table 2.

2   Wolfgang Lutz, "The Future of World Population," *Population Bulletin*, Vol. 49, No. 1 (June 1994), p. 4, table 1 [hereafter: Lutz, "The Future of World Population"].

3   Michael P. Todaro, *Economic Development of the Third World*, fourth edition (New York and London: Longman, 1990), pp. 214–15; John C. Caldwell and Pat Caldwell, "Fertility Transition with Special Reference to the ECWA Region," in ECWA (UN Economic Commission for Western Asia), *Population and Development in the Middle East* (Beirut, 1982), pp. 97–8.

4   Lutz, "The Future of World Population," pp. 4–6.

5   Charles Issawi, *An Economic History of the Middle East and North Africa* (New York: Columbia University Press, 1982), p. 94, table 6.1.

6   The World Bank, *World Development Report – 1996* (Oxford and New York: Oxford University Press, 1996), pp. 188–9, table 1 [hereafter: World Bank, *World Development Report*]; ESCWA (UN Economic and Social Commission for Western Asia), *Demographic and Related Socio-Economic Data Sheets for the Countries of the Economic and Social Commission for Western Asia*, No. 8 (1995), p. 4, table 1 [hereafter: ESCWA, *Demographic Data Sheets*]; see also: Abdel R. Omran and Farzaneh Roudi, "The Middle East Population Puzzle," *Population Bulletin*, Vol. 48, No. 1 (July 1993), p. 4, table 1.

7   "The Middle East: Gets Worse – for Who?," *The Middle East* (October 1994), p. 5.

8   ESCWA, *Survey of Economic and Social Developments in the ESCWA Region in The 1980s* (New York, 1989), p. 172, table 12.1.

9   Gad G. Gilbar, *The Economic Development of the Middle East in Modern Times* (Tel Aviv: Ministry of Defense, 1990), pp. 30–1 (in Hebrew) [hereafter: Gilbar, *The Economic Development of the Middle East*].

10 See: ESCWA and FAO (Food and Agriculture Organization of the UN), *Agriculture & Development in Western Asia*, No. 15 (Amman, December 1993), pp. 5–6.

_____

11 Lynn Simarsky, "The Fabric Cracks: Urban Crisis in the Arab World," *The Middle East* (January 1988), p. 5.
12 Gilbar, *The Economic Development of the Middle East*, p. 40.
13 Regarding the changes in the Egyptian economic policy during the mid-1970s, see: John Waterbury, *The Egypt of Nasser and Sadat: The Political Economy of Two Regimes* (Princeton: Princeton University Press, 1983), pp. 123–57 [hereafter: Waterbury, *The Egypt of Nasser and Sadat*]; Ali Hillal Dessouki, "The Politics of Income Distribution in Egypt," in Gouda Abdel-Khalek and Robert Tignor (eds), *The Political Economy of Income Distribution in Egypt* (New York and London: Meier Publishers, 1982), pp. 75–82.
14 Regarding the changing economic policy in Syria during the late 1980s and the early 1990s, see chapter 6: Conclusions.
15 Alfred Bonné, *The Economic Development of the Middle East – An Outline of Planned Reconstruction After the War* (London: Kegan Paul, Trench, Trubner & Co., 1945), p. 10 [hereafter: Bonné, *The Economic Development of the Middle East*].
16 Regarding the emigration of Syrians during the second half of the nineteenth century and the beginning of the twentieth century, see chapter 4.
17 Kemal H. Karpat, *Ottoman Population 1830–1914: Demographic and Social Characteristics* (Wisconsin: The University of Wisconsin Press, 1985), p. 117, section 1, table 1.6.
18 Robert Widmer, "Population," in Said B. Himadeh (ed.), *Economic Organization of Syria* (Beirut: The American University of Beirut Press, 1936), p. 5, table 1 [hereafter: Widmer, "Population"].
19 Étienne De-Vaumas, "La Population de la Syrie," *Annales de Geographie*, Vol. 64, No. 341 (Jan.–Feb. 1955), p. 74.
20 EIU, *Country Profile – Syria, 1998–99*, p. 15.
21 See in this regard: Saad Eddin Ibrahim, "Urbanization in the Arab World: The Need for an Urban Strategy," in Saad Eddin Ibrahim and Nicholas Hopkins (eds), *Arab Society – Social Science Perspectives* (Cairo: The American University in Cairo Press, 1985), pp. 129–31 [hereafter: Saad Eddin Ibrahim, "Urbanization in the Arab World].

1 Sources for Syrian Demographic Trends and Developments

1 Georges Sabagh, "The Demography of the Middle East," *Middle East Studies Association Bulletin*, Vol. 4, No. 2 (15 May 1972), pp. 1–2 [hereafter: Sabagh, "The Demography of the Middle East"].
2 Stanford J. Shaw, "The Ottoman Census System and Population, 1831–1914," *IJMES*, Vol. 9 (1978), p. 325 [hereafter: Shaw, "The Ottoman Census"].
3 Haim Gerber, "The Population of Syria and Palestine in the Nineteenth Century," *Asian and African Studies*, Vol. 13, No. 1 (1979), p. 58 [hereafter: Gerber, "The Population of Syria and Palestine"].
4 Shaw, "The Ottoman Census," pp. 325–7; Bernard Lewis, *The Emergence of*

Modern Turkey, second edition (Oxford and New York: Oxford University Press, 1968), p. 90.

5   Kemal H. Karpat, "Ottoman Population Records and the Census of 1881/82–1893," *IJMES*, Vol. 9 (1978), p. 242.

6   Uri M. Kupferschmidt, "A Note on the Muslim Religious Hierarchy towards the end of the Ottoman Period," in David Kushner (ed.), *Palestine in the Late Ottoman Period* (Jerusalem: Yad Yzhak Ben-Zvi Press, 1986), p. 123.

7   Justin McCarthy, "The Population of Ottoman Syria and Iraq, 1878–1914," *Asian and African Studies*, Vol. 15, No. 1 (1981), p. 11.

8   Mohamed Chafic Dibbs, "The Relationship between Censuses and Civil Registration in the Syrian Arab Republic," *Population Bulletin of ECWA*, No. 18 (June 1980), pp. 81–2 [hereafter: Dibbs, "The Relationship between Censuses and Civil Registration"]; M. N. Al-Hallak, "Demographic Situation in the Syrian Arab Republic," paper presented at the Expert Group Meeting on the Application of Demographic Data and Studies in Development Planning of the UN Economic and Social Office in Beirut, Beirut, 7–12 December 1970, p. 5 [hereafter: Al-Hallak, "Demographic Situation in the Syrian Arab Republic "].

9   Shaw, "The Ottoman Census," p. 336.

10 Al-Hallak, "Demographic Situation in the Syrian Arab Republic," p. 5.

11 See, for example: U. O. Schmelz, "Population Characteristics of Jerusalem and Hebron Regions According to Ottoman Census of 1905," in Gad. G. Gilbar (ed.), *Ottoman Palestine 1800–1914: Studies in Economic and Social History* (Leiden: E. J. Brill, 1990), pp. 15–67.

12 Dibbs, "The Relationship between Censuses and Civil Registration," p. 82.

13 Widmer, "Population," p. 3.

14 Ibid.

15 Dibbs, "The Relationship between Censuses and Civil Registration," p. 84.

16 UN Fund for Population Activities (UNFPA), *Syrian Arab Republic, Report on Mission on Needs Assessment for Population Assistance*, Report No. 24 (New York, 1980), p. 30 [hereafter: UNFPA, *Syrian Arab Republic*]; Population Division of the UN Department of International Economic and Social Affairs and UNFPA, *Population Policy Compendium, Syrian Arab Republic* (New York, 1980), p. 2 [hereafter: *Population Policy Compendium, Syrian Arab Republic*]; Syrian Arab Republic, State Planning Commission, Central Bureau of Statistics, *Composition and Growth of Population in the Syrian Arab Republic* (Damascus, September 1979), p. 20 [hereafter: Syria, *Composition and Growth of Population*].

17 Al-Hallak, "Demographic Situation in the Syrian Arab Republic," no page, table 5.

18 ECWA, *The Population Situation in the ECWA Region – Syrian Arab Republic* (Beirut, 1980), p. 2 [hereafter: ECWA, *The Population Situation – Syrian Arab Republic*].

19 UNFPA, *Syrian Arab Republic*, pp. 30–1.

20 Al-Hallak, "Demographic Situation in the Syrian Arab Republic," pp. 7–8; see also: UNFPA, *Syrian Arab Republic*, pp. 30–1.

21 Farid El-Boustani, "The Levels of Demographic Data in the Syrian Arab Republic

and Future Trends," in CBS, *Factors of Population Growth and Their Future Trends,* Papers Presented at a Seminar Held in Damascus, 16–20 September 1978, Under the Auspices of the Syrian CBS and UNFPA (Damascus: CBS Press, 1979), p. 3 [hereafter: El-Boustani, "The Levels of Demographic Data" and CBS, *Factors of Population Growth*].

22 UNFPA, *Syrian Arab Republic*, pp. 26–7; *Population Policy Compendium, Syrian Arab Republic*, p. 2; Ahmad Zein El-Din, "Achievements, Plans and Recommendations Relating to Population and Housing Censuses in the Syrian Arab Republic," paper presented at the Expert Group Meeting on Census Techniques of the UN Economic and Social Council, Beirut, 12–16 December 1977, p. 16 [hereafter: El-Din, "Achievements, Plans and Recommendations"].

23 Eliane Domschke and Doreen S. Goyer, *The Handbook of National Population Censuses: Africa and Asia* (New York, Westport and London: Greenwood Press, 1986), p. 835 [hereafter: Domschke and Goyer, *The Handbook of National Population Censuses*].

24 Al-Hallak, "Demographic Situation in the Syrian Arab Republic," p. 5.

25 The unification of Egypt and Syria (February 1958–September 1961).

26 El-Din, "Achievements, Plans and Recommendations," p. 15.

27 Domschke and Goyer, *The Handbook of National Population Censuses*, p. 837; Regarding the definitions of the census, see: Ibid, pp. 837–8.

28 Ibid., p. 837; Syrian Arab Republic, State Planning Commission and CBS, in collaboration with the Population Council, by Nader M. Hallak, *Rates of Natural Increase in the Syrian Regions* (Damascus, September 1979), pp. 1–2 [hereafter: Syria, *Rates of Natural Increase*].

29 El-Din, "Achievements, Plans and Recommendations," p. 17; Mohamed S. El-Khodary, "Organization and Conduct of the Syrian Housing and Population Census of 1970," *Population Bulletin of the UN Economic and Social Office in Beirut*, No. 2 (January 1972), pp. 20–2.

30 Domschke and Goyer, *The Handbook of National Population Censuses*, p. 838.

31 ECWA, *The Population Situation – Syrian Arab Republic*, p. 2.

32 El-Boustani, "The Levels of Demographic Data," p. 5.

33 UNFPA, *Syrian Arab Republic*, p. 34.

34 *MEED*, 8 May 1981, p. 46; 11 September 1981, p. 52; See also: *Tishrin*, 20, 21 October 1982.

35 UNFPA, *Syrian Arab Republic*, p. 29.

36 Eyal Zisser, "Syria," *Middle East Contemporary Survey* (MECS), Vol. 18 (1994), p. 619.

37 See: *al-Thawra*, 14 July, 31 August 1994.

38 See: Sabagh, "The Demography of the Middle East," p. 2.

39 Syria, *Composition and Growth of Population*, p. 22; UNFPA, *Syrian Arab Republic*, p. 33.

40 Syrian Arab Republic, Office of the Prime Minister, CBS, *Follow-Up Demographic Survey, Final Report, 1976–79* (Damascus, November 1981), pp. 3–7 and 29–31 [hereafter: *Follow-Up Demographic Survey, 1976–79*].

41 Syrian Arab Republic, Office of the Prime Minister, CBS in collaboration with The

World Fertility Survey, *Syria Fertility Survey – 1978*, Final Report, Vol. 1 (Damascus, 1982), p. 3 [hereafter: *Syria Fertility Survey – 1978*].

42   World Fertility Survey, *The Syrian Fertility Survey – 1978: A Summary of Findings* (London: International Statistical Institute, February 1982), p. 2.

43   Syrian Arab Republic, Office of the Prime Minister, CBS and Pan Arab Project for Child Development, *Maternal and Child Health Survey in the Syrian Arab Republic*, Summary Report (Damascus, 1995), p.1 [hereafter: *Syrian Maternal and Child Health Survey, 1993*]; "Syria 1993: Results from the PAPCHILD Survey," *Studies in Family Planning*, Vol. 25, No. 4 (July/August 1994), p. 248 [hereafter: "Syria 1993: Results from the PAPCHILD Survey"].

44   The Hashemite Kingdom of Jordan, Department of Statistics, *Statistical Yearbook – 1989* (Amman, 1990), p. 83, table 4/2/3.

45   *MEED*, 18 April 1975, p. 39.

46   Susannah Tarbush, "The New Nomads: Manpower in the Gulf," *The Middle East* (February 1983), p. 33.

47   Domschke and Goyer, *The Handbook of National Population Censuses*, pp. 807–9.

48   EIU, *Country Profile – Saudi Arabia, 1987–88*, p. 7; *MEED*, 18 April 1975, p. 39.

49   Gil Feiler, "The Number of Egyptian Workers in the Arab Oil Countries, 1974–1983: A Critical Discussion," *Occasional Papers* (Tel Aviv University, The Dayan Center, October 1986), p. 2.

50   See: Volker Perthes, *The Political Economy of Syria under Asad* (London and New York: I. B. Tauris, 1994), pp. 13–14 [hereafter: Perthes, *The Political Economy of Syria under Asad*].

51   Eliyahu Kanovsky, "What's Behind Syria's Current Economic Problems?" *Occasional Papers* (Tel Aviv University, The Dayan Center, May 1985), p. 45.

52   See: Moshe Ma'oz, *Asad: The Sphinx of Damascus* (Tel Aviv: Dvir Publishing House, 1988), p. 92 (in Hebrew) [hereafter: Ma'oz, *Asad*].

53   Regarding the unofficial exchange rate of the LS and the scale of workers' remittances transfer via unofficial channels, see chapters 4 and 5.

2 Population Growth

1   K. Hameed, "Manpower and Employment Planning in Iraq and the Syrian Arab Republic," in ECWA, *Studies on Development Problems in Countries of Western Asia, 1975* (New York, 1977), p. 26 [hereafter: Hameed, "Manpower and Employment Planning"].

2   Syria, *Composition and Growth of Population*, p. 3, table 1.2.

3   Regarding the family planning activities of the Syrian authorities, see chapter 5.

4   CAPMAS (Central Agency for Public Mobilisation and Statistics), *Statistical Yearbook of the Arab Republic of Egypt – 1952–1992* (Cairo, June 1993), p. 28, table 1–18 [hereafter: CAPMAS, *Statistical Yearbook*].

5   ESCWA, *Demographic Data Sheets*, No. 7 (1993), p. 36, table 3.

6   Ibid., p. 60, table 3.

7   *Syrian Maternal and Child Health Survey, 1993*, p. 16; Syria, *Statistical Abstract – 1995*, p. 56, table 4/2.

8   UN, *Demographic Yearbook – 1994*, p. 406.
9   CAPMAS, *Statistical Yearbook – 1985*, p. 30.
10 See in this regard: Gad G. Gilbar, *Population Dilemmas in the Middle East* (London and Portland: Frank Cass, 1997), pp. 84–5 [hereafter: Gilbar, *Population Dilemmas*].
11 CAPMAS, *Statistical Yearbook – 1989*, p. 24, table 1–15.
12 *Syrian Maternal and Child Health Survey, 1993*, p. 16.
13 Syria, *Statistical Abstract – 1987*, p. 59, table 3/2.
14 Mahmoud Farag, "Differentials in Age at Marriage in Syria," in S. A. Huzayyin and G. T. Acsadi (eds), *Family and Marriage in some African and Asiatic Countries*, Research Monograph Series, No. 6 (Cairo: Cairo Demographic Centre, 1976), p. 502, table 24.6 [hereafter: Farag, "Differentials in Age at Marriage in Syria," and Huzayyin and Acsadi (eds), *Family and Marriage*].
15 K. S. Seetharam and M. Bdrud Duza, "Nuptiality and Fertility in Selected Areas of Four Arab and African Cities," in Huzayyin and Acsadi (eds), *Family and Marriage*, p. 344, table 17.4.
16 Hamed Abou-Gamrah, "Fertility Levels and Differentials by Mother's Education in some Countries of the ECWA Region," in Cairo Demographic Centre, *Determinants of Fertility in some African and Asian Countries*, Research Monograph Series, No. 10 (Cairo, 1982), p. 199 [hereafter: Abou-Gamrah, "Fertility Levels"].
17 Farag, "Differentials in Age at Marriage in Syria," p. 503, table 24.7.
18 Abou-Gamrah, "Fertility Levels," pp. 199–201.
19 See: S. A. Huzayyin, "Mortality Situation in Some Arab and African Countries: An Overview," in Cairo Demographic Centre, *Mortality Trends and Differentials in some African and Asian Countries*, Research Monograph Series, No. 8 (Cairo, 1982), p. 3.
20 UN Department of International Economic and Social Affairs, "Mortality of Children Under Age 5, World Estimates and Projections, 1950–2025," *Population Studies*, No. 105 (New York, 1988), p. 40, table A.2.
21 Ibid., p. 34, table A.1.
22 *MEED*, 27 June 1987, p. 19.
23 UNICEF, *The State of the World's Children – 1992*, p. 89, table 9.
24 *MEED*, 27 June 1987, p. 19.
25 UNICEF, *The State of the World's Children – 1995*, p. 83, table 9.
26 World Bank, *World Tables*, the third edition, p. 87.
27 ESCWA, *Demographic Data Sheets*, No. 9 (1997), p. 111, table 4.
28 World Bank, *World Tables*, the third edition, p. 87.
29 The data on the population is taken from: Appendix 1. The data on the number of nurses in 1993 is taken from: Syria, *Statistical Abstract – 1994*, p. 360, table 1.11.
30 Syria, *Statistical Abstract – 1983*, p. 332, table 3/11.
31 Syria, *Statistical Abstract – 1994*, p. 361, table 2/11.
32 See in this regard: *Tishrin*, 14 July 1980.
33 World Bank, *World Tables*, 1989–90 edition, p. 544.
34 World Bank, *World Tables, 1995* edition, p. 649.

35 Regarding the overall economic development in Syria during the early 1990s, see chapter 6: Conclusions.

36 *Syria Fertility Survey – 1978*, p. 73, table 6.12.

37 *Syrian Maternal and Child Health Survey, 1993*, p. 3, figure 3.

38 Regarding the development of the public services in the rural areas, see chapter 5.

39 *Tishrin*, 14 April 1984.

40 *Syria Fertility Survey – 1978*, pp. 70–2.

41 *Syrian Maternal and Child Health Survey, 1993*, p. 3, figure 3.

42 The Hashemite Kingdom of Jordan, Department of Statistics and Ministry of Health, by Abdallah Abdel-Aziz Zou'bi, Sri Poedjastoeti, and Mohamed Ayad, *Jordan Population and Family Health Survey – 1990* [JPFHS] (Amman, August 1992), p. 79, table 7.2.

43 Hussein El-Baradei, "Household Structure and Age at Marriage in Damascus, Syria," in Huzayyin and Acsadi (eds), *Family and Marriage*, p. 192 and p. 193, table 9.8 [hereafter: El-Baradei, "Household Structure and Age at Marriage"].

44 UNFPA, *Syrian Arab Republic*, Annex A/2, table 1.

45 *Syria Fertility Survey – 1978*, p. 36, table 4.2 and p. 37.

46 *Syrian Maternal and Child Health Survey, 1993*, p. 15.

47 El-Baradei, "Household Structure and Age at Marriage," p. 195, table 9.9.

48 *Syrian Maternal and Child Health Survey, 1993*, p. 15.

49 *Syria Fertility Survey – 1978*, pp. 40–1, tables 4.7 and 4.8.

50 *Syrian Maternal and Child Health Survey, 1993*, p. 15.

51 Syria, *Statistical Abstract – 1991*, p. 66, table 16/2.

52 Sultanate of Oman, Ministry of Development, *General Census of Population, Housing and Establishments, 1993* (Muscat, 1995), p. 41, table 2–8.

53 UN, *Demographic Yearbook – 1990*, pp. 214–15.

54 K. E. Vaidyanathan and M. A. Alwany, "Population and Labour Force in Syria," in Cairo Demographic Centre, *Demographic Aspects of Manpower in Arab Countries*, Research Monograph Series, No. 3 (Cairo, 1972), p. 225 [hereafter: Vaidyanathan and Alwany, "Population and Labour Force in Syria"].

55 ESCWA, *Population Situation, 1990*, p. 190, table 11.8.

56 ILO, *Yearbook of Labour Statistics – 1992* (Geneva, 1993), p. 37, table 1.

57 ILO, *Yearbook of Labour Statistics – 1994*, pp. 22–3, table 1.

58 Ibid., pp. 22–6, table 1.

59 Syria, *Statistical Abstract – 1992*, pp. 484–5, table 21/16.

60 Ibid., pp. 504–5, table 39/16.

61 Regarding the urbanization process taking place in Syria since the late 1950s, see chapter 3.

62 Alasdair Drysdale, "The Asad Regime and its Troubles," *Merip Reports*, Vol. 12, No. 9 (November–December 1982), p. 6 [hereafter: Drysdale, "The Asad Regime and its Troubles"].

63 *MEED*, 29 January 1993, p. 8; 1 March 1996, p. 3; *Jordan Times*, 11 May 1996.

64 See chapter 5.

65 Hameed, "Manpower and Employment Planning," p. 26.

66   *Syria Fertility Survey – 1978*, p. 88, table 8.1.
67   Ibid., p. 91.

3   The Spatial Distribution of the Population

1   See: Nabil Khoury, "Inter-Relationship between Urbanization and Socio-Economic Change: The Case of Syria," in CBS, *Factors of Population Growth*, p. 57.
2   Richard Hay, "Patterns of Urbanization and Socio-Economic Development in the Third World," in Janet Abu-Lughod and Richard Hay (eds), *Third World Urbanization* (Chicago: Maaroufa Press, 1977), p. 71 [hereafter: Hay, "Patterns of Urbanization"]; Mary E. Morris, "Regional Economic Cooperation in the Middle East: Prospects and Problems," in Joseph Ginat and Onn Winckler (eds), *The Jordanian–Palestinian–Israeli Triangle: Smoothing the Path to Peace* (Brighton: Sussex Academic Press, 1998), p. 142 [hereafter: Ginat and Winckler (eds), *The Jordanian–Palestinian–Israeli Triangle*]; Gregory D. Foster, "Global Demographic Trends to the year 2010: Implications for US Security," T*he Washington Quarterly*, Vol. 12, No. 2 (Spring 1989), p. 7.
3   Michael P. Todaro, "Urbanization in Developing Nations: Trends, Prospects and Policies," in Pradip K. Ghosh (ed.), *Urban Development in the Third World* (Westport and London: Greenwood Press, 1984), p. 7.
4   Saad Eddin Ibrahim, "Urbanization in the Arab World," p. 131; see also: idem, "Urbanization in the Arab World," *Population Bulletin of the UN ECWA*, No. 7 (July 1974), pp. 74–102.
5   Bonné, *The Economic Development of the Middle East*, p. 11.
6   Gerber, "The Population of Syria and Palestine," p. 68, table C.
7   Regarding the agricultural development in Syria during the late 1940s and early 1950s, see chapter 5.
8   Bent Hansen, *Economic Development in Syria* (California: Rand Corporation, December 1969), p. 29.
9   Ibid.; see also: Yusif A. Sayigh, *The Economies of the Arab World: Development Since 1945* (London: Croom Helm, 1982), p. 232, table 6.3 [hereafter: Sayigh, *The Economies of the Arab World*].
10   Regarding the July 1961 Decrees, see: Tabitha Petran, *Syria* (London: Ernest Benn, 1972), pp. 139–40 [hereafter: Petran, *Syria*]; Waterbury, *The Egypt of Nasser and Sadat*, pp. 73–9.
11   Petran, *Syria*, p. 234; see also: Edmund Y. Asfour, *Syria: Development and Monetary Policy* (Cambridge, Mass.: Harvard University Press, 1967), pp. 13–15.
12   Muhammad Nadir Hallak, "The Impact of Migration on the Demographic Structure of the Syrian Arab Republic," in CBS, *Factors of Population Growth*, pp. 77–9 [hereafter: Hallak, "The Impact of Migration"].
13   E. Kanovsky, *The Economic Development of Syria* (Tel Aviv: University Publishing Projects, 1977), p. 27, table 6.
14   The cropped area included all the cultivated area which is actually under crops in a given year.

15 Regarding the implementation of the Syrian Agrarian Reform after September 1958 and the frequent changes of the Agrarian Reform Law during the period between September 1961–March 1963, see chapter 5.

16 *MEED*, 4 February 1972, p. 120.

17 See chapter 4.

18 *Tishrin*, 5 June 1985; see also: *al-Ba'th*, 5 November 1987.

19 See: Syria, *Statistical Abstract – 1984*, p. 56, table 2/2.

20 Winckler, *Population Growth and Migration in Jordan, 1950–1994* (Brighton: Sussex Academic Press, 1997), pp. 104–7, Appendices 1 and 3.

21 CAPMAS, *Statistical Yearbook, 1952–1992*, p. 16, table 1–9; Janet Abu-Lughod, "Urbanization in Egypt: Present State and Future Prospects," *Economic Development and Cultural Change*, Vol. 13, No. 3 (April 1965), pp. 318–19, table 1.

22 UN, *Demographic Yearbook – 1993*, pp. 156, 284.

23 UN, *Demographic Yearbook – 1957*, pp. 129, 151.

24 Kais Firro, "The Syrian Economy under the Assad Regime," in Mosh Ma'oz and Avner Yaniv (eds), *Syria under Assad: Domestic Constraints and Regional Risks* (London and Sydney: Croom Helm, 1986), p. 57.

25 Regarding the implementation of this project, see chapter 5.

26 EIU, *Country Profile – Jordan, 1995–96*, p. 10.

27 Regarding the agricultural development plans in the northeastern provinces of Syria, see chapter 5.

28 See: J. P. Bhattacharjee, "On Balance," in Thomas T. Poleman and Donald K. Freebairn (eds), *Food, Population and Employment: The Impact of the Green Revolution* (New York: Praeger Publishers, 1973), pp. 257–9.

29 Vaidyanathan and Alwany, "Population and Labour Force in Syria," p. 233, table 5.

30 ESCWA, *Demographic Data Sheets*, No. 5 (1987), p. 213, table 11.

31 Syria, *Statistical Abstract – 1992*, p. 77, table 6/3.

32 *al-Iqtisad,* March 1991, p. 8, table 1; May 1989, pp. 7–8, tables 2 and 3.

33 Ahmad Mouhamad Al-Zoobi, *The Agricultural Extension and Rural Development in Syria, 1955–1968* (Ph.D. Thesis, The Ohio State University, 1971), p. 74, table 19.

34 See: Richard I. Lowless, "The Agricultural Sector in Development Policy," in Peter Beaumont and Keith McLachlan (eds), *Agricultural Development in the Middle East* (Chichester: John Wiley & Sons, 1985), pp. 112–13 [hereafter: Beaumont and McLachlan (eds), *Agricultural Development in the Middle East*].

35 Alan George, "Syria: An Economy Saved by Circumstances," *The Middle East* (December 1988), p. 28 [hereafter: *The Middle East* (December 1988)]; see also: *Nidal al-Falahin*, 25 March 1981, p. 6.

36 See below, pp. 80–1.

37 *al-Thawra*, 7 July 1977; see also: 19 June 1975.

38 Mustafa Al-Shihabi, "Rural Population and Agriculture in the Syrian Arab Republic," Paper presented at the First ECWA Regional Population Conference, Beirut, 18 February–1 March 1974, p. 6.

39   Regarding the governmental development projects in the countryside and in the remote provinces, see chapter 5.

40   UNICEF, *The State of the World's Children – 1986*, p. 137, table 3; see also: UNDP (UN Development Programme), *Human Development Report – 1992* (Oxford and New York: Oxford University Press, 1992), p. 146, table 10.

41   UNICEF, *The State of the World's Children – 1996*, p. 85, table 3.

42   *al-Thawra*, 28 September 1980.

43   For example: *al-Thawra*, 26 May 1982; *Nidal al-Falahin*, 13 February 1980; 25 March; 25 May 1981; 10 July 1985.

44   Foreign Areas Studies Division, *Area Handbook for Syria* (Washington, D.C.: Special Operations Research Office, The American University, July 1965), p. 143.

45   *Agriculture in the Syrian Arab Republic*, Serié Etudes No. 178 (Office Arabe de Presse et de Documentation, 1978), p. 1.

46   *Tishrin*, 14 July 1980.

47   *Tishrin*, 5 July 1989.

48   Elisabeth Longuenesse, "The Syrian Working Class Today," *Merip Reports*, No. 134 (July/August 1985), p. 18; See also: *al-Thawra*, 7 July 1977.

49   "The Industrial Situation in Syria," in *Industrial Development in the Arab Countries*, Selected Document Presented to the Symposium on Industrial Development in the Arab Countries, Kuwait, 1–10 March 1966 (New York, 1967), p. 116.

50   "MEED Special Report – Syria," *MEED*, March 1980, p. 7.

51   World Bank, *World Development Report – 1983*, p.151, table 3.

52   World Bank, *World Development Report – 1985*, p. 179, table 3.

53   See in this regard chapter 6: Conclusions.

54   World Bank, *World Development Report – 1994*, p. 167, table 3.

55   Regarding the urbanization process in the Gulf countries, see for example: Ishaq Y. Qutub, "Urbanization in Contemporary Arab Gulf States," *Ekistics*, Vol. 53 May/June 1983), pp. 170–82; N. C. Grill, *Urbanisation in the Arabian Peninsula* (Durham: Centre for Middle Eastern and Islamic Studies, 1984).

56   Hallak, "The Impact of Migration," p. 73.

57   CBS, *Socio-Economic Development in Syria, 1960–1970*, p. 44.

58   Syria, *Statistical Abstract – 1991*, p. 67, table 17/2.

59   *Tishrin*, 24 May 1976; see also: *al-Thawra*, 19 June 1975.

60   "Development Planning and Social Objectives in Syria," in United Nations Economic and Social Office in Beirut (UNESOB), *Studies on Selected Development Problems in Various Countries in the Middle East* (New York, 1971), pp. 16–17 [hereafter: "Development planning and Social Objectives in Syria"].

61   Ibid., p. 17; UNESOB, *Studies on Social Development in the Middle East, 1971* (New York, 1973), p. 57; see also: *Nidal al-Falahin*, 25 June 1975.

62   CBS, *Socio-Economic Development in Syria, 1960–1970*, pp. 32–3.

63   *Tishrin*, 24 June 1978.

64   Ibid.; CBS, *Socio-Economic Development in Syria, 1960–1970*, p. 33; see also: *Tishrin*, 24 April 1978.

65   *Tishrin*, 24 May 1976.

66 *Tishrin*, 20 October 1982; *al-Ba'th*, 2 April 1984.
67 *al-Ba'th*, 24 March 1977; *Nidal al-Falahin*, 25 June 1975.
68 See: *Tishrin*, 19 March 1990.
69 *Tishrin*, 13 January 1990.
70 K. E. Vaidyanathan, "Urbanization and the Development Process in the Arab World," in S. A. Huzayyin and T. E. Smith (eds), *Demographic Aspects of Socio-Economic Development in some Arab and African Countries*, Research Monograph Series, No. 5 (Cairo: Cairo Demographic Centre, 1974), pp. 129–30.
71 Faul Bairoch, *Urban Unemployment in Developing Countries* (Geneva: ILO, 1973), p. 49, table 15.
72 EIU, *Country Profile – Syria, 1991–92*, p. 19.
73 Marvin G. Weinbaum, *Food, Development and Policies in the Middle East* (Boulder: Westview Press and London: Croom Helm, 1982), p. 37 [hereafter: Weinbaum, *Food, Development and Policies in the Middle East*].
74 See in this regard: *al-Thawra*, 23 January 1980; *Tishrin*, 5 July 1989; 17 September 1990.

4 Syrian Migration Abroad

1 A. Ruppin, "Migration from and to Syria," in Charles Issawi (ed.), *The Economic History of the Middle East, 1800–1914* (Chicago and London: The University of Chicago Press, 1966), p. 269.
2 See: Najib E. Saliba, "Emigration from Syria," *Arab Studies Quarterly*, Vol. 3, No. 1 (1981), p. 56.
3 Great Britain, Naval Intelligence Division, *Syria* (London: H.M. Stationery Office, April 1943), p. 206.
4 Widmer, "Population," p. 14.
5 Thomas Philipp, "Demographic Patterns of Syrian Immigration to Egypt in the Nineteenth Century – An Interpretation," *Asian and African Studies,* Vol. 16, No. 2 (July 1982), p. 171.
6 Regarding the Syrian emigration to America, both north and south, see: Kemal H. Karpat, "The Ottoman Emigration to America, 1860–1914," *IJMES,* Vol. 17 (1985), pp. 175–209; Philip M. Kayal and Joseph M. Kayal, *The Syrian – Lebanese in America: A Study in Religion and Assimilation* (New York: Twayne Publishers, 1975).
7 M. A. El-Badry, "Trends in the Components of Population Growth in the Arab Countries of the Middle East: A Survey of Present Information," *Demography*, Vol. 2 (1965), p. 173; see also: Mouna Liliane Samman, *La Population de la Syrie: Étude Géo – Démographiqe* (Paris: ORSTOM, 1978), pp. 128–9.
8 Regarding the nationalization and other social and economic measures which took place in Syria during the 1960s, see: Ziad Keilany, "Socialism and Economic Change in Syria," *Middle Eastern Studies*, Vol. 9, No. 1 (1973), pp. 65–9.
9 M. E. Sales (Co-Directors and Principal Researchers: J. S. Birks and C. A. Sinclair), *International Migration Project, Country Case Study: Syrian Arab Republic*

(Durham: University of Durham, Department of Economics, October 1978), p. 59 [hereafter: Sales, *International Migration Project: Syrian Arab Republic*].

10   *al-Khalij*, 11 January 1985.

11   Syria, *Statistical Abstract – 1992*, p. 63, table 13/2; see also: Hallak, "The Impact of Migration," p. 75.

12   Gad G. Gilbar, *The Middle East Oil Decade and Beyond* (London and Portland: Frank Cass, 1997), p. 1.

13   M. G. Quibria, "Migrant Workers and Remittances: Issues for Asian Developing Countries," *Asian Development Review,* Vol. 4, No. 1 (1986), p. 82, table 1.

14   World Bank, *World Tables,* 1989–90 edition, pp. 334–5, 472–3.

15   The Kingdom of Saudi Arabia, Central Planning Organization, *Development Plan, 1390 AH* (Riyadh, 1970), p. 23.

16   Sultanate of Oman, Development Council, *The Five-Year Development Plan, 1976–1980* (Muscat, 1976), p. 13.

17   Gilbar, *The Economic Development of the Middle East*, pp. 112–13.

18   See: United Nations Department of International Economic and Social Affairs, *Case Studies in Population Policy: Kuwait,* Population Policy Paper, No. 15 (New York, 1988), pp. 7–8 [hereafter: UN, *Kuwait*].

19   Onn Winckler, "The Immigration Policy of the Gulf Cooperation Council (GCC) States," *Middle Eastern Studies*, Vol. 33, No. 3 (July 1997), pp. 489–90, table 1 [hereafter: Winckler, "The Immigration Policy"].

20   ESCWA, *Survey of Economic and Social Developments in the ESCWA Region - 1992* (New York, October 1993), p. 119, table 48.

21   See: ECWA, *Demographic Data Sheets*, No. 2 (1978), country pages; Robert E. Looney, *Manpower Policies and Development in the Persian Gulf Region* (Westport and London: Praeger, 1994), pp. 29–34.

22   See for example: Roger Owen, *Migrant Workers in the Gulf* (London: Minority Rights Group, 1985), p. 4; *al-Thawra*, 23 January 1980; *MEED*, 11 March 1977, p. 9; Bent Hansen and Samir Radwan, *Employment Opportunities and Equity in A Changing Economy: Egypt in the 1980s. A Labour Market Approach* (Geneva: ILO, 1982), pp. 91–2.

23   Allan M. Findlay, "Return to Yemen: The End of the Old Migration Order in the Arab World," in W. T. S. Gould and A. M. Findlay (eds), *Population Migration and the Changing World Order* (Chichester and New York: John Wiley & Sons, 1994), p. 206 [hereafter: Findlay, "Return to Yemen"].

24   Tyseer Abdel-Jaber, "Inter-Arab Labor Movements: Problems and Prospects," in Said El-Naggar (ed.), *Economic Development of the Arab Countries: Selected Issues*, Papers presented at a seminar held in Bahrain, February 1–3, 1993 (Washington, D.C.: IMF, 1993), pp. 150–1.

25   Nabeel A. Khoury, "The Politics of Intra-Regional Migration in the Arab World," *Journal of South Asian and Middle Eastern Studies*, Vol. 6, No. 2 (1982), pp. 5–6.

26   Gil Feiler, Gideon Fishelson, and Roby Nathanson, *Labour Force and Employment in Egypt, Syria and Jordan* (Tel Aviv: Histadrut, April 1993), pp. 67–8.

27   Nazli Choucri, "Migration in the Middle East: Transformation and Change,"

Middle East Review, Vol. 16, No. 2 (Winter 1983/4), p. 18, table 1 [hereafter: Choucri, "Migration in the Middle East"].

28 Birks et al., "Who is Migrating Where?" p. 114, table 1.
29 Richards and Waterbury, *A Political Economy of the Middle East*, p. 382, table 14.3.
30 Choucri, "Migration in the Middle East," p. 27, table 4.
31 ESCWA, Proceedings, *Expert Group Meeting on the Absorption of Returnees in the ESCWA Region with Special Emphasis on Opportunities in the Industrial Sector*, Amman, 16–17 December 1991 (Amman, October 1992), pp. 3, 7; *MEED*, 4 October 1991, p. 6; EIU, *Country Profile – Syria, 1993–94*, p. 22.
32 *MEED*, 11 March 1977, p. 9.
33 *Nidal al-Falahin*, 12 July 1978; see also: *al-Thawra*, 23 January 1980.
34 *Nidal al-Falahin*, 12 July 1978.
35 Annika Rabo, *Change on the Euphrates: Villagers, Townsmen and Employees in Northeast Syria* (Stockholm: Studies in Social Anthropology, 1986), p. 101.
36 Ibid.
37 *al-Thawra*, 23 January 1980.
38 U. Shmeltz, "Hahitpathut Hademographit shel Hamedinot Ha'arviyot" [The Demographic Development of the Arab Countries], *Hamizrah Hehadash* [The New East], Vol. 22 (1972), p. 451 (in Hebrew).
39 Choucri, "Migration in the Middle East," p. 18, table 1.
40 Hameed, "Manpower and Employment Planning," p. 28.
41 *al-Khalij*, 11 January 1985.
42 Hameed, "Manpower and Employment Planning," p. 28.
43 *al-Ishtiraqi*, 19 September 1980.
44 Regarding these two agreements and their influence on the Syrian's position in Lebanon, see: William W. Harris, "Lebanon," *Middle East Contemporary Survey (MECS)*, Vol. 14 (1990), pp. 528–32; Eyal Zisser, "Syria," *MECS*, Vol. 15 (1991), pp. 680–2.
45 *The Wall Street Journal*, 19 July 1995.
46 *Yedioth Ahronoth*, 25 July 1997.
47 See: *Financial Times*, 6 June 1995, p. 4; 18 March 1997, p. 7.
48 *Yedioth Ahronoth*, 20 March 1998.
49 *Ha'aretz*, 29 June 1998.
50 *The Wall Street Journal*, 19 July 1995.
51 Birks and Sinclair, *International Migration*, pp. 134–8, tables 10 and 14.
52 UNFPA, *Syrian Arab Republic*, p. 49.
53 Ian J. Seccombe, "Immigrant Workers in an Emigrant Economy: An Examination of Replacement Migration in the Middle East," *International Migration*, Vol. 24, No. 2 (June 1986), p. 380 [hereafter: Seccombe, "Immigrant Workers in an Emigrant Economy"].
54 HRD, S*ocio-Demographic Profiles*, pp. 44–5, tables 3.2 and 3.3.
55 *al-Ra'y*, 7 January 1989.
56 Jordan, *Statistical Yearbook – 1996*, p. 78, table 4/2/3.
57 "Jordan – The Demographic Time Bomb," *The Middle East* (February 1988), p. 29.

58 Regarding the economic situation in Syria during the second half of the 1980s, see chapter 6: Conclusions.

59 Sales, *International Migration Project: Syrian Arab Republic*, p. 63.

60 Birks and Sinclair, *International Migration*, p. 85.

61 J. S. Birks and C. A. Sinclair, "The Libyan Arab Jamahiriya: Labour Migration Sustains Dualistic Development," *Maghreb Review*, Vol. 4, No. 3 (May/June 1979), p. 99, table 8 [hereafter: Birks and Sinclair, "The Libyan Arab Jamahiriya"].

62 Saad Eddin Ibrahim, *The New Arab Social Order: A Study of the Social Impact of Oil Wealth* (Boulder: Westview Press and London: Croom Helm, 1982), p. 33, table 3.3 [hereafter: Saad Eddin Ibrahim, *The New Arab Social Order*].

63 Birks and Sinclair, "The Libyan Arab Jamahiriya," p. 99, table 8.

64 Eliyahu Kanovsky, "Migration from the Poor to the Rich Arab Countries," *Occasional Papers* (Tel Aviv University – The Dayan Center, June 1984), p. 35 [hereafter: Kanovsky, "Migration from the Poor to the Rich Arab Countries"].

65 Ibrahim Abdussalem and Richard Lawless, "Immigrant Workers in the Libyan Labour Force," *Immigrants & Minorities*, Vol. 7. No. 2 (July 1988), p. 211, table 3.

66 "Qaddafi's War of Words," *The Middle East* (October 1985), p. 12.

67 Richard J. Ward, "The Long Run Employment Prospects for Middle East Labor," *The Middle East Journal*, Vol. 24 (1970), p. 153, table 1.

68 Choucri, "Migration in the Middle East," p. 18, table 1.

69 Fouad Al-Farsy, *Saudi Arabia: A Case Study in Development* (London and Boston: Kegan Paul International, 1986), p. 90, table 3.3.

70 *GCC Market Report – 1990*, p.133, table 5.3; p. 135, table 6.3.

71 See: J. Addleton, "The Impact of the Gulf War on Migration and Remittances in Asia and the Middle East," *International Migration*, Vol. 29, No. 4 (1991), pp. 514–15; Nicholas Van Hear, "Mass Flight in the Middle East: Involuntary Migration and the Gulf Conflict, 1990–1991," in Richard Black and Vaughan Robinson (eds), *Geography and Refugees: Patterns and Processes of Change* (London and New York: Belhaven Press, 1993), pp. 68–9 [hereafter: Van Hear, "Mass Flight in the Middle East"]; "Asian Expatriates – Coming Back," *The Middle East* (October 1991), p. 36.

72 See: Shamlan Y. Alessa, *The Manpower Problem in Kuwait* (London and Boston: Kegan Paul International, 1981) p. 32; David E. Long, *The Persian Gulf: An Introduction to Its Peoples, Politics, and Economics* (Boulder: Westview Press, 1976), pp. 13–14; *MEED*, 25 October 1991, p. 15.

73 Kuwait, *Annual Statistical Abstract – 1976*, p. 31, table 17.

74 See: Ragaei El-Mallakh, *Economic Development and Regional Cooperation: Kuwait* (Chicago and London: The University of Chicago Press, 1970), p. 173, table 7.

75 Kuwait, *Annual Statistical Abstract – 1978*, p. 22, table 21; p. 23, table 23.

76 *MEED*, 4 October 1991, p. 6; see also: Van Hear, "Mass Flight in the Middle East," p. 67; Elizabeth N. Offen, "Migrants and Refugees: The Human Toll," in Gad Barzilai, Aharon Klieman, and Gil Shidlo (eds), *The Gulf Crisis and its Global Aftermath* (London and New York: Routledge, 1993), pp. 105–12.

77 *Gulf States Newsletter*, 14 December 1992, p. 5.
78 EIU, *Country Report – Kuwait*, 3rd Quarter (1993), p. 17.
79 Bahrain, *Statistical Abstract – 1972*, p. 10, table 6.
80 Bahrain, *Statistical Abstract – 1992*, p. 16, table 2.01.
81 EIU, *Country Profile – Bahrain, Qatar, 1989–90*, p. 24.
82 ECWA, *The Population Situation – Qatar*, p. 9, table 10.2.
83 EIU, *Country Profile – Bahrain, Qatar, 1992–93*, p. 24.
84 EIU, *Country Profile – Bahrain, Qatar, 1995–96*, p. 31.
85 Birks and Sinclair, *International Migration*, pp. 138–9, table 14.
86 HRD base, *Socio-Demographic Profiles*, p. 116, table 1.1.
87 Saad Eddin Ibrahim, *The New Arab Social Order*, p. 33, table 3.3.
88 ECWA, *The Population Situation – UAE*, p. 4, table 13.1.
89 ECWA, *Demographic Data Sheets*, No. 3 (1982), p. 179, table 1.
90 ESCWA, *Survey of Economic and Social Development in the ESCWA Region - 1992*, p. 119, table 48.
91 Winckler, "The Immigration Policy," pp. 489–90, table 1.
92 ESCWA, *Survey of Economic and Social Developments in the ESCWA Region - 1992*, p. 119, table 48.
93 EIU, *Country Profile – United Arab Emirates, 1994–95*, p. 15.
94 See: *Population Policy Compendium, Syrian Arab Republic*, p. 5. Regarding the distribution of the Syrian migrant workers in the Arab labor-receiving countries in 1975 according to occupations, see: Ismail Serageldin, James A. Socknat, Stace Birks, Bob Li, and Clive A. Sinclair, *Manpower and International Labor Migration in the Middle East and North Africa* (Oxford and New York: Oxford University Press, 1983), p. 73, table 8.3 [hereafter: Serageldin et al., *Manpower and International Labor Migration*].
95 Hallak, "The Impact of Migration," p. 74.
96 Regarding the economic damages caused by this emigration, see: *al-Iqtisad*, 1 February 1973; *al-Ba'th*, 12 June 1973; *Tishrin*, 27 February, 14 June 1977.
97 *MEED*, 21 September 1973, p. 1108.
98 "Special Report on Syria: Characteristics of the National Economy," *The Arab Economist*, Vol. 11 (October 1979), p. xv [hereafter: "Special Report on Syria"].
99 Hameed, "Manpower and Employment Planning," p. 28.
100 *Tshrin*, 8 August 1978.
101 *MEED*, 11 March 1977, p. 9.
102 See: Suleiman Farag Yeslam, "Major Issues in Sending Countries," in ECWA, *International Migration in the Arab World*, Proceedings of an ECWA Population Conference, Nicosia, Cyprus, 11–16 May 1981, Vol. 1 (Beirut, 1982), pp. 409–10.
103 Mostafa H. Nagi, "Labor Immigration and Development in the Middle East: Patterns, Problems, and Policies," *International Review of Modern Sociology*, Vol. 12, No. 2 (1982), p. 204 [hereafter: Nagi, "Labor Immigration and Development"].
104 Tayseer Abdel-Jaber, "Trends and Prospects of Brain Drain from Arab Countries," in ECWA, *International Migration in the Arab World*, Proceedings of an ECWA Population Conference, Nicosia, Cyprus, 11–16 May 1981, Vol. 2 (Beirut, 1982), p. 781 [hereafter: Abdel-Jaber, "Trends and Prospects of Brain Drain"]; Hassan

Bin Talal (His Royal Highness Prince Hassan Bin Talal is the Crown Prince of the Hashemite Kingdom of Jordan), "Manpower Migration in the Middle East: An Overview," *The Middle East Journal*, Vol. 38, No. 1 (1984), p. 614.

105 World Bank, *World Tables*, 1995 edition, pp. 258–9, 386–7.

106 Findlay, "Return to Yemen," p. 215.

107 World Bank, *World Tables*, 1995 edition, pp. 650–1.

108 Allan Findlay and Musa Samha, "Return Migration and Urban Change: A Jordanian Case Study," in Russell King (ed.), *Return Migration and Regional Economic Problems* (London: Croom-Helm, 1986), p. 179, table 8.4.

109 Roger Owen, "The Arab Economies in the 1970s," *Merip Reports*, Vol. 11 (October–December 1981), p. 8; see also: Nagi, "Labor Immigration and Development," p. 202.

110 *The New York Times Magazine*, 1 April 1990; *Financial Times*, 11 May 1993, p. 4.

111 *MEED*, 18 November 1994, p. 12.

112 World Bank, *World Tables*, 1995 edition, p. 650.

113 M. Samha, "Population Spatial Distribution Policies in Jordan," in ESCWA, *Population Spatial Distribution* (Amman, August 1993), p. 93.

114 Nazli Choucri, "Migration in the Middle East: Old Economics or New Politics?" *Journal of Arab Affairs*, Vol. 7, No. 1 (1988), p. 12 [hereafter: Choucri, "Migration in the Middle East: Old Economics or New Politics?"].

115 Serageldin et al., *Manpower and International Labor Migration*, p. 68.

116 Nagi, "Labor Immigration and Development," p. 205.

117 See: Seccombe, "Immigrant Workers in an Emigrant Economy," pp. 377–8.

118 Kanovsky, "Migration from the Poor to the Rich Arab Countries," p. 56, table 1.

119 World Bank, *World Tables*, 1989–90 edition, p. 227.

120 Choucri, "Migration in the Middle East: Old Economics or New Politics?" p. 12.

121 Regarding the development of the Egyptian migration policy, see: A. Dessouki, "The Shift in Egypt's Migration Policy, 1952–78," *Middle Eastern Studies*, Vol. 18, No. 1 (1982), pp. 53–68.

122 *al-Musawwar*, 30 June 1989, p. 17.

123 World Bank, *World Tables*, 1989–90 edition, pp. 226–7.

5 Demographic Policies of the Syrian Authorities

1 Gabriel Baer, *The Arabs of the Middle East: Population and Society* (Tel Aviv: Hakibbutz Hameuchad, 1973), p. 39 (in Hebrew).

2 Regarding the rapid urbanization process and its socioeconomic consequences in developing countries, see: Hay, "Patterns of Urbanization," pp. 71–101; Saad Eddin Ibrahim, "Arab Cities: Present Situation and Future Prospects," Paper presented at the Second Regional Population Conference of ECWA, Damascus, 1–6 December 1979.

3 Richard Symonds and Michael Carder, *The United Nations and the Population Question, 1945–1970* (New York: McGraw-Hill, Book Company, 1973), p. xiv.

4 See: Muhammad Faour, "Fertility Policy and Family Planning in the Arab

Countries," *Studies in Family Planning*, Vol. 20, No. 5 (September/October 1989), pp. 256–60; International Planned Parenthood Federation – Middle East and North Africa Region, "Family Planning and Population Policies in the Middle East and North Africa," in James Allman (ed.), *Women's Status and Fertility in the Muslim World* (New York and London: Praeger Publishers, 1981), pp. 37–46.

5   See: Onn Winckler, "Consequences of the Rapid Population Growth and the Fertility Policies in the Arab Countries of the Middle East," paper presented at the conference: "Transformations of Middle Eastern Natural Environment: Legacies and Lessons," Yale University, October 30–1 November 1997, pp. 11–18.

6   Adnan Habbab, "Family Planning in the Syrian Arab Republic," paper presented at the First Regional Population Conference of ECWA, Beirut, 18 February–1 March 1974, pp. 5–6 [hereafter: Habbab, "Family Planning"].

7   CBS, *Socio-Economic Development in Syria, 1960–1970*, p. 47.

8   Ibid., pp. 43–4.

9   *Population Policy Compendium, Syrian Arab Republic*, pp. 4–5.

10 *al-Ba'th*, 14 July 1994.

11 Abou-Gamrah, "Fertility Levels," p. 208.

12 *Tishrin*, 23 August 1982.

13 Habbab, "Family Planning," pp. 8–9; *al-Ba'th*, 28 April 1974; ESCWA, *Population Situation, 1990*, p. 192; *Population Policy Compendium, Syrian Arab Republic*, p. 4.

14 *Tishrin*, 29 June 1979.

15 *Tishrin*, 30 May 1982.

16 *Tishrin*, 22 June 1980.

17 See for example: *Tishrin*, 23 August, 6 September, 20 October, 21 October 1982, 7 December 1983, 27 January 1984, 30 October 1985.

18 *Tishrin*, 21 May 1985.

19 See: Gilbar, *Population Dilemmas*, pp. 122–5.

20 ESCWA, *Population Situation, 1990*, p. 192.

21 See: Eyal Zisser, "Syria," *MECS*, Vol. 18 (1994), p. 619.

22 Regarding the use of religious legitimacy to promote the practice of contraceptives in Egypt, see: Gilbar, *Population Dilemmas*, p. 121; Arab Republic of Egypt, Ministry of Waqfs and Ministry of Information, State Information Service, Information, Education and Communication Center, *Islam's Attitude Towards Family Planning* (Cairo, 1994). This publication was represented during the UN Conference on Population and Development, held in Cairo in September 1994; Regarding Jordan, see: Winckler, *Population Growth and Migration in Jordan*, p. 82.

23 *Tishrin*, 10 April 1994.

24 See for example: *Tishrin*, 4 August 1992; *al-Thawra*, 4 April 1993.

25 *Tishrin*, 23 August 1982.

26 Syrian Arab Republic, Office of the Prime Minister, State Planning Commission, *Fifth Five Year Economic and Social Development Plan of the Syrian Arab Republic, 1981–1985* (Damascus: Arab Office for Press and Documentation, August 1982), p. 30.

27   ESCWA, *Population Situation, 1990*, p. 190, table 11.8.

28 Ibid., p. 99, table 5.8; see also: ESCWA, *Arab Women in ESCWA Member States* (New York, 1994), pp. 155–74, table 18.

29   ILO, *Yearbook of Labour Statistics – 1992*, p. 18, table 1.

30   Syria, *Statistical Abstract – 1971*, p. 337, table 184.

31   UNESCO, *Statistical Yearbook – 1990* (Paris, 1991), p. 3–241, table 3.10.

32   UNESCO, *Statistical Yearbook – 1994*, p. 3–254, table 3.11.

33   Ibid. and UNESCO, *Statistical Yearbook – 1990*, p. 3–241, table 3.10.

34   See also in this regard: Weinbaum, *Food, Development, and Politics in the Middle East*, pp. 47–8.

35   See below, pp. 123.

36   See below, pp. 123–4.

37   Raymond A. Hinnebusch, "Party and Peasant in Syria," *Cairo Papers in Social Science*, Vol. 3, Monograph 1 (November 1979), p. 17 [hereafter: Hinnebusch, "Party and Peasant"].

38   Regarding the joining of Asad to the Ba'th party in 1946, see: Ma'oz, *Asad*, pp. 35–6; Patrick Seale, *Asad of Syria: The Struggle for the Middle East* (London: I. B. Tauris, 1988), pp. 35–7 [hereafter: Seale, *Asad*].

39   John J. Devlin, *The Ba'th Party: A History from its Origins to 1966* (Stanford: Hoover Institution Press, Stanford University, 1979), Appendix D, p. 349; a wide discussion on the socialism policy of the Ba'th party appears in: Kamal Abu-Jaber, *The Arab Ba'th Socialist Party: History, Ideology, and Organization* (New York: Syracuse University Press, 1966), pp. 111–24.

40   Petran, *Syria*, pp. 205–9.

41   Nikolaos Van Dam, "Sectarian and Regional Factionalism in the Syrian Political Elite," *The Middle East Journal*, Vol. 32, No. 2 (1978), p. 202, table I, p. 204, table II.

42   Doreen Warriner, *Land Reform and Development in the Middle East: A Study of Egypt, Syria, and Iraq* (London and New York: Oxford University Press, 1962), pp. 71–2.

43   R. S. Porter, "The Growth of the Syrian Economy," *Middle East Forum*, Vol. 39 (November 1963), p. 20.

44   See also in this regard: IBRD (International Bank for Reconstruction and Development), *The Economic Development of Syria* (Baltimore: The Johns Hopkins University Press, 1955), pp. 354–5; Bishara Khader, "Propriété Agricole et Réforme Agraire en Syrie," *Civilisations*, Vol. 25 (1975), pp. 64–8; Eva Garzouzi, "Land Reform in Syria," *The Middle East Journal*, Vol. 17 (Winter — Spring 1963), p. 83 [hereafter: Garzouzi, "Land Reform"].

45   Garzouzi, "Land Reform," p. 83.

46   UNESOB, *Studies on Social Development in the Middle East, 1971*, p. 95; see also: Doreen Warriner, *Land and Poverty in the Middle East* (London and New York: Royal Institute of International Affairs, 1948), pp. 84–91.

47   See: Françoise Metral, "State and Peasants in Syria: A Local View of A Government Irrigation Project," *Peasant Studies*, Vol. 11, No. 2 (Winter 1984), p. 70 [hereafter: Metral, "State and Peasants in Syria"].

48 UNESOB, *Studies on Social Development in the Middle East, 1971*, pp. 88–9.

49 See: UNESOB, *Studies on Selected Development Problems in Various Countries in the Middle East, 1971* (New York, 1971), p. 7, note 25.

50 Ziad Keilany, "Land Reform in Syria," *Middle Eastern Studies*, Vol. 16, No. 3 (October 1980), pp. 210–11 [hereafter: Keilany, "Land Reform in Syria"]; Garzouzi, "Land Reform," p. 85.

51 UNESOB, *Studies on Social Development in the Middle East, 1971*, p. 95.

52 Ian R. Manners and Tagi Sagafi-Nejad, "Agricultural Development in Syria," in Beaumont and McLachlan (eds), *Agricultural Development in the Middle East*, p. 271 [hereafter: Manners and Sagafi-Nejad, "Agricultural Development in Syria"].

53 Keilany, "Land Reform in Syria," pp. 211–12.

54 Regarding the pace of the implementing of the agrarian reform law, see: Sayigh, *The Economies of the Arab World*, p. 258.

55 Regarding the various irrigation projects conducted in Syria, see below, pp. 127–9.

56 UNESOB, *Studies on Selected Development Problems in Various Countries in the Middle East, 1971*, p. 37, tables 7 and 8.

57 Perthes, *The Political Economy of Syria under Asad*, p. 81.

58 Hinnebusch, *Peasant and Bureaucracy*, p. 98.

59 Manners and Sagafi-Nejad, "Agricultural Development in Syria," p. 273, table 14.7.

60 Perthes, *The Political Economy of Syria under Asad*, pp. 83–6; Garzouzi, "Land Reform," p. 89.

61 Keilany, "Land Reform," p. 218.

62 "Special Report on Syria," pp. x–xi.

63 UNFPA, *Syrian Arab Republic*, pp. 16–17.

64 Regarding the implementation of the *Ghab–Asharneh* project, see: Metral, "State and Peasants in Syria," pp. 71–87; Hinnebusch, *Peasant and Bureaucracy*, pp. 223–32; *All About the Projects of Development in Syria – Present Status – Analytical Study – Figures* (Beirut: Syrian Documentation Papers, 1971), p. 33.

65 Hans Meliczek, "Land Settlement in the Euphrates Basin of Syria," *Ekistics*, Vol. 53, No. 318/319 (May/June–July/August 1986), p. 202 [hereafter: Meliczek, "Land Settlement"].

66 Annika Rabo, "Great Expectations: Perceptions on Development in Northeast Syria," *Ethnos*, Vol. 49, No. 3–4 (1984), p. 212; "Special Report on Syria," p. xi.

67 *MEED*, 31 March 1978, p. 33.

68 *MEED*, 12 May 1978, p. 50.

69 Meliczek, "Land Settlement," p. 211; EIU, *Country Profile – Syria, 1986–87*, p. 21; Seale, *Asad*, p. 445.

70 "Syria's Budget: Where the Cash Flows in '87," *The Middle East* (May 1987), p. 33 [hereafter: *The Middle East* (May 1987)].

71 Regarding the Syrian complaints about the amount of the Euphrates River's water released by Turkey in recent years, see: *Jordan Times*, 11 May 1996.

72 Meliczek, "Land Settlement," p. 211; EIU, *Country Profile – Syria, 1986–87*, p. 26; *The Middle East* (December 1988), p. 27.

73 Alasdair Drysdale, "The Regional Equalization of Health Care and Education in

Syria Since the Ba'thi Revolution," *IJMES*, Vol. 13 (1981), p. 94 [hereafter: Drysdale, "The Regional Equalization of Health Care and Education"].

74 Syrian Arab Republic, Ministry of Planning, *Third Five Year Plan for Economic and Social Development in the Syrian Arab Republic, 1971–1975* (Damascus: Office Arabe de Presse et de Documentation, 1971), p. 2 [hereafter: Syria, *Third Five Year Plan, 1971–75*].

75 Syrian Arab Republic, Ministry of Planning, *Fourth Five Year Economic and Social Development Plan of the Syrian Arab Republic, 1976–1980* (Damascus: Arab Office for Press and Documentation, 1977), Annex No. 1: General and Strategic Aims of the Plan, no page.

76 Delwin A. Roy and Thomas Naff, "Ba'thist Ideology, Economic Development and Educational Strategy," *Middle Eastern Studies*, Vol. 25, No. 4 (October 1989), p. 453.

77 The data for 1970 is taken from: Syria, *Statistical Abstract – 1971*, p. 336, table 183. The data for 1990 is taken from: Syria, *Statistical Abstract – 1991*, p. 315, table 7/10.

78 Syria, *Statistical Abstract – 1994*, p. 76, table 3/3; p. 77, table 3/4.

79 See: Drysdale, "The Regional Equalization of Health Care and Education," pp. 104–5, tables 3 and 4.

80 See: Perthes, *The Political Economy of Syria under Asad*, p. 94.

81 Syria, *Statistical Abstract – 1991*, pp. 74–5, tables 3/3 and 3/4.

82 Drysdale, "The Regional Equalization of Health Care and Education," p. 94.

83 Ibid., p. 95.

84 Petran, *Syria*, p. 219.

85 ESCWA, *Population Situation, 1990*, p. 192.

86 Petran, *Syria*, p. 219; Drysdale, "The Regional Equalization of Health Care and Education," p. 100.

87 UNDP, *Human Development Report – 1994*, p. 148, table 10.

88 See chapter 3.

89 Syria, *Third Five-Year Plan, 1971–75*, p. 10.

90 "MEED Special Report – Syria," *MEED*, March 1980, p. 20.

91 *MEED*, 28 September 1979, p. 42.

92 *MEED*, 24 March 1978, p. 34.

93 *MEED*, 13 February 1981, p. 38.

94 Ibid.; *MEED*, 24 March 1978, p. 34.

95 Ibid.; "MEED Special Report – Syria," *MEED*, March 1980, p. 20.

96 *MEED*, 20 March 1981, p. 41.

97 Alan George, "Syria Transforms its Electricity System," *The Middle East* (December 1995), pp. 29–30 [hereafter: *The Middle East* (December 1995)].

98 *Tishrin*, 6 March 1989.

99 *Tishrin*, 19 November 1990.

100 *al-Ba'th*, 10 March 1991.

101 *The Middle East* (December 1995), p. 29.

102 Seale, *Asad*, p. 447.

103 See: *MEED*, 24 May 1996, p. 11.

104 See in this regard chapter 6: Conclusions.
105 *The Middle East* (December 1995), p. 29.
106 *MEED*, 24 May 1996, p. 11; Alan George, "Syrian Construction Market Expands," *The Middle East* (September 1995), p. 19 [hereafter: *The Middle East* (September 1995)].
107 I. J. Seccombe and R. I. Lawless, "State Intervention and the International Labour Market: A Review of Labour Emigration Policies in the Arab World," in Reginald Appleyard (ed.), *The Impact of International Migration on Developing Countries* (Paris: Development Centre of the Organization for Economic Co-Operation and Development, 1989), pp. 83–4.
108 John M. Wardwell, "Jordan," in William J. Serow, Charles B. Nam, David F. Sly, and Robert H. Weller (eds), *Handbook on International Migration* (New York, Westport, and London: Greenwood Press, 1990), p. 168.
109 World Bank, *World Tables*, 1995 edition, pp. 258–9.
110 See: Abdel-Jaber, "Trends and Prospects of Brain Drain," pp. 783–4.
111 ESCWA, *Population Situation, 1990*, p. 192; see also: Hameed, "Manpower and Employment Planning," p. 28.
112 Ziauddin Sardar, *Science and Technology in the Middle East* (London and New York: Longman, 1982), p. 12.
113 Sales, *International Migration Project: Syrian Arab Republic*, pp. 63–4.
114 *MEED*, 25 May 1979, p. 47.
115 See: *al-Thawra*, 28 June 1988.
116 *MEED*, 1 May 1985, p. 34.
117 Ibid.
118 World Bank, *World Tables*, 1989–90 edition, pp. 544–6.
119 ILO, *Yearbook of Labour Statistics – 1992*, p. 37, table 1.
120 *Tishrin*, 11, 17 September 1990; see also: 6 July 1989.
121 *MEED*, 18 November 1994, p. 10; 24 May 1996, p. 8.
122 *MEED*, 13 April 1979, p. 3.
123 *MEED*, 13 October 1989, pp. 4–5.
124 Peter H. Gleick, "Water, War, and Peace in the Middle East," *Environment*, Vol. 36, No. 3 (April 1994), pp. 12–13 and p. 37, table 3.
125 Syria, *Statistical Abstract – 1987*, pp. 54–7, table 2/2.
126 *MEED*, 20 September 1991, p. 15.
127 World Bank, *World Development Report – 1993*, p. 242, table 3.
128 *Jordan Times*, 14 October 1991.
129 Nasra M. Shah, "Arab Labour Migration: A Review of Trends and Issues," *International Migration*, Vol. 32, No. 1 (1994), p. 10.
130 See for example: *Ha'aretz*, 29 June 1998.

6 Conclusions: Demography, Economy, and Political Changes under Asad

1 Rizkallah Hilan, "The Effects on Economic Development in Syria of a Just and Long-Lasting Peace," in Stanley Fischer, Dani Rodrik, and Elias Tuma (eds), *The*

Economics of Middle East Peace (Cambridge, Mass. and London: The MIT Press, 1993), p. 61 [hereafter: Hilan, "The Effects on Economic Development in Syria;" and Fischer et al. (eds), *The Economics of Middle East Peace*]; see also: Moshe Ma'oz, *Syria and Israel: From War to Peace Making* (Ma'ariv Book Guild: Or Yehuda, 1996), pp. 162–6 (in Hebrew) [hereafter: Ma'oz, *Syria and Israel*].

2 Gilbar, *The Economic Development of the Middle East*, pp. 204–5; see also: Hilan, "The Effects on Economic Development in Syria," p. 60, table 3.1.

3 United States Arms Control and Disarmament Agency (USACDA), *World Military Expenditures and Arms Transfers, 1972–1982* (Washington, D.C.: April 1984), p. 88, table II [hereafter: USACDA, *World Military Expenditures and Arms Transfers*].

4 *The Middle East* (May 1987), p. 33; see also: *The Middle East* (December 1988), p. 27; *Financial Times*, 4 January 1989, p. 3; *MEED*, 28 May 1982, p. 44.

5 *Financial Times*, 2 June 1986, p. 5.

6 *Financial Times*, 8 December 1986, p. 4.

7 Gilbar, *The Economic Development of the Middle East*, p. 204; Ma'oz, *Asad*, p. 193.

8 *Financial Times*, 8 December 1986, p. 4.

9 Nabil Sukkar, "The Crisis of 1986 and Syria's Plan for Reform," in Eberhard Kienle (ed.), *Contemporary Syria: Liberalization between Cold War and Cold Peace* (London: British Academic Press in association with the Centre of Near and Middle Eastern Studies, School of Oriental and African Studies, University of London, 1994), p. 27 [hereafter: Sukkar, "The Crisis of 1986 and Syria's Plan for Reform" and Kienle (ed.), *Contemporary Syria*]; idem, "Economic Liberalization in Syria," in Hans Hopfinger (ed.), *Economic Liberalization and Privatization in Socialist Arab Countries: Algeria, Egypt, Syria and Yemen as Examples* (Gotha: Justus Perthes Verlag, 1996), p. 147 [hereafter: Sukkar, "Economic Liberalization in Syria"].

10 Drysdale, "The Asad Regime and its Troubles," p. 5; *MEED*, 22 May 1981, p. 38.

11 Regarding the effects of the "oil boom" on the Syrian economy, see also: Eliyahu Kanovsky, "Middle East Economies and Arab-Israeli Peace Agreements," *Israel Affairs*, Vol. 1, No. 4 (Summer 1995), p. 28 [hereafter: Kanovsky, "Middle East Economies and Arab-Israeli Peace Agreements"].

12 World Bank, *World Tables*, 1989–90 edition, pp. 544–5.

13 *The Economist*, 3 May 1986, p. 51.

14 Raymond A. Hinnebusch, "Syria," in Tim Niblock and Emma Murphy (eds), *Economic and Political Liberalization in the Middle East* (London and New York: British Academic Press, 1993), p. 188 [hereafter: Hinnebusch, "Syria"].

15 See: *MEED*, 11 April 1987, p. 36.

16 Sukkar, "The Crisis of 1986 and Syria's Plan for Reform," p. 27.

17 *MEED*, 14 November 1987, p. 49.

18 *al-Hayat* (London), 26 January 1992.

19 *MEED*, 14 November 1987, p. 49.

20 Sukkar, "The Crisis of 1986 and Syria's Plan for Reform," p. 28; see also: *Financial Times*, 8 December 1986, p. 4.

21 *Financial Times*, 6 May 1988, p. 3; Volker Perthes, "The Private Sector, Economic Liberalization, and the Prospects of Democratization: The Case of Syria and some Other Arab Countries," in Ghassan Salamé (ed.), *Democracy Without Democrats? The Renewal of Politics in the Muslim World* (London and New York: I. B. Tauris Publishers, 1994), p. 245 [hereafter: Perthes, "The Private Sector, Economic Liberalization, and the Prospects of Democratization"].

22 *The New York Times Magazine*, 1 April 1990, p. 33; see also: *Financial Times*, 4 January 1989, p. 3.

23 Kanovsky, "Middle East Economies and Arab-Israeli Peace Agreements," p. 29.

24 World Bank, *World Tables*, 1995 edition, p. 649.

25 See: *Financial Times*, 8 December 1986, p. 4.

26 *Financial Times*, 6 May 1988, p. 3.

27 Ma'oz, *Syria and Israel*, p. 157; see also: Ze'ev Shif and Ehud Ya'ari, *Milhemet Sholal* [The Misleading War] (Tel Aviv: Schocken Publishing House, 1984), pp. 203–4 (in Hebrew).

28 *The Middle East* (December 1988), p. 27.

29 USACDA, *World Military Expenditures and Arms Transfers, 1996*, p. 93, table I.

30 EIU, *Country Profile – Syria, 1997–98*, p. 8.

31 Regarding to the Soviet–Syrian Treaty of Friendship and Cooperation which was signed in October 1980, see: Galia Golan, *Soviet Policies in the Middle East from World War Two to Gorbachev* (Cambridge and New York: Cambridge University Press, 1991), pp. 153–5; Robert O. Freedman, *Moscow and the Middle East: Soviet Policy since the Invasion of Afghanistan* (Cambridge and New York: Cambridge University Press, 1991), pp. 92–3.

32 See: Volker Perthes, "Incremental Change in Syria," *Current History*, Vol. 92 (1993), p. 24 [hereafter: Perthes, "Incremental Change in Syria"].

33 Yahya M. Sadowski, "Cadres, Guns, and Money: The Eight Regional Congress of the Syrian Ba'th," *Merip Reports* (July/August 1985), p. 6.

34 Alan George, "No Going Back," *The Middle East* (November 1996), p. 20 [hereafter: *The Middle East* (November 1996)]; regarding Law No. 10 of 1986, see: Sylvia Pölling, "Investment Law No. 10: Which Future for the Private Sector?" in Kienle (ed.), *Contemporary Syria*, pp. 15–19 [hereafter: Pölling, "Investment Law No. 10"].

35 Hinnebusch, "Syria," pp. 188–9.

36 Eberhard Kienle, "Syria, the Kuwait War, and the New World Order," in Tarek Y. Ismael and Jacqueline S. Ismael (eds), *The Gulf War and the New World Order* (Gainesville: University Press of Florida, 1994), p. 385.

37 *MEED*, 29 September 1995, p. 10.

38 *MEED*, 18 November 1994, p. 10.

39 *The Jerusalem Post*, 21 January 1992.

40 *MEED*, 29 September 1995, p. 12; 9 February 1996, p. 2; *Ha'aretz*, 9 September 1992.

41 *Jordan Times*, 11–12 April 1996.

42 *MEED*, 24 May 1996, p. 7.

43 ESCWA, *Survey of Economic and Social Developments in the ESCWA Region –*
    1995 (New York, 1996), p. 27.
44 *MEED*, 9 February 1996, p. 2.
45 See also: *Jordan Times*, 13–14 June 1996.
46 ESCWA, *National Accounts Studies of the ESCWA Region*, Bulletin No. 17 (New
    York, 1997), p. 15.
47 Perthes, "The Private Sector, Economic Liberalization, and the Prospects of
    Democratization," p. 249.
48 Pölling, "Investment Law No. 10," p. 20; Sukkar, "Economic Liberalization in
    Syria," p. 148; *The Wall Street Journal*, 4 January 1994; *Financial Times*, 28 July
    1995, p. 16.
49 *MEED*, 29 September 1995, p. 14; see also: "Syria: Secretive Power Play," *The*
    Middle East (January 1994), p. 32; Mariam Shahin, "Syria: Secret to the Economic
    Future," *The Middle East* (February 1995), pp. 27–8 [hereafter: *The Middle East*
    (February 1995)].
50 *Yedioth Ahronoth*, 27 November 1996.
51 *MEED*, 29 September 1995, p. 14.
52 *The Middle East* (November 1996), p. 20; see also: Glenn E. Robinson, "Elite
    Cohesion, Regime Succession and Political Instability in Syria," *Middle East*
    Policy, Vol. 5, No. 4 (January 1988), p. 162.
53 *The Middle East* (February 1995), p. 28.
54 *MEED*, 24 May 1996, p. 8.
55 *Jordan Times*, 7 May 1996.
56 World Tourism Organization, *Yearbook of Tourism Statistics – 1990*, 43rd edition
    (Madrid, 1991), p. 113.
57 *MEED*, 24 May 1996, p. 8; see also: 18 November 1994, p. 8.
58 *The Middle East* (November 1996), p. 20.
59 *MEED*, 9 February 1996, p. 2.
60 *The Wall Street Journal*, 7 November 1996.
61 EIU, *Country Profile – Syria, 1997–98*, p. 10.
62 *The Middle East* (September 1995), p. 20.
63 Perthes, "The Private Sector, Economic Liberalization, and the Prospects of
    Democratization," p. 268.
64   *MEED*, 29 September 1995, p. 10.
65 *MEED*, 24 May 1996, p. 8.
66 EIU, *Country Profile – Syria, 1997–98*, p. 32; *MEED*, 18 November 1994, p. 10.
67 *The Middle East* (February 1995), pp. 28–9.
68 *MEED*, 29 September 1995, p. 11.
69 EIU, *Country Profile – Syria, 1998–99*, p. 29.
70 *MEED*, 9 February 1996, p. 3.
71 EIU, *Country Profile – Syria, 1997–98*, p. 32; *MEED*, 29 September 1995, pp.
    10–11; 18 November 1994, p. 10.
72 EIU, *Country Profile – Syria, 1998–99*, p. 30.
73 See: *MEED*, 8 October 1993, p. 3.

74 Regarding the distribution among the private and the public sectors in the Syrian various economic activities by mid-1996, see: *Jordan Times*, 13–14 June 1996.

75 Regarding Egypt, see: Gilbar, *The Economic Development of the Middle East*, pp. 197–202; Heba Handoussa and Nemat Shafik, "The Economics of Peace: The Egyptian Case," in Fischer et al. (eds), *The Economics of Middle East Peace*, pp. 19–54; Regarding Jordan, see: Onn Winckler, "The Economic Factor of the Middle East Peace Process: The Jordanian Case," in Ginat and Winckler (eds), *The Jordanian–Palestinian–Israeli Triangle* , pp. 156–77.

Appendices

Appendix 1 Distribution of Syria's population, according to sex, 1937–95 (in thousands)

Year	Males	Females	Total	Year	Males	Females	Total
1937	1,186	1,182	2,368	1967	2,913	2,767	5,680
1938	1,251	1,236	2,487	1968	3,008	2,858	5,866
1939	1,280	1,265	2,545	1969	3,107	2,952	6,059
1940	1,336	1,313	2,649	1970	3,233	3,072	6,305
1941	1,363	1,334	2,697	1971	3,310	3,157	6,467
1942	1,417	1,375	2,792	1972	3,421	3,263	6,684
1943	1,411	1,449	2,860	1973	3,536	3,372	6,908
1944	1,471	1,430	2,901	1974	3,655	3,485	7,140
1945	1,496	1,454	2,950	1975	3,777	3,603	7,380
1946	1,524	1,482	3,006	1976	3,904	3,723	7,627
1947	1,544	1,499	3,043	1977	4,035	3,848	7,883
1948	1,571	1,521	3,092	1978	4,170	3,978	8,148
1949	1,619	1,559	3,178	1979	4,310	4,111	8,421
1950	1,656	1,596	3,252	1980	4,455	4,249	8,704
1951	1,696	1,633	3,329	1981	4,622	4,424	9,046
1952	1,752	1,682	3,434	1982	4,749	4,549	9,298
1953	1,869	1,787	3,656	1983	4,909	4,702	9,611
1954	1,949	1,858	3,807	1984	5,074	4,860	9,934
1955	2,007	1,908	3,915	1985	5,244	5,023	10,267
1956	2,066	1,959	4,025	1986	5,420	5,192	10,612
1957	2,130	2,015	4,145	1987	5,603	5,366	10,969
1958	2,263	2,157	4,420	1988	5,793	5,545	11,338
1959	2,385	2,271	4,656	1989	5,986	5,733	11,719
1960	2,344	2,221	4,565	1990	6,189	5,927	12,116
1961	2,400	2,280	4,680	1991	6,400	6,129	12,529
1962	2,487	2,355	4,833	1992	6,620	6,338	12,958
1963	2,560	2,432	4,992	1993	6,842	6,551	13,393
1964	2,644	2,512	5,156	1994	7,005	6,807	13,812
1965	2,731	2,594	5,325	1995	7,194	6,992	14,186
1966	2,820	2,680	5,500				

Note: 1957, 1960, 1970, 1994 – censuses data.

Sources: 1937–59: *Statistiques Syriennes – Comparées 1928–1968*, p. 10
1960–83: Syria, *Statistical Abstract – 1984*, p. 61, table 5/2.
1984–90: Syria, *Statistical Abstract – 1991*, p. 56, table 6/2.
1991–93: Syria, *Statistical Abstract – 1991*, p. 58, table 6/2.
1994–95: Syria, *Statistical Abstract – 1995*, p. 58, table 6/2.

Appendix 2   Syrian cultivated area, 1920–94 (in thousands of hectares*)

Year	Non-Irrigated	Irrigated	Total cropped area	Total cultivated area
1920	–	–	–	700
1921	–	–	–	–
1922	–	86	–	1,050
1923	–	–	–	–
1924	–	–	–	–
1925	–	–	–	–
1926	–	160	–	1,193
1927	–	–	–	–
1928	–	–	–	1,600
1929	–	–	–	864
1930	–	–	–	1,040
1931	–	–	–	956
1932	–	–	–	1,135
1933	–	–	809	1,050
1934	–	–	809	–
1935	–	–	809	–
1936	–	–	809	–
1937	–	–	809	–
1938	–	–	809	–
1942	–	–	939	–
1945	–	–	1,510	2,290
1950	–	333	–	2,500
1951	–	–	–	3,490
1952	–	–	–	3,230
1953	1,931	509	2,440	3,670
1956	3,908	682	4,590	4,590
1957	4,067	583	4,560	4,650
1958	4,862	590	5,452	5,452
1959	2,901	476	3,377	5,491
1960	2,953	527	3,480	6,014
1961	3,256	558	3,814	6,381
1962	2,544	657	3,201	6,263
1963	3,083	670	3,753	6,942
1964	2,761	489	3,250	6,654
1965	2,826	522	3,348	6,341
1966	2,620	507	3,127	6,130
1967	2,800	538	3,338	6,097
1968	2,171	476	2,647	5,864
1969	2,934	546	3,480	5,875
1970	2,841	450	3,291	5,899
1971	2,340	476	2,816	5,908
1972	2,479	625	3,104	6,001
1973	2,778	619	3,397	5,808
1974	2,956	578	3,534	6,027
1976	3,702	547	4,249	5,544
1977	3,336	531	3,867	5,509

1978	3,215	519	3,734	5,588
1979	3,300	539	3,839	5,686
1980	3,354	539	3,893	5,684
1981	3,286	567	3,853	5,759
1982	3,432	555	3,987	5,801
1983	3,490	580	4,070	5,607
1984	3,117	618	3,735	5,655
1985	3,318	652	3,970	5,623
1986	3,251	652	3,903	5,627
1987	3,387	654	4,041	5,630
1988	3,647	650	4,297	5,560
1989	4,727	670	5,397	5,503
1990	4,773	693	5,466	5,626
1991	4,065	788	4,853	5,576
1992	4,215	906	5,121	5,554
1993	3,926	1,013	4,939	5,426
1994	3,770	1,082	4,852	5,487

* Hectare = 2.47 acres.

– No data available.

Sources:

1920–33: Albert Khuri, "Agriculture," in Himadeh (ed.), *Economic Organization of Syria*, pp. 74, 102.

1934–42: UN Department of Economic Affairs, *Review of Economic Conditions in the Middle East* (New York, March 1951), p. 45, table 5.

1945: Hansen, *Economic Development in Syria*, p. 20, table 4.

1950: UN, Department of Economic Affairs, *Review of Economic Conditions in the Middle East, 1951–1952*, Supplement to World Economic Report (New York, March 1953), p. 16, table 5.

1951–52: Adnan Mahhouk, "Recent Agricultural Development and Bedouin Settlement in Syria," *The Middle East Journal*, Vol. 10 (Spring 1956), p. 171, table 11.

1953: Kanovsky, *The Economic Development of Syria*, p. 21, table 4.

1956: "Development Planning and Social Objectives in Syria," p. 36, table 5.

1957–64: Syria, *Statistical Abstract – 1966*, p. 283, table 142.

1965–70: Syria, *Statistical Abstract – 1971*, p. 66, table 26.

1971–72: Syria, *Statistical Abstract – 1973*, p. 154, table 6/4.

1973: Kanovsky, *The Economic Development of Syria*, p. 21, table 4.

1974: EIU, *Syria, Lebanon, Cyprus, Annual Supplement – 1977*, p. 9.

1976–77: EIU, *Syria, Annual Supplement – 1982*, p. 11

1978–81: Syria, *Statistical Abstract – 1983*, p. 118, table 6/4.

1982–86: Syria, *Statistical Abstract – 1987*, p. 117, table 6/4.

1987–90: Syria, *Statistical Abstract – 1992*, p. 102, table 6/4.

1991–94: Syria, *Statistical Abstract – 1995*, p. 104, table 6/4.

Appendix 3: Syria: World bank Demographic Projections, 2000–20

	2000–2005	2005–2010	2010–2015	2015–2020
Population (thousands)	(a) 16,934	(b) 19, 948	(c) 23,331	(d) 30,375
Crude birth rate (per thousand)	38.1	35.1	31.8	28.0
Crude death rate (per thousand)	4.3	3.8	3.6	3.5
Total fertility rate	5.25	4.65	4.05	3.45
Infant mortality rate (per thousand live births)	24.1	19.5	17.9	16.3
Life expectancy at birth (years)	70.29	71.93	72.69	73.48

(a) projection for the year 2000.

(b) projection for the year 2005.

(c) projection for the year 2010.

(d) projection for the year 2020.

Source: The World Bank, by Eduard Bos, My T. Vu, Ernest Massaiah, and Rodolfo A. Bulatao, *World Population Projections, 1994–95 Edition, Estimates and Projections with Related Demographic Statistics* (Baltimore and London: The Johns Hopkins University Press, 1995), p. 464.

Bibliography

OFFICIAL PUBLICATIONS

Arab Republic of Egypt
Central Agency for Public Mobilisation and Statistics (CAPMAS). *Statistical Yearbook*, 1980–1996, Various Issues. Cairo.
Ministry of Waqfs and Ministry of Information, State Information Service, Information, Education and Communication Center. *Islam's Attitude Towards Family Planning*. Cairo, 1994.

Bahrain
Ministry of Finance and National Economy. *Statistical Abstract*, 1975–1994, Various Issues. Manama.

Great Britain
Naval Intelligence Division. *Syria*. London: H.M. Stationery Office. April 1943.

The Hashemite Kingdom of Jordan
Department of Statistics. *Statistical Yearbook*, 1965–1996, Various Issues. Amman.
—— and Ministry of Health, by Abdallah Abdel-Aziz Zou'bi, Sri Poedijastoeti, and Mohamed Ayad. *Jordan Population and Family Health Survey – 1990*. Amman, August 1992.

Kuwait
Ministry of Planning, Central Statistical Office. *Annual Statistical Abstract*, 1968–1994, Various Issues. Kuwait: Government Printing Press.

The Sultanate of Oman
Development Council. *The Five-Year Development Plan, 1976–1980*. Muscat, 1976.
Ministry of Development, Information and Documentation Center. *Statistical Yearbook*, 1980–1994, Various Issues. Muscat: Government Printing Press.
——. *General Census of Population, Housing and Establishments, 1993*. Muscat, 1995.

Qatar
Presidency of the Council of Ministers, Central Statistical Organization. *Statistical*

Bibliography

Abstract, 1981–1993, Various Issues. Doha.

Kingdom of Saudi Arabia
Central Planning Organization. *Development Plan, 1390 AH*. Riyadh, 1970.
Ministry of Planning. *The Third Development Plan, 1980–1985*. Riyadh, 1980.

Syrian Arab Republic
Agriculture in the Syrian Arab Republic. Serié Etudes No. 178. Office Arabe de Presse et de Documentation, 1978.
All About the Projects of Development in Syria – Present Status – Analytical Study – Figures. Beirut: Syrian Documentation Papers, 1971.
Statistiques Syriennes, Comparées 1928–1968. Damas: Office Arabe de Presse et de Documentation, Avril 1970.
Office of the Prime Minister, Central Bureau of Statistics. *Statistical Abstract*, 1949–1995, Various Issues. Damascus: Government Printing Press.
——. *Composition and Growth of Population in the Syrian Arab Republic*. Damascus, September 1979.
——. *Factors of Population Growth and Their Future Trends*. Papers Presented at a Seminar Held in Damascus, 16–20 September 1978, Under the Auspices of the Syrian Central Bureau of Statistics and UNFPA. Damascus: Central Bureau of Statistics Press, 1979.
——. *Follow-Up Demographic Survey*, Final Report, 1976–1979. Damascus, November 1981.
——. *Socio-Economic Development in Syria, 1960–1970*. Studies Series, No. 73. Damascus, 1973.
——. *Syria Fertility Survey – 1978*. 2 Vols. Damascus, 1982.
—— and Pan Arab Project for Child Development. *Maternal and Child Health Survey in the Syrian Arab Republic*, Summary Report. Damascus, 1995.
—— by Hallak, Nader M. *Rates of Natural Increase in the Syrian Regions*. Damascus, December 1979.
Ministry of Planning. *Second Five Year Development Plan, 1966–1970*. Damascus: Office Arabe de Presse at de Documentation, 1966.
—— *Third Five Year Plan for Economic and Social Development in the Syrian Arab Republic, 1971–1975*. Damascus: Office Arabe de Presse at de Documentation, 1971.
——. *Fourth Five Year Economic and Social Development Plan of the Syrian Arab Republic, 1976–1980*. Damascus: Arab Office for Press and Documentation, 1977.
——. *Fifth Five Year Economic and Social Development Plan of the Syrian Arab Republic, 1981–1985*. Damascus: Arab Office for Press and Documentation, August, 1981.

United States Arms Control and Disarmament Agency (USACDA)
World Military Expenditures and Arms Transfers, 1972–1996, Various Issues. Washington, D.C.

Bibliography

The World Bank

World Development Report, 1978–1996, Various Issues. Oxford and New York: Oxford University Press.

Bos, Eduard, My T. Vu, Ernest Massaiah, and Rodolfo A. Bulatao. *World Population Projections, 1994–95 Edition, Estimates and Projections with Related Demographic Statistics*. Published for the World Bank by the Johns Hopkins University Press, 1995.

World Tables, 1984–1995 editions, Various Issues. Baltimore and London: The Johns Hopkins University Press.

Serageldin, Ismail, James A. Socknat, Stace Birks, Bob Li, and Clive A. Sinclair. *Manpower and International Labor Migration in the Middle East and North Africa.* Published for the World Bank by Oxford University Press, 1983.

International Bank for Reconstruction and Development (IBRD)

The Economic Development of Syria. Baltimore: The Johns Hopkins University Press, 1955.

International Monetary Fund (IMF)

International Financial Statistics Yearbook, 1980–1995, Various Issues. Washington, D.C.

The United Nations (UN)

GENERAL PUBLICATIONS

Demographic Yearbook, 1960–1996, Various Issues. New York.

"The Industrial Situation in Syria." In *Industrial Development in the Arab Countries.* Selected Documents Presented to the Symposium on Industrial Development in the Arab Countries, Kuwait, 1–10 March 1967. New York, 1967, pp. 116–35.

——. *Review of Economic Conditions in the Middle East, 1951–52*. New York, March 1953.

——. *Review of Economic Conditions in the Middle East, 1958–59*. New York, 1960.

Department of Economic Affairs. *Economic Developments in the Middle East, 1959–61*. New York, 1962.

——. *Economic Developments in the Middle East, 1961–63*. New York, 1964.

Department of International Economic and Social Affairs. *Case Studies in Population Policy: Kuwait.* Population Policy Paper, No. 15. New York, 1988.

——. *Compendium of Statistics and Indicators of the Situation of Women, 1986*, Series No. 5. New York, 1989.

——. "Mortality of Children Under Age 5, World Estimates and Projections, 1950–2025." *Population Studies*, No. 105. New York, 1988.

——. Population Division, and UNFPA. *Population Policy Compendium: Syrian Arab Republic.* New York, 1980.

——. Statistical Office, Centre for Social Development and Humanitarian Affairs.

——. "World Population at the Turn of the Century." *Population Studies*, No. 111. New York, 1989.

——. *The World's Women, 1970–1990: Trends and Statistics*. New York, 1991.

World Fertility Survey. *The Syrian Fertility Survey – 1978: A Summary of Findings.* London: International Statistical Institute, February 1982.

United Nations Conference on Trade and Development (UNCTAD)
Hand-Book of International Trade and Development Statistics, 1980–1993, Various Issues. New York.

United Nations Development Programme (UNDP)
Human Development Report, 1992–1995, Various Issues. Oxford and New York: Oxford University Press.

United Nations Economic and Social Office in Beirut (UNESOB)
Studies on Selected Development Problems in Various Countries in the Middle East, 1969–71, Various Issues. New York.
Studies on Social Development in the Middle East, 1971. New York, 1973.

Economic Commission for Western Asia (ECWA)
Hameed, K. "Manpower and Employment Planning in Iraq and the Syrian Arab Republic." In ECWA. *Studies on Development Problems in Countries of Western Asia,* 1975. New York, 1977, pp. 22–44.
"Review and Appraisal of Progress in Housing Building and Urban Planning in Selected Countries of Western Asia." In ECWA. *Studies on Development Problems in Countries of Western Asia, 1974.* New York, 1975, pp. 70–95.
Demographic and Related Socio-Economic Data Sheets for Countries of the Economic Commission for Western Asia, 1978–1982, Various Issues. Beirut.
Population Bulletin of the United Nations Economic Commission for Western Asia. Special Issue, Nos. 10 and 11 (January–July 1976).
Population and Development in the Middle East. Beirut, 1982.
The Population Situation in the ECWA Region – Bahrain, Kuwait, Saudi Arabia, Syrian Arab Republic. Beirut, 1979–1981.
Studies on Development Problems in Countries of Western Asia, 1975. New York, 1977.
Survey of Economic and Social Developments in the ECWA Region, 1982–1984. Baghdad.
—— and the League of Arab States. *Statistical Indicators of the Arab World for the Period 1970–1979.* Beirut, 1981.

Economic and Social Commission for Western Asia (ESCWA)
Arab Women in ESCWA Member States. New York, 1994.
Demographic and Related Socio-Economic Data Sheets for Countries of the Economic and Social Commission for Western Asia, 1985–1996, Various Issues. Baghdad, Amman and Beirut.
Expert Group Meeting on the Absorption of Returnees in the ESCWA Region with Special Emphasis on Opportunities in the Industrial Sector. Amman, 16–17 December 1991. Amman, October 1992.

191

National Accounts Studies of the ESCWA Region, 1990–1996, Various Issues. New York.

Population Situation in the ESCWA Region – 1990. Amman, 20 May 1992.

Population Spatial Distribution. Amman, August 1993.

Return Migration Profiles, Impact and Absorption in Home Countries. New York, December 1993.

Statistical Abstract of the Region of the Economic and Social Commission for Western Asia, 1977–1986, 1978–1987, 1981–1990, 1984–1993. Baghdad and Amman.

Statistical Abstract of the ESCWA Region, Sixteenth Issue. New York, 1996.

Survey of Economic and Social Developments in the ESCWA Region, 1985–1995, Various Issues. New York and Baghdad.

Survey of Economic and Social Developments in the ESCWA Region in the 1980s. New York, 1989.

—— and FAO (Food and Agriculture Organization of the UN). *Agriculture & Development in Western Asia*, No. 15. Amman, December 1993.

United Nations Children's Fund (UNICEF)

The State of the World's Children, 1984–1997, Various Issues. Oxford and New York: Oxford University Press.

United Nations Educational Scientific and Cultural Organization (UNESCO)

Statistical Yearbook, 1975–94, Various Issues. Paris.

United Nations Fund for Population Activities (UNFPA)

The Arab World and Population. New York, 1979.

Omran, Abdel Rahim. *Population Problem and Prospects in the Arab World*. New York, July 1984.

Syrian Arab Republic, Report on Mission on Needs Assessment for Population Assistance. Report No. 24. New York, April 1980.

International Labour Office (ILO)

Yearbook of Labour Statistics, 1970–1995, Various Issues. Geneva.

Bairoch, Paul. *Urban Unemployment in Developing Countries*. Geneva, 1973.

Birks, J. S. and C. A. Sinclair, *International Migration and Development in The Arab Region*. Geneva, 1980.

Hansen, Bent and Samir Radwan. *Employment Opportunities and Equity in Egypt in A Changing Economy: Egypt in the 1980s. A Labour Market Approach*. Geneva, 1982.

World Tourism Organization

Yearbook of Tourism Statistics, 1980–1995, Various Issues. Madrid.

Bibliography

PAPERS SUBMITTED TO INTERNATIONAL CONFERENCES

UN Economic and Social Office in Beirut, Expert Group Meeting on the Application of Demographic Data and Studies in Development Planning, Beirut, 7–12 December 1970
Al-Hallak, M. N. "Demographic Situation in the Syrian Arab Republic."

ECWA First Regional Population Conference, Beirut, 18 February–1 March 1974
Habbab, Adnan. "Family Planning in the Syrian Arab Republic."
Safadi, Safouh. "Population and Labour Force."
Al-Shihabi, Mustafa. "Rural Population and Agriculture in the Syrian Arab Republic."

UN Economic and Social Council, Expert Group Meeting on Census Techniques, Beirut, 12–16 December 1977
Zein El-Din, Ahmad. "Achievements, Plans and Recommendations Relating to Population and Housing Censuses in the Syrian Arab Republic."

ECWA Second Regional Population Conference, Damascus, 1–6 December 1979
Mroueh, Adnan M. "Family Planning and Family Welfare."
Saad Eddin, Ibrahim. "Arab Cities: Present Situation and Future Prospects."

ECWA Population Conference, Nicosia, Cyprus, 11–16 May 1981
Abdel-Jaber, Tayseer. "Trends and Prospects of Brain Drain from Arab Countries." In ECWA. *International Migration in the Arab World*, Vol. 2. Beirut, 1982, pp. 779–90.
Yeslam, Suleiman Farag. "Major Issues in Sending Countries." In ECWA. *International Migration in the Arab World*, Vol. 1. Beirut, 1982, pp. 395–411.

The Economic Development in the Arab World Conference, Bahrain, 1–3 February 1993
Abdel-Jaber, Tayseer. "Inter-Arab Labor Movements: Problems and Prospects." In Said El-Naggar (ed.). *Economic Development of the Arab Countries: Selected Issues*. Washington, D.C., 1993, pp. 145–62.
El-Naggar, Said. "Economic Development of the Arab Countries: The Basic Issues." In Said El-Naggar (ed.). *Economic Development of the Arab Countries: Selected Issues*. Washington, D.C., 1993, pp. 1–25.

Transformations of the Middle Eastern Natural Environments: Legacies and Lessons, Yale University, 30 October – 1 November 1997
Winckler, Onn. "Consequences of the Rapid Population Growth and the Fertility Policies in the Arab Countries of the Middle East."

Bibliography

DISSERTATIONS (PH.D. THESIS)

Bendardaf, Ibrahim Bushnaf. *Socioeconomic Modernization and Demographic Changes in Syria.* Unpublished Ph.D. Thesis, University of Missouri, 1988.

Al-Zoobi, Ahmad Mouhamad. *The Agricultural Extension and Rural Development in Syria, 1955–1968.* Unpublished Ph.D Thesis, The Ohio State University, 1971.

Winckler, Onn. *Demographic Developments and Population Policy in Syria, 1960–1990.* Unpublished Ph.D. Thesis, University of Haifa, 1994 (in Hebrew).

COMMERCIAL COMPANIES PUBLICATIONS

Birks and Sinclair Ltd. *GCC Market Report,* 1990 and 1992. Durham: Mountjoy Research Centre.

HRD base Ltd., Lloyds Bank Chambers. *Socio-Demographic Profiles of Key Arab Countries.* Newcastle, May 1987.

BOOKS

Abdel-Khalek, Gouda and Robert Tignor (eds). *The Political Economy of Income Distribution in Egypt.* New York and London: Meier Publishers, 1982.

Abu-Jaber, Kamal. *The Arab Ba'th Socialist Party: History, Ideology, and Organization.* New York: Syracuse University Press, 1966.

Abu-Lughod, Janet and Richard Hay (eds). *Third World Urbanization.* Chicago: Maaroufa Press, 1977.

Alessa, Shamlan Y. *The Manpower Problem in Kuwait.* London and Boston: Kegan Paul International, 1981.

Allan, J. A. (ed.). *Politics and the Economy in Syria.* London: The School of Oriental and African Studies, University of London, 1987.

Allman, James (ed.). *Women's Status and Fertility in the Muslim World.* New York and London: Praeger Publishers, 1978.

Appleyard, Reginald (ed.). *The Impact of International Migration on Developing Countries.* Paris: Development Centre of the Organization for Economic Co-Operation and Development, 1989.

Asfour, Edmund Y. *Syria: Development and Monetary Policy.* Cambridge: Harvard University Press, 1969.

Ayalon, Ami and Gad G. Gilbar (eds). *Demography and Politics in the Arab Countries.* Tel Aviv: Hakibbutz Hameuchad, 1995 (in Hebrew).

Baer, Gabriel. *The Arabs of the Middle East: Population and Society.* Tel Aviv: Hakibbutz Hameuchad, 1973 (in Hebrew).

Barzilai, Gad, Aharon Klieman, and Gil Shidlo (eds). *The Gulf Crisis and its Aftermath.* London and New York: Routledge, 1993.

Beaumont, Peter and Keith McLachlan (eds). *Agricultural Development in the Middle East.* Chichester: John Wiley & Sons, 1985.

194

Bibliography

Birks, J. S. and C. A. Sinclair. *International Migration Project, Country Case Study: The Kingdom of Saudi-Arabia*. Durham: The University of Durham, Department of Economics, March 1979.

——. *International Migration Project, Country Case Study: Libyan Arab Jamahiriya*. Durham: The University of Durham, Department of Economics, July 1978.

——. *International Migration Project, Country Case Study: The Sultanate of Oman*. Durham: The Universitty of Durham, Department of Economics, May 1977.

Black, Richard and Vaughan Robinson (eds). *Geography and Refugees: Patterns and Processes of Change*. London and New York: Belhaven Press, 1993.

Bonné, Alfred. *The Economic Development of the Middle East – An Outline of Planned Reconstruction After the War*. London: Kegan Paul, Trench, Trubner & Co., 1945.

Cairo Demographic Centre. *Demographic Aspects of Manpower in Arab Countries*. Research Monograph Series, No. 3. Cairo, 1972.

——. *Demographic Measures and Population Growth in Arab Countries*. Research Monograph Series, No. 1. Cairo, 1970.

——. *Determinants of Fertility in some African and Asian Countries*. Research Monograph Series, No. 10. Cairo, 1982.

——. *Mortality Trends and Differentials in some African and Asian Countries*. Research Monograph Series, No. 8. Cairo, 1982.

——. *Population and Development*. Research Monograph Series, No. 14. Cairo, 1986.

Clarke, J. I. and H. Bowen-Jones (eds). *Change and Development in the Middle East*. London and New York: Methuen, 1981.

—— and W. B. Fisher (eds). *Populations of the Middle East and North Africa*. London: University of London Press Ltd., 1972.

Devlin, John F. *The Ba'th Party: A History from its Origins to 1966*. Stanford: Hoover Institution Press, Stanford University, 1979.

Domschke, Eliane and Doreen S. Goyer. *The Handbook of National Population Censuses: Africa and Asia*. New York, Westport, and London: Greenwood Press, 1986.

Al-Farsy, Fouad. *Saudi Arabia: A Case Study in Development*. London and Boston: Kegan Paul International, 1986.

Feiler, Gil, Gideon Fishelson, and Roby Nathanson. *Labour Force and Employment in Egypt, Syria and Jordan*. Tel Aviv: Histadrut, April 1993.

Fenelon, K. G. *The United Arab Emirates: An Economic and Social Survey*. London: Longman, 1978.

Fischer, Stanley, Dani Rodrik, and Elias Tuma (eds). *The Economics of Middle East Peace*. Cambridge, Mass. and London: The MIT Press, 1993.

Foreign Areas Studies Division. *Area Handbook for Syria*. Washington, D.C.: Special Operations Research Office, The American University, July 1965.

Freedman, Robert O. *Moscow and the Middle East: Soviet Policy Since the Invasion of Afghanistan*. Cambridge and New York: Cambridge University Press, 1991.

Ghosh, Pradip K. (ed.). *Urban Development in the Third World*. Westport and London: Greenwood Press, 1984.

Gilbar, Gad G. *The Economic Development of the Middle East in Modern Times*. Tel Aviv: Ministry of Defense, 1990 (in Hebrew).

——. *The Middle East Oil Decade and Beyond*. London and Portland: Frank Cass, 1997.

—— (ed.). *Ottoman Palestine 1800–1914: Studies in Economic and Social History*. Leiden: E. J. Brill, 1990.

——. *Population Dilemmas in the Middle East*. London and Portland: Frank Cass, 1997.

Ginat, Joseph and Onn Winckler (eds.). *The Jordanian–Palestinian–Israeli Triangle: Smoothing the Path to Peace*. Brighton: Sussex Academic Press, 1998.

Golan, Galia. *Soviet Policies in the Middle East from World War Two to Gorbachev*. Cambridge and New York: Cambridge University Press, 1991.

Gould, W. T. S. and A. M. Findlay (eds). *Population Migration and the Changing World Order*. Chichester: John Wiley & Sons, 1994.

Grill, N. C. *Urbanisation in the Arabian Peninsula*. Durham: Centre for Middle Eastern and Islamic Studies, 1984.

Hansen, Bent. *Economic Development in Syria*. California Rand Corporation, December 1969.

Himadeh, Said B. (ed.). *Economic Organization of Syria*. Beirut: The American University of Beirut Press, 1936.

Hinnebusch, Raymond A. *Authoritarism Power and State Formation in Ba'thist Syria: Army, Party, and Peasant*. Boulder: Westview Press, 1990.

——. *Peasant and Bureaucracy in Ba'thist Syria: The Political Economy of Rural Development*. Boulder: Westview Press, 1989.

Hopfinger, Hans (ed.). *Economic Liberalization and Privatization in Socialist Arab Countries: Algeria, Egypt, Syria and Yemen as Examples*. Gotha: Justus Perthes Verlag, 1996.

Hopwood, Derek. *Syria 1945–1986: Politics and Society*. London: Unwin Hyman, 1988.

Huzayyin, S. A. and G. T. Acsadi (eds). *Family and Marriage in some African and Asiatic Countries*. Research Monograph Series, No. 6. Cairo: Cairo Demographic Centre, 1976.

—— and T. E. Smith (eds). *Demographic Aspects of Socio-Economic Development in some Arab and African Countries*. Research Monograph Series, No. 5. Cairo: Cairo Demographic Centre, 1974.

Ismael, Tarek Y. and Jacqueline S. Ismael (eds). *The Gulf War and the New World Order*. Gainesville: University Press of Florida, 1994.

Issawi, Charles. *An Economic History of the Middle East and North Africa*. New York: Columbia University Press, 1982.

—— (ed.). *The Economic History of the Middle East, 1800–1914*. Chicago and London: The University of Chicago Press, 1966.

Kanovsky, Eliyahu. *The Economic Development of Syria*. Tel-Aviv: University Publishing Projects, 1977.

Karpat, Kemal H. *Ottoman Population 1830–1914: Demographic and Social Characteristics*. Wisconsin: The University of Wisconsin Press, 1985.

Kayal, Philip M. and Joseph M. Kayal. *The Syrian – Lebanese in America: A Study in Religion and Assimilation*. New York: Twayne Publisher, 1975.

Khalidi, Trif (ed.). *Land Tenure and Social Transformation in the Middle East*. Beirut: The American University of Beirut Press, 1984.

Bibliography

Khouri, Philip S. *Syria Under the Franch Mandate*. Princeton: Princeton University Press, 1987.

Kienle, Eberhard (ed.). *Contemporary Syria: Liberalization between Cold War and Cold Peace*. London: British Academic Press in association with the Centre of Near and Middle Eastern Studies, School of Oriental and African Studies, University of London, 1994.

Kushner, David (ed.). *Palestine in the Late Ottoman Period*. Jerusalem: Yad Yizhak Ben-Zvi Press, 1986.

Lewis, Bernard. *The Emergence of Modern Turkey*, second edition. Oxford and New York: Oxford University Press, 1968.

Long, David E. *The Persian Gulf: An Introduction to Its Peoples, Politics, and Economics*. Boulder: Westview Press, 1976.

Looney, Robert E. *Manpower Policies and Development in the Persian Gulf Region*. Westport and London: Praeger, 1994.

Luciani, Giacomo (ed.). *The Arab State*. London: Routledge, 1990.

El-Mallakh, Ragaei. *Economic Development and Regional Cooperation: Kuwait*. Chicago and London: The University of Chicago Press, 1970.

Ma'oz, Moshe. *Asad: The Sphinx of Damascus*. Tel Aviv: Dvir Publishing House, 1988 (in Hebrew).

——. *Syria and Israel: From War to Peace Making*. Or Yehuda: Ma'ariv Book Guild, 1996 (in Hebrew).

—— and Avner Yaniv (eds). *Syria under Assad: Domestic Constraints and Regional Risks*. London and Sidney: Croom-Helm, 1986.

Niblok, Tim and Emma Murphy (eds). *Economic and Political Liberalization in the Middle East*. London and New York: British Academic Press, 1993.

Owen, Roger. *Migrant Workers in the Gulf*. London: Minority Rights Group Ltd., 1985.

Perthes, Volker. *The Political Economy of Syria under Asad*. London and New York: I. B. Tauris, 1994.

Petran, Tabitha. *Syria*. London: Ernest Benn, 1972.

Poleman, Thomas and Donald Freebairn (eds). *Food, Population and Employment: The Impact of the Green Revolution*. New York: Praeger, 1973.

Rabinovich, Itamar. *Syria Under the Ba'th, 1963–1966: The Army – Party Symbiosis*. Jerusalem: Israel Universities Press, 1972.

Rabo, Annika. *Change on the Euphrates: Villagers, Townsmen and Employees in Northeast Syria*. Stockholm: Studies in Social Anthropology, 1986.

Raymond, André (ed.). *La Syrie D'Aujourd'hui*. Paris: Centre National de la Recherche Scientifique, 1980.

Richards, Alan and Philip L. Martin (eds). *Migration, Mechanization, and Agricultural Labor Markets in Egypt*. Boulder: Westview Press, 1983.

—— and John Waterbury. *A Political Economy of the Middle East*. Boulder: Westview Press, 1990.

Russell, King (ed.). *Return Migration and Regional Economic Problems*. London: Croom Helm, 1986.

Saad Eddin, Ibrahim. *The New Arab Social Order: A Study of the Social Impact of Oil Wealth*. Boulder: Westview Press and London: Croom Helm, 1982.

—— and Nicholas S. Hopkins (eds). *Arab Society – Social Science Perspectives*. Cairo: The American University in Cairo Press, 1985.

Salamé, Ghassan (ed.). *Democracy Without Democrats? The Renewal of Politics in the Muslim World*. London and New York: I. B. Tauris Publishers, 1994.

Sales, M. E. (Co-Directors and Principal Researchers: J. S. Birks and C. A. Sinclair). *International Migration Project, Country Case Study: Syrian Arab Republic*. Durham: University of Durham, Department of Economics, October 1978.

Samman, Mouna Liliane. *La Population de la Syrie: Étude Géo – Démographique*. Paris: ORSTOM, 1978.

Sardar, Ziauddin. *Science and Technology in the Middle East*. London and New York: Longman, 1982.

Sayigh, Yussif A. *The Economies of the Arab World: Development Since 1945*. London: Croom Helm, 1978.

Seale, Patrick. *Asad of Syria: The Struggle for the Middle East*. London: I. B. Tauris, 1988.

Serow, William J., Charles B. Nam, David F. Sly, and Robert H. Weller (eds). *Handbook on International Migration*. New York, Westport and London: Greenwood Press, 1990.

Shif, Ze'ev and Ehud Ya'ari. *Milhemet Sholal* [The Misleading War]. Tel Aviv: Schocken Publishing House, 1984 (in Hebrew).

Symonds, Richard and Michael Carder. *The United Nations and the Population Question, 1945–1970*. New York: McGraw-Hill, Book Company, 1973.

Todaro, Michael P. *Economic Development in the Third World*, Fourth Edition. New York and London: Longman, 1990.

Warriner, Doreen. *Land and Poverty in the Middle East*. London and New York: Royal Institute of International Affairs, 1948.

——. *Land Reform and Development in the Middle East: A Study on Egypt, Syria and Iraq*. London and New York: Oxford University Press, 1962.

Waterbury, John. *The Egypt of Nasser and Sadat: The Political Economy of Two Regimes*. Princeton: Princeton University Press, 1983.

Weinbaum, Marvin G. *Food, Development and Policies in the Middle East*. Boulder: Westview Press and London: Croom Helm, 1982.

Winckler, Onn. *Population Growth and Migration in Jordan, 1950–1994*. Brighton: Sussex Academic Press, 1997.

Ziadeh, Nicola. *Syria and Lebanon*. London: Ernest Benn Limited, 1957.

ARTICLES

Abdussalem, Ibrahim and Richard Lawless. "Immigrant Workers in the Libyan Labour Force." *Immigrants & Minorities*, Vol. 7, No. 2 (July 1988), pp. 206–23.

Abou-Gamrah, Hamed. "Fertility Levels and Differentials by Mother's Education in some Countries of the ECWA Region." In Cairo Demographic Centre. *Determinants of Fertility in some African and Asian Countries*. Research Monograph Series, No. 10. Cairo, 1982, pp. 191–211.

Bibliography

Abu-Lughod, Janet. "Urbanization in Egypt: Present State and Future Prospects." *Economic Development and Cultural Change*, Vol. 13, No. 3 (April 1965), pp. 313–43.

Acsadi, George. T. "Design of the Comparative Surveys." In S. A. Huzayyin and G. T. Acsadi (eds). *Family and Marriage in some African and Asiatic Countries*. Research Monograph Series, No. 6. Cairo: Cairo Demographic Centre, 1976, pp. 3–21.

——. "Selected Characteristics of the Survey Population." In S. A. Huzayyin and G. T. Acsadi (eds). *Family and Marriage in some African and Asiatic Countries*. Research Monograph Series, No. 6. Cairo: Cairo Demographic Centre, 1976, pp. 51–63.

Addleton, J. "The Impact of the Gulf War on Migration and Remittances in Asia and the Middle East." *International Migration*, Vol. 29, No. 4 (1991), pp. 509–25.

"Asian Expatriates – Coming Back." *The Middle East* (October 1991), p. 36.

El-Badry, M. A. "Trends in the Components of Population Growth in the Arab Countries of the Middle East: A Survey of Present Information." *Demography*, Vol. 2 (1965), pp. 140–86.

El-Baradei, Hussein. "Household Structure and Age at Marriage in Damascus, Syria." In S. A. Huzayyin and G. T. Acsadi (eds) *Family and Marriage in some African and Asiatic Countries*. Research Monograph Series, No. 6. Cairo: Cairo Demographic Centre, 1976, pp. 175–97.

Bhattacharjee, J. P. "On Balance." In Thomas T. Poleman and Donald K. Freebairn (eds). *Food, Population and Employment: The Impact of the Green Revolution*. New York: Praeger Publishers, 1973, pp. 245–68.

Birks, J. S., I. Serageldin, C. A. Sinclair, and J. A. Socknat. "Who is Migrating Where? An Overview of International Labor Migration in the Arab World." In Alan Richards and Philip L. Martin (eds). *Migration, Mechanization and Agricultural Labor Markets in Egypt*. Boulder, Colorado: Westview Press, 1983, pp. 103–16.

——, I. J. Seccombe, and C. A. Sinclair. "Labour Migration in the Arab Gulf States: Patterns, Trends and Prospects." *International Migration*, Vol. 26 (1988), pp. 267–86.

—— and C. A. Sinclair. "The Libyan Arab Jamahiriya: Labour Migration Sustains Dualistic Development." *Maghreb Review*, Vol. 4, No. 3 (May/June 1979), pp. 95–102.

Caldwell, John C. and Pat Caldwell. "Fertility Transition with Special Reference to the ECWA Region." In ECWA. *Population and Development in the Middle East*. Beirut, 1982, pp. 97–118.

Choucri, Nazli. "Migration in the Middle East: Old Economics or New Politics?" *Journal of Arab Affairs*, Vol. 7, No. 1 (1988), pp. 1–18.

——. "Migration in the Middle East: Transformation and Change." *Middle East Review*, Vol. 16, No. 2 (Winter 1983/4), pp. 16–27.

Dessouki, Ali Hilal. "The Politics of Income Distribution in Egypt." In Gouda Abdel-Khalek and Robert Tignor (eds). *The Political Economy of Income Distribution in Egypt*. New York and London: Meier Publishers, 1982, pp. 55–87.

——. "The Shift in Egypt's Migration Policy, 1952–78." *Middle Eastern Studies*, Vol. 18, No. 1 (1982), pp. 53–68.

Dibbs, Mohamed Chafic. "The Relationship between Censuses and Civil Registration in the Syrian Arab Republic." *Population Bulletin of ECWA*, No. 18 (June 1980), pp.

81–101.

Drysdale, Alasdair. "The Asad Regime and its Troubles." *Merip* (Middle East Research and Information Project) *Reports*, Vol. 12, No. 9 (November–December 1982), pp. 3–11.

——. "Regional Growth and Change in Syria Since 1963." In J. A. Allan (ed.). *Politics and the Economy in Syria*. London: The School of Oriental and African Studies, University of London, 1987, pp. 64–87.

——. "The Regional Equalization of Health Care and Education in Syria Since the Ba'thi Revolution." *IJMES*, Vol. 13 (1981), pp. 93–111.

Durand, John D. "Historical Estimate of World Population: An Evaluation." *Population and Development Review*, Vol. 3, No. 3 (1977), pp. 253–96.

"L'Explosion Demographique en Syrie," *Syrie & Monde Arabe*, Vol. 22 (Fevrier 1975), pp. 4–11.

Faour, Muhammad. "Fertility Policy and Family Planning in the Arab Countries." *Studies in Family Planning*, Vol. 20, No. 5 (September/October 1989), pp. 254–63.

Farag, Mahmoud. "Differentials in Age at Marriage in Syria." In S. A. Huzayyin and G. T. Acsadi (eds). *Family and Marriage in some African and Asiatic Countries*. Research Monograph Series, No. 6. Cairo: Cairo Demographic Centre, 1976, pp. 493–504.

——. "Mortality Level and Differentials Associated with Socio-Economic Development in Syria." In Cairo Demographic Centre. *Mortality Trends and Differentials in some African and Asian Countries*. Research Monograph Series, No. 8. Cairo, 1982, pp. 317–51.

Fargues, Philippe. "The Decline of Arab Fertility." *Population*, Vol. 44, No. 1 (1989), pp. 147–75.

Feiler, Gil. "The Number of Egyptian Workers in the Arab Oil Countries, 1974–1983: A Critical Discussion." *Occasional Papers*. Tel Aviv University – The Dayan Center, October 1986.

Findlay, Allan M. "Return to Yemen: The End of the Old Migration Order in the Arab World." In W. T. S. Gould and A. M. Findlay (eds). *Population Migration and the Changing World Order*. Chichester and New York: John Wiley & Sons, 1994, pp. 205–23.

—— and Musa Samha. "Return Migration and Urban Change: A Jordanian Case Study." In King Russell (ed.). *Return Migration and Regional Economic Problems*. London: Croom Helm, 1986, pp. 171–84.

Firro, Kais. "The Syrian Economy under the Assad Regime." In Moshe Ma'oz and Avner Yaniv (eds). *Syria under Assad: Domestic Constraints and Regional Risks*. London and Sidney: Croom Helm, 1986, pp. 36–68.

Foster, Gregory D. "Global Demographic Trends to the Year 2010: Implications for US Security." *The Washington Quarterly*, Vol. 12, No. 2 (Spring 1989), pp. 5–24.

Franklin, Bob. "Migrant Labor and the Politics of Development in Bahrain." *Merip Reports*, Vol. 15, No. 4 (May 1985), pp. 7–13, 32.

Garzouzi, Eva. "Land Reform in Syria." *The Middle East Journal*, Vol. 17 (Winter–Spring 1963), pp. 83–90.

George, Alan. "No Going Back." *The Middle East* (November 1996), p. 20.

Bibliography

——. "Syria – An Economic Saved by Circumstances." *The Middle East* (December 1988), pp. 27–9.

——. "Syrian Construction Market Expands." *The Middle East* (September 1995), pp. 19–20.

——. "Syria Transforms its Electricity System." *The Middle East* (December 1995), pp. 29–30.

Gerber, Haim. "The Population of Syria and Palestine in the Nineteenth Century." *Asian and African Studies*, Vol. 13, No. 1 (1979), pp. 58–80.

Gleick, Peter H. "Water, War, and Peace in the Middle East." *Environment*, Vol. 36, No. 3 (April 1994), pp. 6–15, 35–42.

Hallak, Muhammad Nadir. "The Impact of Migration on the Demographic Structure of the Syrian Arab Republic." In CBS. *Factors of Population Growth and Their Future Trends*. Papers presented at a seminar held in Damascus, 16–20 September 1978, under the auspices of the Syrian Central Bureau of Statistics and UNFPA. Damascus: Central Bureau of Statistics Press, 1979, pp. 72–84.

Hameed, K. "Manpower and Employment Planning in Iraq and the Syrian Arab Republic." In ECWA. *Studies on Development Problems in Countries of Western Asia, 1975*. New York, 1977, pp. 22–44.

Handoussa, Heba and Nemat Shafik. "The Economics of Peace: The Egyptian Case." In Stanley Fischer, Dani Rodrik, and Elias Tuma (eds). *The Economics of Middle East Peace*. Cambridge and London: The MIT Press, 1993, pp. 19–54.

Harris, William W. "Lebanon." *Middle East Contemporary Survey* (MECS), Vol. 14 (1990), pp. 520–56.

Hassan Bin Talal (His Royal Highness Prince Hassan Bin Talal is the Crown Prince of the Hashemite Kingdom of Jordan). "Manpower Migration in the Middle East: An Overview." *The Middle East Journal*, Vol. 38, No. 4 (Autumn 1984), pp. 610–14.

Hay, Richard. "Patterns of Urbanization and Socio-Economic Development in the Third World: An Overview." In Janet Abu-Lughod and Richard Hay (eds). *Third World Urbanization*. Chicago: Maaroufa Press, 1977, pp. 71–101.

Hilan, Rizkallah. "The Effects on Economic Development in Syria of a Just and Long-Standing Peace." In Stanley Fischer, Dani Rodrik, and Elias Tuma (eds). *The Economics of Middle East Peace*. Cambridge and London: The MIT Press, 1993, pp. 56–79.

Hill, Allan G. "Population Growth in the Middle East Since 1945 with Special Reference to the Arab Countries of West Asia." In J. I. Clarke and H. Bowen-Jones (eds). *Change and Development in the Middle East*. London and New York: Methuen, 1981, pp. 131–53.

——. "Population Growth in the Middle East and North Africa: Selected Policy Issues." In A. L. Udovich (ed.). *The Middle East: Oil, Conflict and Hope*. Lexington, Mass.: Lexington Book, 1976, pp. 7–57.

Hinnebusch, Raymond A. "Party and Peasant in Syria." *Cairo Papers in Social Science*, Vol. 3, Monograph 1 (November 1979).

——. "Rural Politics in Ba'thist Syria: A Case Study in the Role of the Countryside in the Political Development of Arab Societies." *The Review of Politics*, Vol. 44, No. 1 (1982), pp. 110–30.

——. "Syria." In Tim Niblok and Emma Murphy (eds). *Economic and Political Liberalization in the Middle East*. London and New York: British Academic Press, 1993, pp. 177–202.

Huzayyin, S. A. "Mortality Situation in some Arab and African Countries." In Cairo Demographic Centre. *Mortality Trends and Differentials in some African and Asian Countries*. Research Monograph Series, No. 8. Cairo, 1982, pp. 3–17.

International Planned Parenthood Federation – Middle East and North Africa Region. "Family Planning and Population Policies in the Middle East and North Africa." In James Allman (ed.). *Women's Status and Fertility in the Muslim World*. New York and London: Praeger Publishers, 1981, pp. 33–53.

Jean-Claude, David. "Alep." In André Raymond (ed.). *La Syrie D'Aujourd'Hui*. Paris: Centre National de la Recherche Scientifique, 1980, pp. 385–406.

"Jordan – The Demographic Time Bomb." *The Middle East* (February 1988), pp. 28–9.

Kanovsky, Eliyahu. "Middle East Economies and Arab-Israeli Peace Agreements." *Israel Affairs*, Vol. 1, No. 4 (Summer 1995), pp. 22–39.

——. "Migration from the Poor to the Rich Arab Countries." *Occasional Papers*. Tel Aviv University – The Dayan Center, June 1984.

——. What's Behind Syria's Current Economic Problems?" *Occasional Papers*. Tel Aviv University – The Dayan Center, May 1985.

Karpat, Kemal H. "The Ottoman Emigration to America, 1860–1914." *IJMES*, Vol. 17 (1985), pp. 175–209.

——. "Ottoman Population Records and the Census of 1881/2–1893." *IJMES*, Vol. 9 (1978), pp. 237–74.

Keilany, Ziad. "Land Reform in Syria." *Middle Eastern Studies*, Vol. 16, No. 3 (October 1980), pp. 209–24.

——. "Socialism and Economic Change in Syria." *Middle Eastern Studies*, Vol. 9, No. 1 (1973), pp. 61–72.

Kelidar, A. R. "Religion and State in Syria." *Asian Affairs*, Vol. 61, No. 1 (February 1974), pp. 16–22.

Khader, Bichara. "Propriété Agricole et Réforme Agraire en Syrie." *Civilisations*, Vol. 25 (1975), pp. 62–82.

——. "Structures et Réforme Agraires en Syrie." *Maghreb Machrek,* No. 65 (September–October 1974), pp. 45–55.

El-Khodary, Mohamed S. "Organization and Conduct of the Syrian Housing and Population Census of 1970." *Population Bulletin of the United Nations Economic and Social Office in Beirut*, No. 2 (January 1972), pp. 20–3.

Khoury, Nabeel A. "The Politics of Intra-Regional Migration in the Arab World." *Journal of South Asian and Middle Eastern Studies,* Vol. 6, No. 2 (Winter 1982), pp. 3–20.

——. "Inter Relationship between Urbanization and Socio-Economic Change: The Case of Syria." In CBS. *Factors of Population Growth and Their Future Trends*. Papers presented at a seminar held in Damascus, 16–20 September 1978, under the auspices of the Syrian Central Bureau of Statistics and UNFPA. Damascus: Central Bureau of Statistics Press, 1979, pp. 57–71.

Kienle, Eberhard. "Syria, the Kuwait War, and the New World Order." In Tarek Y.

Bibliography

Ismael and Jacqueline S. Ismael (eds). *The Gulf War and the New World Order*. Gainesville: University Press of Florida, 1994, pp. 383–98.

Kupperschmidt, Uri M. "A Note on the Muslim Religious Hierarchy towards the End of the Ottoman Period." In David Kushner (ed.). *Palestine in the Late Ottoman Period*. Jerusalem: Yad Izhak Ben-Zvi Press, 1986, pp. 123–9.

"Kuwait: Expatriate Workers Outnumber Nationals." *The Arab Economist*, Vol. 11 (April 1979), pp. 31–2.

Longuenesse, Elisabeth. "The Syrian Working Class Today." *Merip Reports*, No. 134 (July/August 1985), pp. 17–24.

Lowless, Richard I. "The Agricultural Sector in Developing Policy." In Peter Beaumont and Keith McLachlan (eds). *Agricultural Development in the Middle East*. Chichester: John Wiley & Sons, 1985, pp. 107–22.

Lutz, Wolfgang. "The Future of World Population." *Population Bulletin*, Vol. 49, No. 1 (June 1994), pp. 1–45.

Mahhouk, Adnan. "Recent Agricultural Development and Bedouin Settlement in Syria." *The Middle East Journal*, Vol. 10 (Spring 1956), pp. 167–76.

Manners, Ian R. and Tagi Sagafi-Nejad. "Agricultural Development in Syria." In Peter Beaumont and Keith McLachlan (eds). *Agricultural Development in the Middle East*. Chichester: John Wiley & Sons, 1985, pp. 255–78.

McCarthy, Justin. "The Population of Ottoman Syria and Iraq, 1878–1914." *Asian and African Studies*, Vol. 15, No. 1 (1981), pp. 3–44.

Meliczek, Hans. "Land Settlement in the Euphrates Basin of Syria." *Ekistics*, Vol. 53, No. 318/19 (May/June–July/August 1986), pp. 202–12.

Metral, Françoise. "Land Tenure and Irrigation Projects in Syria: 1948–82." In Tarif Khalidi (ed.). *Land Tenure and Social Transformation in the Middle East*. Beirut: American University of Beirut, 1984, pp. 465–81.

———. "State and Peasants in Syria: A Local View of A Government Irrigation Project." *Peasant Studies*, Vol. 11, No. 2 (Winter 1984), pp. 69–90.

"The Middle East: Gets Worse – for Who?" *The Middle East* (October 1994), p. 5.

Morris, Mary E. "Regional Economic Cooperation in the Middle East: Prospects and Problems." In Joseph Ginat and Onn Winckler (eds). *The Jordanian –Palestinian–Israeli Triangle: Smoothing the Path to Peace*. Brighton: Sussex Academic Press, 1998, pp. 137–55.

Nagi, Mostafa H. "Labor Immigration and Development in the Middle East: Patterns, Problems, and Policies." *International Review of Modern Sociology*, Vol. 12, No. 2 (1982), pp. 185–240.

Al-Najjar, Baquer Salman. "Population Policies in the Countries of the Gulf Co-Operation Council: Politics and Society." *Immigrants & Minorities*, Vol. 12, No. 2 (July 1993), pp. 200–18.

Offen, Elizabeth N. "Migration and Refugees: The Human Toll." In Gad Barzilai, Aharon Klieman, and Gil Shidlo (eds). *The Gulf Crisis and its Global Aftermath*. London and New York: Routledge, 1993, pp. 103–26.

Omran, Abdel R. and Farzaneh Roudi. "The Middle East Population Puzzle." *Population Bulletin*, Vol. 48, No.1 (July 1993).

Owen, Roger. "The Arab Economies in the 1970s." *Merip Reports*, Vol. 11

(October–December 1981), pp. 3–13.

Perthes, Volker. "Incremental Change in Syria." *Current History*, Vol. 92 (1993), pp. 23–6.

——. "The Private Sector, Economic Liberalization, and the Prospects of Democratization: The Case of Syria and some Other Arab Countries." In Ghassan Salamé (ed.). *Democracy Without Democrats? The Renewal of Politics in the Muslim World*. London and New York: I. B. Tauris Publishers, 1994, pp. 243–69.

Philipp, Thomas. "Demographic Patterns of Syrian Immigration to Egypt in the Nineteenth Century – An Interpretation." *Asian and African Studies*, Vol. 16, No. 2 (July 1982), pp. 171–95.

Pölling, Sylvia. "Investment Law No. 10: Which Future for the Private Sector?" In Eberhard Kienle (ed.). *Contemporary Syria: Liberalization between Cold War and Cold Peace*. London: British Academic Press in association with the Centre of Near and Middle Eastern Studies, School of Oriental and African Studies, University of London, 1994, pp. 14–25.

Porter, R. S. "The Growth of the Syrian Economy." *Middle East Forum*, Vol. 39 (November 1963), pp. 17–22.

"Qaddafi's War of Words." *The Middle East* (October 1985), pp. 12–13.

Quibria, M. G. "Migrant Workers and Remittances: Issues for Asian Developing Countries." *Asian Development Review*, Vol. 4, No. 1 (1986), pp. 79–99.

Qutub, Ishaq Y. "Urbanization in Contemporary Arab Gulf States." *Ekistics*, Vol. 53 (May/June 1983), pp. 170–82.

Rabo, Annika. "Great Expectations: Perceptions on Development in Northeast Syria." *Ethnos*, Vol. 49, No. 3–4 (1984), pp. 211–25.

Roberts, Ann Milnes. "Why Syrian Agriculture is a Top Priority." *The Middle East* (July 1984), pp. 28–30.

Robinson, Glenn E. "Elite Cohesion, Regime Succession and Political Instability in Syria." *Middle East Policy*, Vol. 5, No. 4 (January 1998), pp. 159–79.

Roy, Delwin A. and Thomas Naff. "Ba'thist Ideology, Economic Development and Educational Strategy." *Middle Eastern Studies*, Vol. 25, No. 4 (October 1989), pp. 451–79.

Ruppin, A. "Migration from and to Syria." In Charles Issawi (ed.). *The Economic History of the Middle East, 1800–1914*. Chicago and London: The University of Chicago Press, 1966, pp. 269–73.

Russell, Sharon Stanton. "Politics and Ideology in Migration Policy Formulation: The Case of Kuwait." *International Migration Review*, Vol. 23, No. 1 (1989), pp. 24–47.

Ryan, Miriam. "Boosting Syrian's Food Potential." *The Middle East* (August 1986), pp. 20–1.

Saad Eddin, Ibrahim. "Urbanization in the Arab World: The Need for an Urban Strategy." In Saad Eddin Ibrahim and Nicholas S. Hopkins (eds). *Arab Society – Social Science Perspectives*. Cairo: The American University in Cairo Press, 1985, pp. 123–47.

——. "Urbanization in the Arab World." *Population Bulletin of the UN ECWA*, No. 7 (July 1974), pp. 74–102.

Sabagh, Georges. "The Demography of the Middle East." *Middle East Studies*

Association Bulletin, Vol. 4, No. 2 (15 May 1970), pp. 1–19.

Sadowski, Yehya M. "Cadres, Guns and Money: The Eighth Regional Congress of the Syrian Ba'th." *Merip Reports* (July/Augost 1985), pp. 3–8.

Saliba, Najib E. "Emigration From Syria." *Arab Studies Quarterly,* Vol. 3, No. 1 (1981), pp. 56–67.

Samha, Musa. "Population Spatial Distribution Policies in Jordan." In ESCWA. *Population Spatial Distribution.* Amman, August 1993, pp. 83–105.

"Saudi Arabia: Jobs for the Boys." *The Middle East* (July 1993), p. 25.

Schmelz, U. O. "Population Characteristics of Jerusalem and Hebron Regions According to Ottoman Census of 1905." In Gad. G. Gilbar (ed.). *Ottoman Palestine 1800–1914: Studies in Economic and Social History.* Leiden: E. J. Brill, 1990, pp. 15–67.

——. "Hahitpathut Hademographit shel Hamedinot Ha'arviot" [The Demographic Development of the Arab Countries]. *Hamizrah Hehadash* [The New East], Vol. 22 (1972), pp. 424–61 (in Hebrew).

Seccombe, Ian J. "Immigrant Workers in an Emigrant Economy: An Examination of Replacement Migration in the Middle East." *International Migration,* Vol. 24, No. 2 (June 1986), pp. 377–96.

—— and R. I. Lawless. "State Intervention and the International Labour Market: A Review of Labour Emigration Policies in the Arab World." In Reginald Appleyard (ed.). *The Impact of International Migration on Developing Countries.* Paris: Development Centre of the Organization for Economic Co-Operation and Development, 1989, pp. 69–89.

Seetharam, K.S. and Badrud M. Duza. "Nuptiality and Fertility in Selected Areas of Four Arab and African Cities." In S. A. Huzayyin and G. T. Acsadi (eds). *Family and Marriage in Some African and Asiatic Countries.* Research Monograph Series, No. 6. Cairo: Cairo Demographic Centre, 1976, pp. 337–55.

Shah, Nasra, M. "Arab Labour Migration: A Review of Trends and Issues." *International Migration,* Vol. 32, No. 1 (1994), pp. 3–28.

—— and Sulayman S. Al-Qudsi. "The Changing Characteristics of Migrant Workers in Kuwait." *IJMES,* Vol. 21, No. 1 (1989), pp. 31–55.

Shahin, Mariam. "Syria: Secret to the Economic Future." *The Middle East* (February 1995), pp. 27–8.

Shaw, Stanford J. "The Ottoman Census System and Population, 1831–1914." *IJMES,* Vol. 9 (1978), pp. 325–38.

Simarsky, Lynn. "The Fabric Crack: Urban Crisis in the Arab World." *The Middle East* (January 1988), pp. 5–7.

Sivamurthy, M. and K. S. Seetharam. "Age at First Marriage in Selected Areas of Four Arab and African Cities." In S. A. Huzayyin and G. T. Acsadi (eds). *Family and Marriage in Some African and Asiatic Countries.* Research Monograph Series, No. 6. Cairo: Cairo Demographic Centre, 1976, pp. 285–309.

"Special Report of Syria: Characteristics of the National Economy." *The Arab Economics,* Vol. 11 (October 1979).

Sukkar, Nabil. "The Crisis of 1986 and Syria's Plan for Reform." In Eberhard Kienle (ed.). *Contemporary Syria: Liberalization between Cold War and Cold Peace.*

London: British Academic Press in association with the Centre of Near and Middle
Eastern Studies, School of Oriental and African Studies, University of London, 1994,
pp. 26–43.

——. "Economic Liberalization in Syria." In Hans Hopfinger (ed.). *Economic
Liberalization and Privatization in Socialist Arab Countris: Algeria, Egypt, Syria and
Yemen as Examples*. Gotha: Justus Perthes Verlag, 1996, pp. 147–64.

"Syria: Secretive Power Play." *The Middle East* (January 1994), 32–3.

"Syria's Budget: Where the Cash Flows in '87." *The Middle East* (May 1987), p. 33.

"Syria 1993: Results from the PAPCHILD Survey." *Studies in Family Planning*, Vol.
25, No. 4 (July/August 1994), pp. 248–52.

Tarbush, Susanna. "The New Nomads: Manpower in the Gulf." *The Middle East*
(February 1983), pp. 29–34.

Todaro, Michael P. "Urbanization in Developing Nations: Trends, Prospects and
Policies." In Pradip K. Ghosh (ed.). *Urban Development in the Third World*. Westport
and London: Greenwood Press, 1984, pp. 7–26.

Vaidyanathan, K. E. "Demographic Aspects of Unemployment in Arab Countries." In
Cairo Demographic Centre. *Demographic Aspects of Manpower in Arab Countries*.
Research Monograph Series, No. 3. Cairo, 1972, pp. 361–73.

——. "Urbanization and Development Process in the Arab World." In S. A. Huzayyin
and T. E. Smith (eds). *Demographic Aspects of Socio-Economic Development in some
Arab and African Countries*. Research Monograph Series, No. 5. Cairo: Cairo
Demographic Centre, 1974, pp. 117–31.

—— and M. A. Alwany. "Population and Labour Force in Syria." In Cairo Demographic
Centre. *Demographic Aspects of Manpower in Arab Countries*. Research Monograph
Series, No. 3. Cairo, 1972, pp. 221– 52.

Van Dam, Nikolaos. "Sectarian and Regional Factionalism in the Syrian Political Elite."
The Middle East Journal, Vol. 32, No. 2 (1978), pp. 201–10.

Van Hear, Nicholas. "Mass Flight in the Middle East: Involuntary Migration and the
Gulf Conflict, 1990–1991." In Richard Black and Vaughan Robinson (eds).
Geography and Refugees: Patterns and Processes of Change. London and New York:
Belhaven Press, 1993, pp. 64–83.

De-Vaumas, Étienne. "La Population de la Syrie." *Annales de Geograpgie*, Vol. 64, No.
341 (Jan.–Feb. 1955), pp. 74–80.

Ward, Richard J. "The Long Run Employment Prospects for Middle East Labor." *The
Middle East Journal*, Vol. 24 (1970), pp. 147–61.

Wardwell, John M. "Jordan." In William J. Serow, Charles B. Nam, David F. Sly, and
Robert H. Weller (eds). *Handbook on International Migration*. New York, Westport,
and London: Greenwood Press, 1990, pp. 167–87.

Widmer, Robert. "Population." In Said B. Himadeh (ed.). *Economic Organization of
Syria*. Beirut: The American University of Beirut Press, 1936, pp. 3–26.

Winckler, Onn. "The Economic Factor of the Middle East Peace Process: The Jordanian
Case." In Joseph Ginat and Onn Winckler (eds). *The Jordanian–Palestinian–Israeli
Triangle: Smoothing the Path to Peace*. Brighton: Sussex Academic Press, 1998, pp.
156–77.

——. "The Immigration Policy of the Gulf Cooperation Council (GCC) States." *Middle*

Eastern Studies, Vol. 33, No. 3 (July 1997), pp. 480–93.
——. "Syria: Population Growth and Family Planning, 1960–1990." *Orient*, Vol. 36, No. 4 (1995), pp. 663–72.
——. "Syrian Migration to the Arab Oil-Producing Countries." *Middle Eastern Studies*, Vol. 33, No. 1 (January 1997), pp. 107–18.
Zisser, Eyal. "Syria." *MECS*, Vol. 15 (1991), pp. 664–89.
——. "Syria." *MECS*, Vol. 17 (1993), pp. 633–69.
——. "Syria." *MECS*, Vol. 18 (1994), pp. 610–53.
——. "Syria." *MECS*, Vol. 19 (1995), pp. 591–621.

WEEKLIES, MONTHLIES, QUARTERLIES AND ANNUALS

Arabic
al-Ahram al-Iqtisadi, Weekly (Cairo).
al-Iqtisad, Monthly (Damascus).
al-Ishtiraqi, Weekly (Damascus).
al-Musawwar, Weekly (Cairo).
Nidal al-Falahin, Weekly (Damascus).

English
The Arab Economist, Monthly (London).
Gulf States Newsletter, bi-Weekly (West Sussex).
The Middle East, Monthly (London).
The Middle East and North Africa, Annual (London).
(MEED) *Middle East Economic Digest*, Weekly and Special Reports (London).
The New York Times Magazine, Weekly (New York).
The World of Learning, Annual (London).
EIU, QER (Quarterly Economic Review) *Syria, Jordan*, Quarterly and Annuals supplements (London).
EIU, *Country Profile*, *Syria*, 1986/87–1998/99, Annual (London).

DAILY NEWSPAPERS

Arabic
al-Ba'th (Damascus).
al-Hayat (London).
al-Khalij (Sharja).
al-Ra'y (Amman).
al-Thawra (Damascus).
Tishrin (Damascus).
Hebrew
Ha'aretz (Tel Aviv).
Yedioth Ahronoth (Tel Aviv).

English
Arab Times (Safat).
The Economist (London).
Emirates News (Abu-Dhabi).
Financial Times (London).
The Jerusalem Post (Jerusalem).
Jordan Times (Amman).
The Wall Street Journal (New York).

Index

Index